UNDERSTANDING FINANCIAL STATEMENTS

SIXTH EDITION

UNDERSTANDING FINANCIAL STATEMENTS

LYN M. FRASER
AILEEN ORMISTON

Prentice
Hall

Upper Saddle River, New Jersey 07458

Library of Congress Cataloging-in-Publication Data
Fraser, Lyn M.
    Understanding financial statements / Lyn M. Fraser, Aileen Ormiston.—6th ed.
      p. cm.
    Includes bibliographical references and index.
    ISBN 0-13-027782-7
    1. Financial statements. 2. Corporation reports. I. Ormiston, Aileen. II. Title.

HF5681.B2 F764 2000
657′.3—dc21   00-036214

Editor-in-Chief: PJ Boardman
Acquisitions Editor: Thomas Sigel
Editorial Assistant: Fran Toepfer
Assistant Editor: Kasey Sheehan
Executive Marketing Manager: Beth Toland
Production/Manufacturing Manager: Gail Steier de Acevedo
Production Coordinator: Maureen Wilson
Manufacturing Buyer: Natacha St. Hill Moore
Senior Prepress/Manufacturing Manager: Vincent Scelta
Cover Design: Karen Salzbach
Cover image: Ed Honowitz/Tony Stone Images
Composition: Impressions Book and Journal Services, Inc.

1 0 9 8 7 6 5
ISBN 0-13-027782-7

For Eleanor
—Lyn M. Fraser

For my father, Mike, Josh and Jacqui
—Aileen Ormiston

Contents

CHAPTER 2   The Balance Sheet   50

Preface

For readers of previous editions anxiously awaiting important updates, I am pleased to report that Aileen Ormiston's hair is also turning grey. My daughter Eleanor has completed three fascinating and challenging years as an analyst for Enron Corporation, and she is now heading back to graduate school for an MBA in international business. The smartest move I have ever made on this book over its many years and editions is to involve Aileen as a co-author, beginning with the fifth edition. She, however, still refers to the text as "the Fraser book," much to the dismay of her students and delight of her co-author.

Lyn M. Fraser

Uses for the Sixth Edition

Understanding Financial Statements is designed to serve a wide range of readers and purposes, which include:

1. Text or supplementary text for financial statement analysis courses.
2. Supplementary text for accounting, finance, and business management classes which cover financial statement analysis.
3. Study material for short courses on financial statements in continuing education and executive development programs.
4. Self-study guide or course material for bank credit analysis training programs.
5. Reference book for investors and others who make decisions based on the analysis of financial statements.

Features of the Sixth Edition

In revising the text, we have paid close attention to the responses received from faculty who teach from the book, from students who take courses using the book as a primary or supplementary text, and from other readers of the book. Our primary objective remains to convey to readers the conceptual background and analytical tools necessary to understand and interpret business financial statements. Readers and reviewers of earlier editions have commented that the strengths of this book are its readability, concise coverage, and accessibility. We have attempted to retain these elements in the sixth edition.

The sixth edition incorporates the many new requirements and changes in accounting reporting and standards.

- The financial statements of R.E.C. Inc. have been updated to include the following changes in Appendix B: "The Analysis of Segmental Data," has been rewritten to reflect the new segment standard implemented by the FASB since the last edition. As a result of the many changes that impacted chapter 3, the minicases have been updated.
- Three new problems have been added to each chapter and are identified with icons to indicate the problem type: writing skills problems, Internet problems, and PETsMART problems. The writing skills problems have been added as a result of the emphasis employers place on communication skills. The Internet problems allow the student to explore a variety of Web sites on the Internet. The PETsMART problems offer the opportunity to the student to analyze a real company throughout the use of the text. Information for the PETsMART problems, as well as some of the Internet problems is available on the Prentice Hall Web site: www.prenhall.com/fraser.
- The footnotes provided through the text contain resources that may be used by instructors to form the basis of a reading list for students.
- The sixth edition includes other features of earlier editions that readers have found useful: appendixes on earnings quality, the analysis of segmental data and understanding bank financial statements; self-tests at the ends of chapters, with solutions provided; chapter-end study questions and problems; minicases using real company information, and a glossary of key terms used in the text.
- The Instructor's Manual, which is available as a supplement, contains solutions to study questions, problems, and minicases; a sample course project with

assignment outline and resources. New to the sixth edition Instructor's Manual is a test bank for chapters 1 through 5. Both objective and short-answer test questions are included.

- A Web site for the text has been created as mentioned above.
- Power point slides can be downloaded for use in class from this site.

We hope that readers will continue to find material in *Understanding Financial Statements* accessible, relevant, and useful.

Lyn M. Fraser
Aileen Ormiston

Acknowledgments

We would like to acknowledge with considerable appreciation those who have contributed to the publication of this book.

Several individuals have made critical comments and suggestions on the manuscript. In particular, we would like to thank:

Eric L. Blazer	Millersville University
Richard Brunell	Concordia University
Corolyn E. Clark	St. Joseph's University
Stanley W. Davis	St. Joseph's University
John Erickson	California State University at Fullerton
Charles Fazzi	Robert Morris College
Ted M. Hammett	Southwestern State
George Hruby	University of Akron
Dianne R. Morrison	University of Wisconsin at La Crosse
Solomon S. Smith	Langston University

We would also like to thank the editorial, production, and marketing departments of Prentice Hall for their assistance at each stage of the writing and production process. Special thanks goes to Annie Todd, our original editor, who offered great advice and was not only helpful but also cheerful throughout the revision process. In addition, Annie's assistant, Fran Toepfer, was invaluable. She was at our beck and call and made sure every question we had was immediately answered and kept all of us on task. Thanks also goes to PJ Boardman, who took over as editor, Kasey Sheehan, assistant editor and Beth Toland, Executive Marketing Manager.

The list would be incomplete without mentioning the pets in our households who helped keep us in good humor throughout the revision of this edition. Little Bit, Picadilly Circus, Babe, R.T., and Ruthie kept Lyn smiling. Dieter's constant whining as Aileen worked on the revision (he thinks the computer is a major obstacle to playing) helped move her quickly through the revision. Fortunately, the rest of the animals were able to play with other members of the household.

Lyn M. Fraser
Aileen Ormiston

UNDERSTANDING FINANCIAL STATEMENTS

Financial Statements: An Overview

*Managing may be giving way to manipulation;
integrity may be losing out to illusion.*

—ARTHUR LEVITT
*From his speech "The Numbers Game,"
NYU Center for Law and Business,
September 28, 1998*

Map or Maze

One of the major purposes of a *map* is to help its user reach a desired destination through clarity of representation. A *maze,* on the other hand, attempts to confuse its user by purposefully introducing conflicting elements and complexities that prevent reaching the desired goal. Business financial statements have the potential for being both map and maze.

As a map, financial statements form the basis for understanding the financial position of a business firm and for assessing its historical and prospective financial performance. Financial statements have the capability of presenting clear representations of a firm's financial health, leading to informed business decisions.

Unfortunately, there are mazelike interferences in financial statement data that hinder understanding the valuable information they contain. The sheer quantity of information contained in financial statements can be overwhelming and intimidating. Independent auditors attest to the fairness of financial statement presentation, but many lawsuits have been filed and won against accounting firms for issuing "clean" auditors' reports on companies that subsequently failed. The complexity of accounting policies underlying the preparation of financial statements can lead to confusion and variations in the quality of information presented. In addition, these rules are constantly evolving and changing. Management discretion in a number of areas influences financial statement content and presentation in ways that affect and even impede evaluation. Changing prices can erode the usefulness of financial statement numbers. Some key information needed to evaluate a company is not available in the financial statements, some is difficult to find, and much is impossible to measure.

One of the main objectives of this book is to ensure that financial statements serve as a map, not a maze; that they lead to a determination of the financial health of a business enterprise that is as clear as possible for purposes of making sound business decisions about the firm.

The material in this book will convey information about how to read and evaluate business financial statements, and the authors will attempt to present the material in a straightforward manner that will be readily accessible to any reader, regardless of background or perspective. The book is designed for use by those who would like to learn more about the content and interpretation of financial statements for such purposes as making investment or credit decisions about a company, evaluating a firm for current or prospective employment, advancing professionally in the current business environment, or even passing an examination or course.

The reader can expect more than a dull exposition of financial data and accounting rules. Throughout these pages we will attempt with examples, illustrations, and explanations to get behind the numbers, accounting policies, and tax laws to assess how well companies are actually performing. The chapters and appendixes in the book show how to approach financial statements in order to obtain practical, useful information from their content. Although the examples in the book are based on corporate financial statements, the discussion also applies to the financial statements of small business firms that use generally accepted accounting principles.

The emphasis throughout the book is on *analysis*. We will break financial statements into parts for individual study in order that we might better understand the whole of their content as a map to intelligent decision making.

FIGURE 1.1

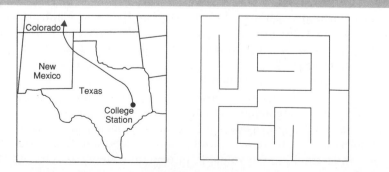

ORGANIZATION

Chapter 1 provides an overview of financial statements and presents approaches to overcoming some of the challenges, obstacles, and blind alleys that may confront the user of financial statements: (1) the volume of information, with examples of specific problems encountered in such areas as the auditor's report and the management discussion and analysis section as well as material that is sometimes provided by management but is not useful for the analyst; (2) the complexity of the accounting rules that underlie the preparation and presentation of financial statements; (3) the variations in quality of financial reporting, including management discretion in some important areas that affect analysis; (4) the impact of inflation on financial statement data; and (5) the importance of financial information that is omitted or difficult to find in conventional financial statement presentations.

Chapters 2 through 5 describe and analyze financial statements for a mythical but potentially real company, Recreational Equipment and Clothing, Incorporated (R.E.C. Inc.), that sells recreational products through retail outlets in the southwestern United States. The specifics of this particular firm should be helpful in illustrating how financial statement analysis can provide insight into a firm's strengths and weaknesses. But the principles and concepts covered throughout the book apply to any set of published financial statements (other than for specialized industries, such as financial institutions and public utilities; the interpretation of financial statements for commercial banks is covered in appendix C.)

Because one company cannot provide every account and problem the user will encounter in financial statements, additional company examples are introduced throughout the text where needed to illustrate important accounting and analytical issues.

Chapters 2 through 4 discuss in detail a basic set of financial statements: the balance sheet in chapter 2; the income (earnings) statement, including the evaluation of earnings quality, and statement of stockholders' equity in chapter 3; and the statement of cash flows in chapter 4. The emphasis in each of these chapters is on what the financial statements convey about the condition and performance of a business firm as well as how the numbers have been derived.

With this material as background, chapter 5 covers the interpretation and analysis of the financial statements discussed in chapters 2 through 4. This process involves the calculation and interpretation of financial ratios, an examination of trends over time, a comparison of the firm's condition and performance with its competitors, and an assessment of the future potential of the company based on its historical record. Chapter 5 also reviews additional sources of information that can enhance the analytical process.

Self-tests at the ends of chapters 1 through 5 provide an opportunity for the reader to assess comprehension (or its absence) of major topics; solutions to the self-tests are given in appendix D. For more extensive student assignments, study questions and problems are placed at the ends of the chapters. Minicases drawn from actual company annual reports are used to highlight in a case-problem format many of the key issues discussed in the chapters.

Appendix A discusses and illustrates issues that relate to the quality, and thus the usefulness, of financial reporting. Appendix A contains a step-by-step checklist of key items to help the analyst assess the quality of reporting, and examples of each step are provided.

Appendix B shows how to evaluate the segmental accounting data reported by diversified companies that operate in several unrelated lines of business.

Appendix C presents a guide to understanding and analyzing the financial statements of commercial banks. Given the impact of commercial banking on all aspects of financial operations in the United States, it is important for a well-informed financial statement user to develop a working knowledge of bank financial statements. The financial statements of commercial banking institutions in the United States are, like their nonbank counterparts, based on generally accepted accounting principles. Because of the nature of a bank's assets and liabilities, however, the financial statements are quite different in organization, content, and appearance from other types of business organizations.

Appendix D contains solutions to self-tests for chapters 1 through 5.

Appendix E covers the computation and definition of the key financial ratios that are used in chapter 5 to evaluate financial statements.

Appendix F presents a glossary of the key terms used throughout the book.

The ultimate goal of this book is to improve the reader's ability to translate financial statement numbers into a meaningful map for business decisions. It is hoped that the material covered in the chapters and the appendixes will enable each reader to approach financial statements with enhanced confidence and understanding of a firm's historical, current, and prospective financial condition and performance.

USEFULNESS

Financial statements and their accompanying notes contain a wealth of useful information regarding the financial position of a company, the success of its operations, the policies and strategies of management, and insight into its future performance. The objective of the financial statement user is to find and interpret this information to answer questions about the company, such as the following:

- Would an investment generate attractive returns?
- What is the degree of risk inherent in the investment?
- Should existing investment holdings be liquidated?
- Will cash flows be sufficient to service interest and principal payments to support the firm's borrowing needs?
- Does the company provide a good opportunity for employment, future advancement, and employee benefits?
- How well does this company compete in its operating environment?
- Is this firm a good prospect as a customer?

The financial statements and other data generated by corporate financial reporting can help the user develop answers to these questions as well as many others. The remainder of this chapter will provide an approach to using effectively the information contained in a corporate annual report. Annual reports in this book will refer to the information package published primarily for shareholders and the general public. The Securities and Exchange Commission requires large, publicly held companies to file annually a 10-K report, which is generally a more detailed document and is used by regulators, analysts, and researchers. The basic set of financial statements and supplementary data is the same for both documents, and it is this basic set of information—financial statements, notes, and required supplementary data—that is explained and interpreted throughout this book.

Volume of Information

The user of a firm's annual report can expect to encounter a great quantity of information that encompasses the required information—financial statements, notes to the financial statements, the auditor's report, a five-year summary of key financial data, high and low stock prices, management's discussion and analysis of operations—as well as material that is included in the report at the imagination and discretion of management.

THE FINANCIAL STATEMENTS

A corporate annual report contains four basic financial statements, illustrated in Exhibit 1.1 for R.E.C. Inc.

FIGURE 1.2

EXHIBIT 1.1

R.E.C. INC.
CONSOLIDATED BALANCE SHEETS AT DECEMBER 31, 2002 AND 2001
(IN THOUSANDS)

	2002	2001
Assets		
Current Assets		
Cash	$ 4,061	$ 2,382
Marketable securities (Note A)	5,272	8,004
Accounts receivable, less allowance for doubtful accounts of $448 in 2002 and $417 in 2001	8,960	8,350
Inventories (Note A)	47,041	36,769
Prepaid expenses	512	759
Total current assets	65,846	56,264
Property, Plant, and Equipment (Notes A, C, and E)		
Land	811	811
Buildings and leasehold improvements	18,273	11,928
Equipment	21,523	13,768
	40,607	26,507
Less accumulated depreciation and amortization	11,528	7,530
Net property, plant, and equipment	29,079	18,977
Other Assets (Note A)	373	668
Total Assets	$95,298	$75,909
Liabilities and Stockholders' Equity		
Current Liabilities		
Accounts payable	$14,294	$ 7,591
Notes payable—banks (Note B)	5,614	6,012
Current maturities of long-term debt (Note C)	1,884	1,516
Accrued liabilities	5,669	5,313
Total current liabilities	27,461	20,432
Deferred Federal Income Taxes (Notes A and D)	843	635
Long-Term Debt (Note C)	21,059	16,975
Commitments (Note E)		
Total liabilities	49,363	38,042
Stockholders' Equity		
Common stock, par value $1, authorized, 10,000,000 shares; issued, 4,803,000 shares in 2002 and 4,594,000 shares in 2001 (Note F)	4,803	4,594
Additional paid-in capital	957	910
Retained Earnings	40,175	32,363
Total stockholders' equity	45,935	37,867
Total Liabilities and Stockholders' Equity	$95,298	$75,909

The accompanying notes are an integral part of these statements.

EXHIBIT 1.1 (Continued)

R.E.C. INC.
CONSOLIDATED STATEMENTS OF EARNINGS
AND RETAINED EARNINGSFOR THE YEARS ENDED
DECEMBER 31, 2002, 2001, AND 2000
(IN THOUSANDS EXCEPT PER SHARE AMOUNTS)

	2002	*2001*	*2000*
Net sales	$215,600	$153,000	$140,700
Cost of goods sold (Note A)	129,364	91,879	81,606
Gross profit	86,236	61,121	59,094
Selling and administrative expenses (Notes A and E)	45,722	33,493	32,765
Advertising	14,258	10,792	9,541
Depreciation and amortization (Note A)	3,998	2,984	2,501
Repairs and maintenance	3,015	2,046	3,031
Operating profit	19,243	11,806	11,256
Other income (expense)			
Interest income	422	838	738
Interest expense	(2,585)	(2,277)	(1,274)
Earnings before income taxes	17,080	10,367	10,720
Income taxes (Notes A and D)	7,686	4,457	4,824
Net earnings	$ 9,394	$ 5,910	$ 5,896
Basic earnings per common share (Note G)	$1.96	$1.29	$1.33
Diluted earnings per common share (Note G)	$1.93	$1.26	$1.31

The accompanying notes are an integral part of these statements.

1. The *balance sheet* shows the financial position—assets, liabilities, and stockholders' equity—of the firm on a particular date, such as the end of a quarter or a year.
2. The *income or earnings statement* presents the results of operations—revenues, expenses, net profit or loss, and net profit or loss per share—for the accounting period.
3. The *statement of stockholders' equity* reconciles the beginning and ending balances of all accounts that appear in the stockholders' equity section of the balance sheet. Some firms prepare a *statement of retained earnings,* frequently combined with the income statement, which reconciles the beginning and ending balances of the retained earnings account. Companies choosing the latter format will generally present the statement of stockholders' equity in a footnote disclosure.
4. The *statement of cash flows* provides information about the cash inflows and outflows from operating, financing, and investing activities during an accounting period.

EXHIBIT 1.1 (Continued)

R.E.C. INC.
CONSOLIDATED STATEMENTS OF CASH FLOWS
FOR THE YEARS ENDED DECEMBER 31, 2002, 2001, AND 2000
(IN THOUSANDS)

	2002	2001	2000
Cash Flows from Operating Activities—Direct Method			
Cash received from customers	$214,990	$149,661	$140,252
Interest received	422	838	738
Cash paid to suppliers for inventory	(132,933)	(99,936)	(83,035)
Cash paid to employees (S & A expenses)	(32,664)	(26,382)	(25,498)
Cash paid for other operating expenses	(29,728)	(21,350)	(20,848)
Interest paid	(2,585)	(2,277)	(1,274)
Taxes paid	(7,478)	(4,321)	(4,706)
Net cash provided (used) by operating activities	$ 10,024	($ 3,767)	$ 5,629
Cash Flows from Investing Activities			
Additions to property, plant, and equipment	(14,100)	(4,773)	(3,982)
Other investing activities	295	0	0
Net cash provided (used) by investing activities	($ 13,805)	($ 4,773)	($ 3,982)
Cash Flows from Financing Activities			
Sales of common stock	256	183	124
Increase (decrease) in short-term borrowings (includes current maturities of long-term debt)	(30)	1,854	1,326
Additions to long-term borrowings	5,600	7,882	629
Reductions of long-term borrowings	(1,516)	(1,593)	(127)
Dividends paid	(1,582)	(1,862)	(1,841)
Net cash provided (used) by financing activities	$ 2,728	$ 6,464	$ 111
Increase (decrease) in cash and marketable securities	($ 1,053)	($ 2,076)	$ 1,758
Supplementary Schedule			
Cash Flows from Operating Activities—Indirect Method			
Net income	$ 9,394	$ 5,910	$ 5,896
Noncash revenue and expense included in net income			
Depreciation and amortization	3,998	2,984	2,501
Deferred income taxes	208	136	118
Cash provided (used) by current assets and liabilities			
Accounts receivable	(610)	(3,339)	(448)
Inventories	(10,272)	(7,006)	(2,331)
Prepaid expenses	247	295	(82)
Accounts payable	6,703	(1,051)	902
Accrued liabilities	356	(1,696)	(927)
Net cash provided (used) by operations	$ 10,024	($ 3,767)	$ 5,629

The accompanying notes are an integral part of these statements.

EXHIBIT 1.1 (Continued)

R.E.C. INC.
CONSOLIDATED STATEMENTS OF STOCKHOLDERS' EQUITY
FOR THE YEARS ENDED DECEMBER 31, 2002, 2001, AND 2000
(IN THOUSANDS)

| | Common Stock | | | | |
	Shares	Amount	Paid-In Capital	Additional Earnings	Retained Total
Balance at December 31, 1999	4,340	$4,340	$857	$24,260	$29,457
Net earnings				5,896	5,896
Proceeds from sale of shares from exercise of stock options	103	103	21		124
Cash dividends				(1,841)	(1,841)
Balance at December 31, 2000	4,443	$4,443	$878	$28,315	$33,636
Net earnings				5,910	5,910
Proceeds from sale of shares from exercise of stock options	151	151	32		183
Cash dividends				(1,862)	(1,862)
Balance at December 31, 2001	4,594	$4,594	$910	$32,363	$37,867
Net earnings				9,394	9,394
Proceeds from sale of shares from exercise of stock options	209	209	47		256
Cash dividends				(1,582)	(1,582)
Balance at December 31, 2002	4,803	$4,803	$957	$40,175	$45,935

Each of these statements will be illustrated, described, and discussed in detail in later chapters of the book.

NOTES TO THE FINANCIAL STATEMENTS

Immediately following the four financial statements is the section entitled Notes to the Financial Statements (Exhibit 1.2). The notes are, in fact, an integral part of the statements and must be read in order to understand the presentation on the face of each financial statement.

The first note to the financial statements provides a summary of the firm's accounting policies. If there have been changes in any accounting policies during the reporting period, these changes will be explained and the impact quantified in a financial statement note. Other notes to the financial statements present detail about particular accounts, such as: (*continued on p.12*)

EXHIBIT 1.2

R.E.C. INC.
NOTES TO CONSOLIDATED FINANCIAL STATEMENTS
DECEMBER 31, 2002, DECEMBER 31, 2001, AND DECEMBER 31, 2000

Note A—Summary of Significant Accounting Policies

R.E.C. Inc. is a retailer of recreational equipment and clothing.

Consolidation: The consolidated financial statements include the accounts and transactions of the company and its wholly owned subsidiaries. The company accounts for its investment in its subsidiaries using the equity method of accounting. All significant intercompany transactions have been eliminated in consolidation.

Marketable Securities: Marketable securities consist of short-term, interest-bearing securities.

Inventories: Inventories are stated at the lower of cost—last in, first out (LIFO)—or market. If the first-in, first-out (FIFO) method of inventory accounting had been used, inventories would have been approximately $2,681,000 and $2,096,000 higher than reported at December 31, 2002 and 2001.

Depreciation and Amortization: Property, plant, and equipment is stated at cost. Depreciation expense is calculated principally by the straight-line method based on estimated useful lives of 3 to 10 years for equipment, 3 to 30 years for leasehold improvements, and 40 years for buildings. Estimated useful lives of leasehold improvements represent the remaining term of the lease in effect at the time the improvements are made.

Expenses of New Stores: Expenses associated with the opening of new stores are charged to expense as incurred.

Other Assets: Other assets are investments in properties not used in business operations.

Note B—Short-Term Debt

The company has a $10,000,000 bank line of credit. Interest is calculated at the prime rate plus 1% on any outstanding balance. Any balance on March 31, 2004, converts to a term note payable in quarterly installments over 5 years.

Note C—Long-Term Debt

Long-term debt consists of the following at the end of each year:

	2002	2001
Mortgage notes collateralized by land and buildings (approximate cost of $7,854,000) payable in aggregate monthly installments of $30,500 plus interest at 8 3/4–10 1/2% maturing in 15 to 25 years	$ 3,808,000	$ 4,174,000
Unsecured promissory note due December, 2008, payable in quarterly installments of $100,000 plus interest at 8 1/2%	4,800,000	5,200,000
Promissory notes secured by equipment (approximate cost of $9,453,000) payable in semiannual installments of $375,000 plus interest at 13%, due in January, 2010	6,000,000	6,750,000
Unsecured promissory note payable in three installments of $789,000 in 2004, 2005, and 2006, plus interest at 9 1/4% payable annually	2,367,000	2,367,000
Promissory notes secured by equipment (approximate cost of $8,546,000) payable in annual installments of $373,000 plus interest at 12 1/2% due in June, 2012	5,968,000	—
	22,943,000	18,491,000
Less current maturities	1,884,000	1,516,000
	$21,059,000	$16,975,000

EXHIBIT 1.2 (Continued)

Current maturities for each of the following 5 years are:

December 31, 2003	$ 2,678,000
2004	2,678,000
2005	2,678,000
2006	1,884,000
2007	1,884,000

Note D—Income Taxes

A reconciliation of income tax expense computed by using the federal statutory tax rate to the Company's effective tax rate is as follows:

	2002		2001		2000	
Federal income tax at statutory rate	$7,859,000	46%	$4,769,000	46%	$4,931,000	46%
Increases (decreases)						
State income taxes	489,000	3	381,000	4	344,000	3
Tax credits	(465,000)	(3)	(429,000)	(4)	(228,000)	(2)
Other items, net	(197,000)	(1)	(264,000)	(3)	(223,000)	(2)
Income tax expense reported	$7,686,000	45%	$4,457,000	43%	$4,824,000	45%

Deferred income taxes reflect the net tax effects of temporary differences between the carrying amount of assets and liabilities for financial reporting purposes and the amounts used for income tax purposes.

Significant components of the Company's deferred tax assets and liabilities at fiscal year-ends were as follows:

	2002	2001	2000
Excess of tax depreciation over book depreciation	$628,000	$430,000	$306,000
Temporary differences applicable to installment sales	215,000	205,000	112,000
Total	$843,000	$635,000	$418,000

Note E—Commitments

The company conducts some of its operations in facilities leased under noncancellable operating leases. Certain agreements include options to purchase the property and certain agreements include renewal options with provisions for increased rental during the renewal term. Rental expense was $13,058,000 in 2002, $7,111,000 in 2001, and $7,267,000 in 2000.

Minimum annual rental commitments as of December 31, 2002, are as follows:

2003	$ 14,561,000
2004	14,082,000
2005	13,673,000
2006	13,450,000
2007	13,003,000
Thereafter	107,250,000
	$176,019,000

EXHIBIT 1.2 (Continued)

Note F—Common Stock

The company has a stock option plan providing that options may be granted to key employees at an option price of not less than 100% of the market value of the shares at the time the options are granted. As of December 31, 2002, the company has under option 75,640 shares (2001—96,450, shares). All options expire 5 years from date of grant.

Note G—Earnings Per Share

Basic earnings per share are computed by dividing net income by the weighted average of common shares outstanding during each period. Earnings per share assuming dilution are computed by dividing net income by the weighted average number of common shares outstanding during the period after giving effect to dilutive stock options. A reconciliation of the basic and diluted per share computations for fiscal 2002, 2001, and 2000 is as follows:

FISCAL YEAR ENDED

	December 31, 2002			December 31, 2001			December 31, 2000		
	Net Income	*Weighted Average Shares*	*Per Share Amount*	*Net Income*	*Weighted Average Shares*	*Per Share Amount*	*Net Income*	*Weighted Average Shares*	*Per Share Amount*
Earnings per common share—basic	$9,394	4,793	$1.96	$5,910	4,581	$1.29	$5,896	4,433	$1.33
Effect of dilutive securities: options		76			96			82	
Earnings per common share—assuming dilution	$9,394	4,869	$1.93	$5,910	4,677	$1.26	$5,896	4,515	$1.31

inventory;
property, plant, and equipment;
investments;
long-term debt; and
the equity accounts.

The notes also include information about

- any major acquisitions or divestitures that have occurred during the accounting period;
- officer and employee retirement, pension, and stock option plans;
- leasing arrangements;
- the term, cost, and maturity of debt;
- pending legal proceedings;
- income taxes;
- contingencies and commitments;
- quarterly results of operations; and
- operating segments.

Certain supplementary information is required by the governmental and accounting authorities—primarily the Securities and Exchange Commission (SEC) and the Financial Accounting Standards Board (FASB)—that establish accounting policies. There are, for instance, supplementary disclosure requirements relating to reserves for companies operating in the oil, gas, or other areas of the extractive industries. Firms operating in foreign countries show the effect of foreign currency translations. If a firm has several lines of business, the notes will contain a section to show revenue, expense, operating profit, and capital expenditures for each reportable segment. (The analysis of segmental data is discussed in Appendix B.)

AUDITOR'S REPORT

Related to the financial statements and notes is the report of an independent auditor (Exhibit 1.3). Management has responsibility for the preparation of financial statements, including the notes, and the auditor's report attests to the fairness of the presentation.

An *unqualified* report, illustrated for R.E.C. Inc. in Exhibit 1.3, states that the financial statements present fairly, in all material respects, the financial position, the results of operations, and the cash flows for the accounting period, in conformity with generally accepted accounting principles. Some circumstances warrant reports other than an unqualified opinion and are called *qualified* reports. A departure from generally

---

EXHIBIT 1.3   Auditor's Report

Board of Directors and Stockholders
R.E.C. Inc.

We have audited the accompanying consolidated balance sheets of R.E.C. Inc., and subsidiaries as of December 31, 2002 and 2001, and the related consolidated statements of earnings, shareholders' equity, and cash flows for each of the three years in the period ended December 31, 2002. These financial statements are the responsibility of the Company's management. Our responsibility is to express an opinion on these financial statements based on our audits.

We conducted our audits in accordance with generally accepted auditing standards. Those standards require that we plan and perform the audits to obtain reasonable assurance about whether the financial statements are free of material misstatement. An audit includes examining, on a test basis, evidence supporting the amounts and disclosures in the financial statements. An audit also includes assessing the accounting principles used and significant estimates made by management, as well as evaluating the overall financial statement presentation. We believe that our audits provide a reasonable basis for our opinion.

In our opinion, the financial statements referred to above present fairly, in all material respects, the consolidated financial position of R.E.C. Inc. and subsidiaries at December 31, 2002 and 2001, and the consolidated results of their operations and their cash flows for each of the three years in the period ended December 31, 2002, in conformity with generally accepted accounting principles.

J. J. Michaels and Company
Dime Box, TX
January 27, 2003

accepted accounting principles will result in a qualified opinion and the use of the following language in the opinion sentence: "In our opinion, *except* for the (nature of the departure explained), the financial statements present fairly. . ." If the departure from generally accepted accounting principles affects numerous accounts and financial statement relationships, then an *adverse* opinion is rendered, which states that the financial statements have not been presented fairly in accordance with generally accepted accounting principles. A scope limitation means that the extent of the audit work has been limited. This will result in a qualified opinion unless the limitation is so material as to require a *disclaimer of opinion,* which means the auditor cannot evaluate the fairness of the statements and therefore expresses no opinion on them. Lack of independence by the auditor will also result in a disclaimer of opinion.

Many circumstances warrant an *unqualified opinion with explanatory language* such as: a consistency departure due to a change in accounting principle, uncertainty caused by future events such as contract disputes and lawsuits, or events that the auditor wishes to describe because they may present business risk and going-concern problems. Unqualified reports with explanatory language result in additional paragraphs to the standard three-paragraph report.

Although the auditor's report is independent, the analyst should be aware that the auditor is hired by the firm whose financial statements are under review. Because the auditor must satisfy the client, the potential for conflict of interest always exists. The analyst should be alert to any change in auditors; a change can be a signal that there are problems with a company's disclosures. Firms that change auditors are required to file Form 8-K with the SEC (available to the public from the SEC).

Malpractice suits have become increasingly common in recent years as a result of complaints that auditors protected their clients at the expense of investors. In other cases, auditors claim to have been duped along with the investors. Interesting examples involve W. R. Grace & Company, Cendant Corporation, and SunBeam Corporation.

The accounting games played by chemical company W. R. Grace & Co. during the early 1990s finally came to light in 1999 when the SEC filed a case against the firm for fraudulently manipulating earnings. A whistleblower also filed suit against the company. The whistleblower, a former in-house audit chief for W. R. Grace & Co., claimed he was fired for raising questions. The problem was that earnings were growing too fast, and the chief financial officer feared that the growth could not be sustained. The excess profits were stashed away in a reserve account to be used in later years to mask problems such as declining earnings. Both Grace's in-house audit chief and a half dozen of the company's outside auditors from Price Waterhouse questioned the reserve; however, instead of insisting the company reverse the entries to the reserve account, the auditors gave the financial statements of the company an unqualified, or clean, opinion.[1]

In 1998, major accounting fraud was discovered at Cendant Corporation, a marketing and franchising company created by the merger of CUC International Inc. and HFS Inc. HFS Inc. was a franchising powerhouse built through acquisitions of companies such as Ramada, Howard Johnson, Coldwell Banker, and Avis. CUC International

---

[1] Ann Davis, "Grace Case Illustrates Earnings 'Management,' " *The Wall Street Journal,* April 7, 1999.

Inc. consisted of a diversified group of businesses including software and advertising publications. Both companies offered services and collected fees from memberships in discount shopping, travel, and entertainment clubs. Fictitious revenue had been recorded for more than three years at CUC International Inc. Ernst & Young, CUC's auditor, claimed to have done its job properly and said that the audit firm was also a victim of massive fraud by CUC's management. Despite this claim, Ernst & Young was dismissed by Cendant Corporation, and Arthur Andersen and Deloitte & Touche were hired to investigate the fraud. In addition to fictitious revenue, the audit firms found other accounting errors such as inappropriate depreciation of certain assets, recording revenue before it should have been recognized, and delaying recognition of cancellation of membership club revenues. More than 70 investor lawsuits were filed against the company.[2]

SunBeam Corporation also had to restate earnings because of improper accounting procedures. The company recorded sales before goods were actually delivered. In this case, one has to wonder why the auditors from Arthur Andersen did not notice the surging sales of heating blankets in the summer or barbecue grills in late fall.[3]

In a fraud study of SEC registrants alleged to be involved in fraudulent financial reporting released in 1999, it was found that external auditors were named in 29% of the cases either for being involved in the fraud or for negligent auditing. In 25% of the cases, companies had changed auditors prior to the fraudulent financial reporting period.[4]

Given the rash of lawsuits against accounting firms and the many highly publicized business failures, the SEC with the support of the American Institute of Certified Accountants (AICPA) has attempted to tighten rules to minimize future frauds. Arthur Levitt, chairman of the SEC, offered recommendations on how the SEC can tighten its regulatory oversight and called for the entire financial community to work toward reinforcing the values needed to protect the investor.[5]

OTHER REQUIRED INFORMATION

There is additional material required for inclusion in an annual report that may prove helpful to the financial analyst. The SEC adopted in 1980 an Integrated Disclosure System that mandates a common body of information for both the 10-K report filed with the commission and the annual report prepared for the company's shareholders. The basic package of information includes the audited financial statements; notes to the financial statements; the auditor's report; a five-year summary of selected financial data (net sales or operating revenue, income or loss from continuing operations, income or loss from continuing operations per common share, total assets, long-term

[2] Emily Nelson, "Cendant Notes Wider Accounting Fraud," *The Wall Street Journal,* July 15, 1998; Emily Nelson and JoAnn S. Lublin, "How Whistle-Blowers Set Off a Fraud Probe That Crushed Cendant," *The Wall Street Journal,* August 13, 1998; Steven Lipin and Mitchell Pacelle, "Price of a Scandal? Cendant Corp. Stock Is Weighed Down by Potential Liability," *The Wall Street Journal,* August 31, 1999.

[3] Richard Melcher, "Where Are the Accountants?" *Business Week,* October 5, 1998.

[4] Mark S. Beasley, Joseph V. Carcello, and Dana R. Hermanson, "COSO's New Fraud Study: What It Means for CPAs," *Journal of Accountancy,* May 1999.

[5] "Arthur Levitt Addresses 'Illusions,'" *Journal of Accountancy,* December 1998; for the complete text of Arthur Levitt's speech, see the Web site www.sec.gov/news/speeches/spch220.txt.

obligations and redeemable preferred stock, and cash dividends per common share); market data (high and low sales prices) on common stock each quarter during the past two years; and a revised and expanded form of the Management Discussion and Analysis (MD&A) of Financial Condition and Results of Operations.

The *Management Discussion and Analysis* section, sometimes labeled "Financial Review," is of potential interest to the analyst because it contains information that cannot be found in the financial data. The content of this section includes coverage of any favorable or unfavorable trends and significant events or uncertainties in the areas of liquidity, capital resources, and results of operations. In particular, the analyst can expect to find a discussion of the following:

1. the internal and external sources of liquidity;
2. any material deficiencies in liquidity and how they will be remedied;
3. commitments for capital expenditures, the purpose of such commitments, and expected sources of funding;
4. anticipated changes in the mix and cost of financing resources;
5. unusual or infrequent transactions that affect income from continuing operations;
6. events that cause material changes in the relationship between costs and revenues (such as future labor or materials price increases or inventory adjustments); and
7. a breakdown of sales increases into price and volume components.

Alas, there are problems as well with the usefulness of the MD&A section. One of the SEC goals in mandating this section was to make publicly available information about future events and trends that might affect future business operations. One study to determine whether the data in the MD&A section provides useful clues to future financial performance revealed that companies did a good job of describing historical events, but very few provided accurate forecasts. Many companies provided essentially no forward-looking information at all. [6]

The SEC filed an action in April 1992 against Caterpillar Inc. that accused the company of failing to disclose in the MD&A section of its annual report that about a quarter of its 1989 income, from its Brazilian unit, would be nonrecurring. Caterpillar negotiated a settlement with the SEC, agreeing to not commit the same act in the future but not conceding it had done anything unlawful. A spokesman for the SEC characterized the action against Caterpillar as a message that the SEC takes the MD&A seriously.[7]

PANDORA (A.K.A. "PR FLUFF")

In addition to the material required for presentation, many companies add to the annual report an array of colored photographs, charts, and other items to make the report and the company attractive to current and prospective investors. Some of these

---

[6] Moses L. Parva and Marc J. Epstein, "How Good Is MD&A as an Investment Tool?" *Journal of Accountancy,* March 1993.

[7] "A Disciplinary Message from the SEC," (box on p. 53) *Journal of Accountancy,* March 1993; for additional reading on this subject, also see Karen L. Hooks and James E. Moon, "A Checklist for Management Discussion and Analysis," *Journal of Accountancy,* December 1991.

creations are beginning to show up on corporate Web sites. Getting to what is needed through the "PR Fluff" can be a challenge.

For example, Time Warner reported net losses applicable to common shareholders for all three years shown in its 1998 annual report. Finding the financial section that reports this important information in Time Warner's 1998 income statement requires opening the glossy annual report cover and then getting through 32 pages of glossy pictures and other information about the entertainment and publishing industry. The financial pages that follow include text that attempts to minimize the net loss figures. In the MD&A section, it is suggested that the readers focus on a number called EBITA, or operating income before noncash amortization of intangible assets. Management also suggests ignoring the significant nonrecurring items.[8] Time Warner has a significant amount of goodwill, which is the price paid for acquisitions in excess of the fair market value of assets acquired. By focusing on what management suggests, the reader is being asked to ignore the fact that goodwill (which creates the noncash amortization) comprises more than one-third of the company's assets and is probably largely responsible for the significant amount of interest expense that is included in the overall net loss, but not included in operating income. Further, nonrecurring items appear to occur on a yearly basis at Time Warner.

Complexity

Financial statements are prepared according to generally accepted accounting principles that have been adopted in order to achieve a presentation of financial information that is understandable by users as well as relevant and reliable for decision making. The accounting rules that have been issued in order to achieve these objectives can be complicated and sometimes confusing.

ALPHABET SOUP

The two authorities primarily responsible for establishing generally accepted accounting principles in the United States are the SEC (public sector) and the FASB (private sector).

The SEC regulates U.S. companies that issue securities to the public and requires the issuance of a prospectus for any new security offering. The SEC also requires

- regular filing of annual reports (10-K);
- quarterly reports (10-Q); and
- other reports dependent upon particular circumstances, such as a change in auditor, bankruptcy, or other important events (all filed as 8-K reports).

The SEC has congressional authority to set accounting policies and has issued rulings called *Accounting Series Releases* (ASRs) and *Financial Reporting Rulings* (FRRs). For the most part, however, accounting rule making has been delegated to the FASB.

The FASB is comprised of seven full-time, paid members. The Board issues *Statements of Financial Accounting Standards* (SFAS) and *Interpretations,* usually after a lengthy process of deliberation that includes the following steps:

---

[8] *Time Warner Annual Report 1998,* pp. 39–40.

1. Introduction of topic or project on the FASB agenda.
2. Research and analysis of the problem.
3. Issuance of a discussion memorandum.
4. Public hearings.
5. Board analysis and evaluation.
6. Issuance of an exposure draft.
7. Period for public comment.
8. Review of public response, revision.
9. Issuance of SFAS.
10. Amendments and Interpretations, as needed.

In recent years, the SEC and FASB have worked closely together in the development of accounting policy, with the SEC playing largely a supportive role. But at times the SEC has pressured the FASB to move on the issuance of accounting standards or to change its policies (inflation accounting, oil and gas accounting). Most of the current heat on the FASB stems from the private sector. For example, FASB Statement No. 115, "Accounting for Certain Investments in Debt and Equity Securities," which requires companies—primarily financial institutions and insurance firms—to value some investment securities at current market prices, potentially cutting into profits, was strongly opposed by the industries affected as well as some

FIGURE 1.3

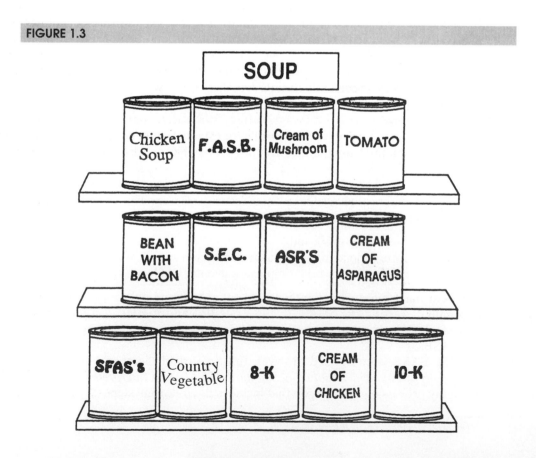

accounting firms.[9] Another measure that was vehemently opposed by the business sector was the FASB's proposal to require companies to deduct from profits compensation to executives in the form of stock options. As a result of the opposition, FASB Statement No. 123, "Accounting for Stock-Based Compensation," only requires that companies disclose in the notes to the financial statements the effects on profits of new employee stock options based on the fair value at the date of grant. The controversy that arose with regard to stock-based compensation caused the SEC to take a closer look at FASB's standard-setting process. In 1996, the SEC made public its concern that the standard-setting process is too slow; however, the SEC rejected suggestions from business executives that the private sector should have more influence in the process. The SEC vowed to maintain FASB's effectiveness and independence.[10]

A GLOBAL MARKETPLACE

The globalization of business activity has resulted in the need for a set of accounting rules that would be uniform in all countries. Unlike the United States, many countries have developed accounting principles to meet legal or tax needs within their countries. Investors and creditors in international markets would benefit from financial statements that are consistent and comparable regardless of the firm's location.

To address this need, the International Accounting Standards Committee (IASC) was formed in 1973 and currently has membership from more than 90 professional accountancy boards worldwide. The goal of the IASC is to eventually have worldwide acceptance of a set of international generally accepted accounting principles. This would allow companies to list securities in any market without having to prepare more than one set of financial statements. Doubt exists as to whether this goal will be met. The United States is currently one of several countries who have not accepted the current international accounting standards. Although financial statements prepared using U.S. accounting principles generally comply with international accounting standards, financial statements prepared according to international accounting standards may not comply with U.S. accounting standards. The SEC and FASB are working closely with the IASC in hopes that international accounting standards will someday meet the high level of standards currently in existence in the United States.[11] The focus throughout this textbook will be on U.S. standards; however, investors interested in foreign investments should take the time to research the accounting standards used in other countries.

MYTHICAL MOUNTAIN

Generally accepted accounting principles—as established by the FASB and the SEC—provide a measure of uniformity, but they also allow considerable discretion in the preparation of financial statements. In order to illustrate the implications of these

---

[9] Lee Berton, "Accounting Rules Board Is Under Fire as It Nears Decision on Two Key Issues," *The Wall Street Journal,* April 6, 1993.

[10] "SEC Calls for More Efficient FASB but Rejects Stronger Outside Influence," *Journal of Accountancy,* May 1996.

[11] "Call Heard for More Independent IASC," *Journal of Accountancy,* June 1999.

issues for financial statement users, the following comprehensive example is provided for the depreciation of *fixed assets* (also called *tangible fixed assets, long-lived assets,* and *capital assets*). Fixed assets are those assets, such as machinery and equipment, that benefit the firm for several years and are generally shown on the balance sheet as property, plant, and equipment. When such an asset is acquired, the cost of the asset is allocated or spread over its useful life rather than expensed in the year of purchase. This allocation process is depreciation. (The exception is land, which is not depreciated because land has a theoretically unlimited useful life.)

Assume that R.E.C. Inc. purchases an artificial ski mountain for its Houston flagship store in order to demonstrate skis and allow prospective customers to test-run skis on a simulated black diamond course. The cost of the mountain is $50,000. Several choices and estimates must be made in order to determine the annual depreciation expense associated with the mountain. For example, R.E.C. Inc. management must estimate how long the mountain will last and the amount, if any, of salvage value at the end of its useful life.

Furthermore, management must choose a method of depreciation: the straight-line method allocates an equal amount of expense to each year of the depreciation period, whereas the accelerated method apportions larger amounts of expense to the earlier years of the asset's depreciable life and lesser amounts to the later years.

If the $50,000 mountain is estimated to have a five-year useful life and $0 salvage value at the end of that period, annual depreciation expense would be calculated as follows for the first year.

Straight line

$$\frac{\text{Depreciable base (cost less salvage value)}}{\text{Depreciation period}} = \text{Depreciation expense}$$

$$\frac{\$50,000 - \$0}{5 \text{ years}} = \$10,000$$

Accelerated[12]

Cost less accumulated depreciation $\times$ twice the straight line rate

$$= \text{Depreciation expense}$$

$$\$50,000 \times (2 \times .2) = \$20,000$$

The choices and estimates relating to the depreciation of equipment affect the amounts shown on the financial statements relating to the asset. The fixed asset account on the balance sheet is shown at historical cost less accumulated depreciation, and the annual depreciation expense is deducted on the income statement to determine net income. At the end of year 1, the accounts would be different according to the method chosen:

---

[12] The example uses the *double-declining balance method* of figuring accelerated depreciation, which is twice the straight-line rate times the net book value (cost less accumulated depreciation) of the asset. Depreciation for year 2 would be:

Straight line $50,000/5 = $10,000   Accelerated $30,000 $\times$ .4 = $12,000

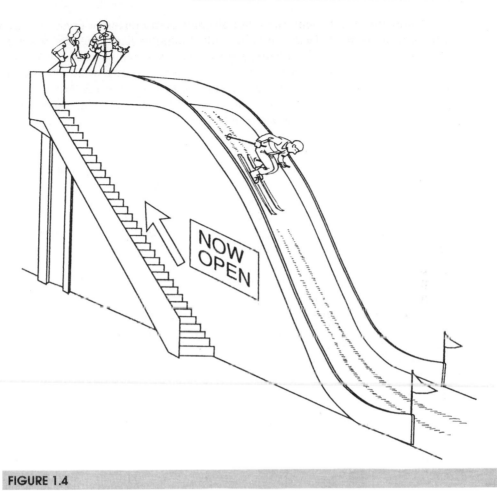

FIGURE 1.4

Straight line

Balance Sheet		*Income Statement*	
Fixed assets	$50,000	Depreciation expense	$10,000
Less accumulated depreciation	(10,000)		
Net fixed assets	$40,000		

Accelerated

Balance Sheet		*Income Statement*	
Fixed assets	$50,000	Depreciation expense	$20,000
Less accumulated depreciation	(20,000)		
Net fixed assets	$30,000		

The amounts would also vary if the estimates were different regarding useful life or salvage value. For example, if R.E.C. Inc. management concludes the mountain could be sold to Denver Mountaineering Co. at the end of five years for use in testing snow shoes, the mountain would then have an expected salvage value that would enter into the calculations. This example is compounded by all of the firm's depreciable assets and by the other accounts that are affected by accounting methods, such as the inventory account (discussed in detail in chapter 2).

OTHER DISCRETIONARY ISSUES

Not only are financial statements encumbered by accounting choices and estimates, such as those regarding depreciation, but they also reflect an attempt to "match" expenses with revenues in appropriate accounting periods. If a firm sells goods on credit, there is a delay between the time the product is sold and the time the cash is collected. Published financial statements are prepared according to the "accrual" rather than the "cash" basis of accounting. The accrual method means that the revenue is recognized in the accounting period when the sale is made rather than when the cash is received. The same principle applies to expense recognition; the expense associated with the product may occur before the cash is paid out. The process of matching expense and revenue to accounting periods involves considerable estimation and judgment and, like the depreciation example, affects the outcome of the financial statement numbers.

If, for instance, the mythical $50,000 mountain needed expensive repairs because one enthusiastic customer tried snowboarding, thereby creating a heretofore nonexistent back bowl in the mountain, management would have to determine whether to recognize the cost of repair in year 2 or to spread it over years 2 through 5.

Furthermore, financial statements are prepared on certain dates at the end of accounting periods, such as a year or a quarter. Whereas the firm's life is continuous, financial data must be appropriated to particular time periods.

More Complications

Because the accounting principles that underlie the preparation of financial statements are complicated, the presentation of data based on the accounting rules can be perplexing. One example of a complex accounting rule that sometimes results in confusion is that for the calculation of *earnings per share*. One typically thinks of earnings per share as the amount of net income earned for every share of common stock outstanding. But the income statement for many companies, those with complex capital structures (which include convertible securities, stock options, and warrants), will show two figures for earnings per share: basic and diluted. Convertible securities, stock options, and warrants represent potential "dilution" of earnings per share; that is, if they were exercised there would be more shares of stock outstanding for every dollar earned. The accounting rules require that this potential for dilution be considered in the computation of earnings per share, and the result is a dual presentation. (This topic is discussed more fully in chapter 3.)

The earnings per share calculation is just one of a vast number of financial statement puzzles. Sorting out the consolidation of a parent and subsidiaries, the accounting for leases and pensions, or the translation of foreign operations of a U.S. company can cause nightmares for the financial analyst. Off–balance sheet financing, a technique used to enable firms to borrow money without recording the debt as a liability on the balance sheet, continues to concern the FASB. As a result, the board issued FASB Statement No. 133, "Accounting for Derivative Instruments and Hedging Activities," which has added to the complexity. Obligations from derivatives, financial instruments that derive their value from an underlying asset or index, such as futures and option contracts,[13] now must be recorded on the balance sheet. Statement No. 133 also requires a company to disclose information about the types of instruments it holds, its objectives in holding the instruments, and its strategies for achieving these objectives.[14]

Another significant change occurred in 1998 when FASB Statement No. 130, "Reporting Comprehensive Income," became effective. Companies must now report an additional income number, comprehensive income, which includes items that previously

---

[13] A futures contract is a contract to buy or sell a commodity or a financial claim at a specified price at a specified future time. An option contract is a contract to buy or sell a fixed number of shares at a specified price over a specified period of time.

[14] "Accounting for Derivative Instruments and Hedging Activities," *FASB Statement of Financial Accounting Standards No. 133,* 1998.

FIGURE 1.5

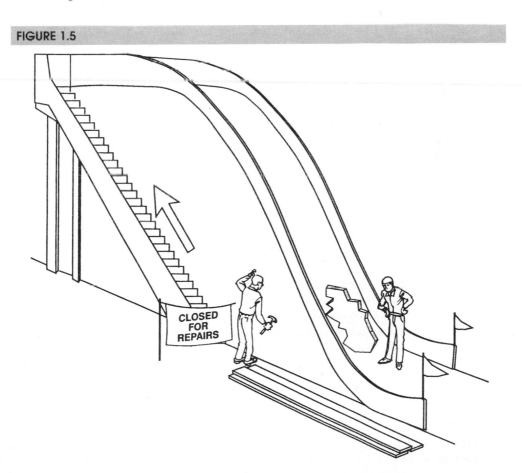

bypassed the income statement and were reported as a component of stockholders' equity.[15] (This important change is discussed more fully in chapter 3.)

Also complicating matters are two sets of accounting rules used by management—one for reporting purposes (preparation of financial statements for the public) and one for tax purposes (calculations of taxes for the Internal Revenue Service [IRS]). In the previous section, there was an example of the choices associated with the depreciation of an asset. Firms typically select one depreciation method for reporting purposes and use the method for tax purposes that is specified by the tax laws (currently the most frequently used tax method is the Modified Accelerated Cost Recovery System [MACRS]). The objective for tax purposes is to pay the smallest amount of tax possible, whereas the objective for reporting purposes is to report the highest possible income but also a smooth earnings stream. Thus, for reporting purposes, the firm might choose the straight-line method because it spreads the expense evenly and results in higher reported income than an accelerated method in the earlier years of an asset's life. Referring to the previous example, the following results were obtained according to the two depreciation methods for year 1:

Straight line		**Accelerated**	
Depreciation expense	$10,000	Depreciation expense	$20,000

Use of the straight-line method produces an expense deduction that is $10,000 less than the accelerated method; net income, therefore, would be $10,000 higher in year 1 under the straight-line method. Assume for purposes of illustration that the accelerated method allowed by the IRS also yields a depreciation expense in year 1 of $20,000. By using the straight-line method, the tax paid to the IRS under the allowed accelerated method would be less than the income tax expense reported in the published income statement because taxable income would be less than reported income.[16] (Eventually this difference would reverse, because in the later years of the asset's useful life, accelerated depreciation would be less than straight line; the total amount of depreciation taken is the same under both methods.) To reconcile the difference between the amounts of tax expense, there is an account on the balance sheet called deferred taxes. This account and its interpretation, discussed in chapter 2, introduce still another challenge to the financial statement user.

Quality of Financial Reporting

It has already been pointed out that management has considerable discretion within the overall framework of generally accepted accounting principles. As a result, the potential exists for management to "manipulate" the bottom line (profit or loss) and other accounts in financial statements. Ideally, financial statements should reflect an accurate picture of a company's financial condition and performance. The information should be useful both to assess the past and predict the future. The sharper and clearer

---

[15] "Reporting Comprehensive Income," *FASB Statement of Financial Accounting Standards No. 130,* 1997.

[16] For a firm with a 34% marginal tax rate, the difference would be $3,400. [Accelerated depreciation expense less straight-line depreciation expense times the marginal tax rate: ($20,000 − $10,000) × .34 = $3,400.]

the picture presented through the financial data and the closer that picture is to financial reality, the higher is the quality of the financial statements and reported earnings.

Many opportunities exist for management to affect the quality of financial statements; some illustrations follow.

ACCOUNTING POLICIES, ESTIMATES—CHOICES AND CHANGES

In preparing financial statements, management makes choices with respect to accounting policies and makes estimations in the applications of those policies. One such choice (others will be discussed in subsequent chapters) was covered in the preceding section related to the depreciation of fixed assets. To continue the depreciation example, in choosing a depreciation method, management decides how to allocate the depreciation expense associated with a fixed asset acquisition.

Assume that the $50,000 ski mountain is more productive in the early years of its operating life, before would-be skiers dig ruts in the simulated runs. Financial reality would argue for the selection of an accelerated depreciation method, which would recognize higher depreciation expense in the early years of its useful life. An environment of rising prices would also support accelerated depreciation because inflation increases the replacement cost of most assets, resulting in an understatement of depreciation based on historical cost. If, however, management wanted to show higher earnings in the early years, the straight-line method would be selected. Note the difference in depreciation expense recognized for year 1:

Straight line	**Accelerated**
Income Statement	*Income Statement*
Depreciation expense $10,000	Depreciation expense $20,000

Remember that the lower the expense, the higher the reported net income. Therefore, under the straight-line method, net income would be $10,000 higher than with the accelerated method. The choice of depreciation method clearly affects the earnings stream associated with the asset, and it also affects the *quality* of the earnings figure reported. Use of accelerated depreciation would produce earnings of higher quality in this particular situation.

Management can also elect to change an accounting policy or estimate if the change can be justified as preferable to what was previously used. In the depreciation example, it was estimated that the mountain had a useful life of five years. It could be argued that competitive sporting goods stores depreciate their mountains over a ten-year rather than a five-year period. If the firm had chosen to use the straight-line method and made this accounting change (called a "change in accounting estimate"), depreciation expense would be decreased from $10,000 to $5,000 per year, and net income would increase by $5,000.

Before change in estimate	**After change in estimate**
Income Statement	*Income Statement*
Depreciation expense $10,000	Depreciation expense $5,000

When a company makes such a change, the quantitative effect of the change must be disclosed in notes to the financial statement. The cumulative effect of accounting changes, net of tax, is shown separately on the income statement and should be considered in making comparisons with future and prior years' earnings because prior years' earnings were computed using a different accounting method.

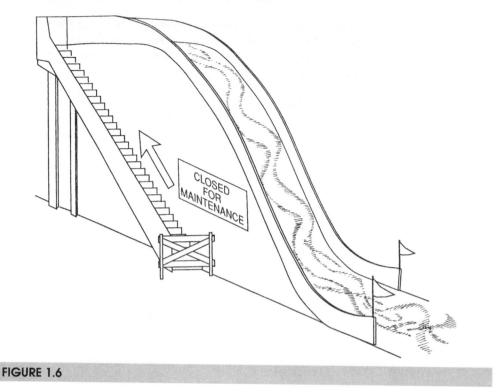

FIGURE 1.6

TIMING OF REVENUE AND EXPENSE RECOGNITION

One of the generally accepted accounting principles that provides the foundation for preparing financial statements is the matching principle: expenses are matched with the generation of revenues in order to determine net income for an accounting period. Reference was made earlier to the fact that published financial statements are based on the accrual rather than the cash basis of accounting, which means that revenues are recognized when earned and expenses are recognized when incurred, regardless of when the cash inflows and outflows occur. This matching process involves judgments by management regarding the timing of expense and revenue recognition. Although accounting rules provide guidelines helpful in making the necessary and appropriate allocations, these rules are not always precise.

For example, suppose that a company learns near the end of an accounting period that a material accounts receivable is probably uncollectible. When will the account be written off as a loss—currently, or in the next accounting period when a final determination is made? Pose the same question for obsolete inventory sitting on the warehouse shelves gathering dust. These are areas involving sometimes arbitrary managerial decisions. Generally speaking, the more conservative management is in making such judgments (conservatism usually implies the choice that is least favorable to the firm), the higher the quality of earnings resulting from the matching of revenues and expenses in a given accounting period.

In recent years, the accounting practices of many companies have been questioned, and in some cases, shareholders have filed lawsuits as a result of abuses in financial reporting. Livent Inc., an entertainment company, filed for Chapter 11 bankruptcy shortly before the SEC brought a civil case against executives of the firm for conducting a massive accounting fraud from 1994 until 1998 when the fraud was discovered. The fraudulent techniques used and discovered by new management of Livent Inc. included (1) erasing expenses in one quarter and entering them in a subsequent quarter; (2) erasing operating expenses from ongoing productions and recording them as preproduction costs (assets) for other shows; and (3) reversing entries for production costs that had been spread over several prior years. All of these techniques resulted in Livent Inc. reporting a higher and inaccurate net income figure. The executives charged in this case face jail terms and extensive fines.[17]

Executives of HBO & Co., a medical software firm, went to great lengths to report higher income prior to being acquired by McKesson Inc. in January 1999. Only after the acquisition did executives learn that sales had been booked sooner than generally accepted accounting principles allowed. In many cases, software was shipped in order to generate a receipt from the customer even though there was no binding sales order from the customer. HBO Inc. also recorded sales of software upgrades, even though a newly released accounting rule forbids the recognition of subscription-type sales until the services are rendered. After reversing the inappropriate entries, McKesson HBOC Inc. revised its 1999 earnings downward from $237.1 million to $84.9 million.[18]

DISCRETIONARY ITEMS

Many of the expenditures made by a business firm are discretionary in nature. Management exercises control over the budget level and timing of expenditures for the repair and maintenance of machinery and equipment, marketing and advertising, research and development, and capital expansion. Policies are also flexible with respect to the replacement of plant assets, the development of new product lines, and the disposal of an operating division. Each choice regarding these discretionary items has both an immediate and a long-term impact on profitability, perhaps not in the same direction. A company might elect to defer plant maintenance in order to boost current period earnings; ultimately, the effect of such a policy could be detrimental.

The nature of a business dictates to a certain extent how discretionary dollars should be spent. For some industries, there is a direct relationship between dollars spent for advertising and market share. Through investment in advertising, Coca-Cola and Pepsi have become the two key players in the soft drink market. As early as 1909, Coca-Cola was winning the advertising war with Pepsi, spending more than $750,000. Although Pepsi struggled in the beginning, the company became a formidable competitor by creating the first-ever fifteen-second radio jingle in 1939. These two companies have used not only radio but television, celebrities, slogans, and on-line advertising to promote their products.[19] By 1997, Coca-Cola controlled 44% of the soft drink market, and Pepsi followed with a 31% share.[20] But a company can also spend too much on advertising. Royal Appliance Manufacturing's stock dropped from $31 to less

---

[17] Joseph Weber and Nanette Byrnes, "Is Fraud the Thing?" *Business Week,* February 15, 1999.

[18] Ralph T. King Jr., "McKesson Restates Income Again as Probe of Accounting Widens," *The Wall Street Journal,* July 15, 1999.

[19] Lawrence Dietz, *Soda Pop.* New York: Simon and Schuster, 1973.

[20] Equity Analytics Ltd., www.e-anlytics.com/ipo/1999/january/pbg.htm.

than $8 a share during 1992, attributed in part to market reaction to excessive adver-
tising expenditures. Royal almost doubled expenditures on advertising and promotion, increasing outlays from $40 million in 1991 to $79 million in 1992; the firm's net
income declined from $33 to $20 million. Advertising and promotion expenses in 1992
accounted for more than 70% of total operating expenses.

Research and development expenditures are of critical importance to some industries, such as high technology. Intense competition in these areas often results in higher
research and development costs while at the same time reducing prices to gain market
share. Roger Ackerman's task as new chief executive officer to Corning in 1996 was to
transform a stodgy old-line conglomerate into a high-tech supplier. Despite the set-
backs, such as a 44% drop in operating earnings and a stock price that dropped by
nearly two-thirds, Ackerman stayed his course and based his decisions on the long-
term success of the firm, rather than short-term profits. The cookware unit was sold off
to make way for Corning to move into the exploding fiber-optic market. Ackerman
wanted Corning to go beyond fiber and become a major supplier of photonic components that increase the amount of information a single strand of fiber can carry.
Unfortunately, the market crash in Southeast Asia in 1997 caused Ackerman to slash
fiber prices by 50%. Despite the decrease in profits, he increased research spending
from $172 million in 1995 to $294 million in 1998, a 71% increase. His efforts paid off;
Corning's share of the world fiber market reached 38% in 1998, compared to 16% for
its closest rival, Lucent.[21]

The financial analyst should carefully scrutinize management's policies with
respect to these discretionary items through an examination of expenditure trends
(absolute and relative amounts) and comparison with industry competitors. Such an
analysis can provide insight into a company's existing strengths and weaknesses and
contribute to an assessment of its ability to perform successfully in the future.

NONRECURRING AND NONOPERATING ITEMS

Business firms may execute financial transactions that are nonrecurring and/or nonoperating in nature. If the analyst is seeking an earnings figure that reflects the *future* operating potential of the firm, such transactions—which are not part of normal ongoing business—should be reviewed and possibly eliminated from earnings. One such example
would be a gain on the sale of a major plant asset, such as a building. Firms sometimes
sell an asset in order to generate cash and/or profits during lean periods; Bank America
Corporation sold its headquarters complex for a huge profit in order to boost earnings in
a bad year.[22] Such a deal is both nonrecurring and nonoperating in nature and should be
ignored in measuring the enterprise's ability to generate future operating profits.

Other transactions that should be considered as nonrecurring and/or nonoperating include write-downs for the impairment of assets, accounting changes, and extraordinary items. In the past, restructuring charges or costs to reorganize a company were
considered to be one-time, nonrecurring expenses. However, in the 1980s and 1990s
companies have used restructuring charges as a way to manipulate their operating
earnings numbers. If a company records restructuring charges on a regular basis, the

---

[21] William C. Symonds, "Has Corning Won Its High-Tech Bet?" *Business Week,* April 5, 1999.
[22] P.B. Gray, "Bank America Agrees to Sell Headquarters," *The Wall Street Journal,* September 16, 1985.

analyst begins to question whether these charges are in fact a recurring operating expense of the company. For example, AT&T claimed that profits had grown annually by 10% from 1985 to 1994. Analysts began to question the profit numbers in 1996 when AT&T announced that the company would be taking a $4 billion restructuring charge, the fourth such charge in the past decade. The total of all restructuring charges taken since 1985 was $14.2 billion, which exceeded the total reported net earnings of $10.3 billion. When calculating the 10% growth rate, the restructuring charges were not considered because it was assumed they were one-time charges. Some descriptions of the charges in AT&T's financial statements sounded a bit too routine to consider these items as nonrecurring.[23]

Exhibit 1.4 presents a checklist for earnings quality that can alert the analyst to some of the key items to consider in the assessment of earnings quality. Appendix A

---

[23] R. Smith, and S. Lipin, "Are Companies Using Restructuring Costs to Fudge the Figures?" *The Wall Street Journal,* January 30, 1996.

EXHIBIT 1.4   A Checklist for Earnings Quality

I. Sales
   1. Allowance for doubtful accounts
   2. Price vs. volume changes
   3. Real vs. nominal growth

II. Cost of goods sold
   4. Cost flow assumption for inventory
   5. Base LIFO layer reductions
   6. Loss recognitions on write-downs of inventory (see also item 13)

III. Operating expenses
   7. Discretionary
       Research and development
       Repair and maintenance
       Advertising and marketing
   8. Depreciation (depletion, amortization)
       Methods
       Estimates
   9. Pension accounting—interest rate assumptions

IV. Nonoperating revenue and expense
   10. Gains (losses) from sales of assets
   11. Interest income
   12. Equity income
   13. Loss recognitions on write-downs of assets (see also item 6)
   14. Accounting changes
   15. Extraordinary items

V. Other Issues
   16. Material changes in number of shares outstanding
   17. Acquisitions and dispositions
   18. Reserves

provides a step-by-step guide to this checklist, with a discussion and illustration of each item.

Impact of Inflation

The historical cost principle of accounting is used to record transactions and to value balance sheet assets and liabilities. Inventory manufactured or purchased for sale is carried on the balance sheet at cost until a different price is established through an arms-length sales transaction. Buildings, machinery, and equipment are recorded at cost and valued on any balance sheet date at their original cost less accumulated depreciation. Land used in the business or held for investment also is valued at the original price paid, regardless of any changes in actual market value. Liabilities are measured by the amount of principal balance outstanding.

The historical cost principle forms the basis of our accounting system because it provides an objective and verifiable method of measurement. During a period of inflation, however, distortions occur in the valuation of assets and the determination of net income. Consider the example of the mountain discussed earlier in this chapter. The original purchase price was $50,000, and the equipment was expected to have a five-year useful life. At the end of year 1, using straight-line depreciation, the asset would be valued as follows:

Cost	$50,000
Less: accumulated depreciation	(10,000)
	$40,000

Depreciation expense would be $10,000 for the year. What if, during that year, the cost to replace the mountain had increased by 10%? The replacement cost would now be 10% higher, $50,000 × 1.10 = $55,000, and inflation-adjusted depreciation expense, based on new replacement cost, would be $10,000 × 1.10 = $11,000. If, at the end of 2 years, inflation had continued at a 10% rate, the asset value at replacement cost would be even further from the original cost. Bear in mind that a firm will continue to purchase new assets and replace old ones. The balance sheet fixed assets category thus reflects assets purchased over many years, with dollars of varying amounts of purchasing power.

To generalize, the balance sheet fixed asset accounts for many firms are understated because prices have risen since the assets were purchased and recorded. Depreciation expense is also understated because depreciation is a cost allocation based on the undervalued historical cost of fixed assets. The effect of inflation on inventory and cost of goods sold, the other major categories of potential inflationary impact, depends on the cost flow assumption used to value inventory (see chapter 2). During a period of inflation, a LIFO[24] company would have undervalued inventory on the balance sheet and currently valued cost of goods sold expense on the income statement, whereas use of FIFO produces an understated cost of goods sold and currently valued inventory. During a period of inflation, the net result—of understated depreci-

---

[24] The LIFO (last in, first out) method assumes that the last goods purchased are the first goods sold; during inflation, the higher cost goods are assumed to be sold first. Under FIFO (first in, first out), the first goods or older, lower cost goods are assumed to be sold first.

ation expense for most firms and understated cost of goods sold for companies that do not use LIFO—is an *overstatement of net income* in the earnings statements of most U.S. companies.

The impact of inflation is uneven. For capital-intensive industries with outdated plant and equipment—such as steel, autos, and paper—the toll taken by inflation has been tremendous. On the other hand, some industries—such as electronics, instruments, and computers—have been virtually unscathed by inflation.

The accounting rule makers wrestled for many years with the challenge of how to account for inflation. Reliance on historical cost renders statements that are objective and verifiable but, in some cases, not meaningful. If the relevant accounts are adjusted for inflation, however, there is controversy over how the adjustments should be made. The *general price level* approach (also called the *constant dollar* approach) adjusts each account by applying the change in a general price index, such as the CPI[25] to the historical cost of the asset. The *current cost* approach considers the specific price change of each asset. Since the general price level method is still based on historical cost, it is considered to be more objective, and it is also less costly and easier to apply because one index is used for all assets. On the other hand, current cost is probably more relevant and useful for analysts, but it is also a more subjective and costly approach, requiring estimates of current value.

In October 1979, the FASB issued for a five-year trial period FASB Statement No. 33, "Financial Reporting and Changing Prices." This statement required large ($1 billion of total assets or $125 million of inventories and gross property, plant, and equipment) publicly traded companies to disclose supplementary schedules to account for the impact of inflation on key balance sheet items and related income statement expenses. The data were supplementary to the primary financial statements and unaudited. In late 1986, the FASB issued Statement No. 89, "Financial Reporting and Changing Prices," which said that companies were no longer required to provide the supplementary disclosures mandated by FASB No. 33. Firms may choose to provide the data on a voluntary basis. Reasons given by the FASB for dropping the requirements were that research studies indicated the information was not widely used, and the costs to provide the data outweighed the benefits.

It should also be noted that the rate of inflation slowed, thus lessening the impact of inflation on earnings relative to the 1970s and reducing the pressure for inflation accounting disclosures. The financial statement user should continue to be aware, however, that any inflation distorts asset valuations and income recognition.

Missing and Hard-to-Find Information

Some of the facts needed to evaluate a company are not available in the financial statements. These include such intangibles as employee relations with management, the morale and efficiency of employees, the reputation of the firm with its customers, its prestige in the community, the effectiveness of management, provisions for management succession, and potential exposure to changes in regulations—such as environmental or

---

[25] The CPI, or consumer price index, is a weighted average of prices of consumer goods relative to base year.

food and drug enforcement. These qualities impact the firm's operating success both directly and indirectly but are difficult to quantify.

Publicity in the media, which affects public perception of a firm, can also impact its financial performance. Research has been conducted to measure the correlation between reputation of a company and its financial performance. Research firm Clark Martire & Bartolomeo found that total return and earnings growth were strongly correlated to reputation.[26] When the publicity is negative, companies often try to counter the damage as soon as possible. Coca-Cola's management moved aggressively in 1999 to offset news of a health scare in Belgium caused by contaminated Coke products. To mitigate the largest product recall in Coke's history, management launched a significant marketing and public relations campaign.[27] After dozens of passenger complaints were lodged against Northwest Airlines in January 1999, Congressman John D. Dingell requested the Secretary of Transportation to review the response of Northwest Airlines and the Wayne County Department of Airports to the January 2–3, 1999, snowstorm in Detroit, which resulted in the stranding of passengers on taxiways for up to eight hours. Actions taken by Northwest Airlines to address the problem included sending a letter of apology and a voucher for a free round trip ticket from Northwest for each passenger who experienced a ground delay of at least two hours while in Detroit on January 2 to 4.[28]

Some relevant facts are available in the financial statements but may be difficult for an average user to find. For example, the amount of long-term debt a firm has outstanding is disclosed on the face of the balance sheet in the noncurrent liability section. However, "long-term" could apply to debt due in 12.5 months or 2 years or 15 years. To determine when cash resources will be required to meet debt principal payments, the user must find and analyze the note to the financial statements on long-term debt with its listing of principal, interest, and maturity of a firm's long-term debt instruments.

All U.S. companies—large, small, public, private, financial, and nonfinancial—are now required by FASB Statement No. 107, "Disclosures about Fair Value of Financial Instruments," to disclose the market value of financial instruments—including receivables, payables, forward contracts, options, guaranties, and equity instruments. Firms are allowed to show this information either on the face of the balance sheet or in financial statement notes.

Many firms have turned toward using complicated financing schemes—leases, product financing arrangements, sales of receivables with recourse, limited partnerships, joint ventures—that do not have to be recorded on balance sheets. Disclosure of information about the extent, nature, and terms of off-balance sheet financing arrangements can be found (though often not easily) in the notes to the financial statements.

Another important form of supplementary information is that reported by diversified companies operating in several unrelated lines of business. These conglomerates

---

[26] Anne B. Fisher, "Corporate Reputations," *Fortune,* March 4, 1996.

[27] "Coca-Cola Says Sales, Case Volume Hurt," Yahoo! Headlines, June 30, 1999, www.yahoo.co.uk/headlines/19990630/business/0930757397-0000003597.html.

[28] Secretary of the Department of Transportation, *Report on the January 1999 Detroit Snowstorm,* June 1999.

report financial information for the consolidated entity on the face of its financial statements. For a breakdown of financial data by individual operating segments, the analyst must use information in notes to the financial statement. Beginning in 1998, companies must comply with FASB Statement No. 131, "Disclosures about Segments of an Enterprise and Related Information." (The analysis of segmental data is discussed in appendix B.)

There are numerous other examples of material that must be extracted from notes, supplementary schedules, or the management discussion and analysis section in order to interpret the financial statement numbers. The facts are there, but finding them may involve a search. The remaining material in this book is directed to helping the reader find and effectively use the information in financial statements and supplementary data.

SELF-TEST

Solutions are provided in appendix D.

_____ 1. What are the basic financial statements provided in an annual report?
  (a) Balance sheet and income statement.
  (b) Statement of financial earnings and statement of shareholders' equity.
  (c) Balance sheet, income statement, and statement of cash flows.
  (d) Balance sheet, income statement, statement of cash flows, and statement of retained earnings or statement of shareholders' equity.

_____ 2. What is the function of the statement of cash flows?
  (a) To provide information about cash receipts and payments during an accounting period.
  (b) To provide information about the operating, investing, and financing activities for an accounting period.
  (c) To reconcile the beginning and ending balance of all equity accounts.
  (d) Both (a) and (b)

_____ 3. What items are included in the notes to the financial statements?
  (a) Summary of accounting policies.
  (b) Changes in accounting policies, if any.
  (c) Detail about particular accounts.
  (d) All of the above.

_____ 4. What does an unqualified auditor's report indicate?
  (a) The financial statements unfairly and inaccurately present the company's financial position for the accounting period.
  (b) The financial statements present fairly the financial position, the results of operations, and the changes in cash flows for the company.
  (c) There are certain factors that might impair the firm's ability to continue as a going concern.
  (d) Certain managers within the firm are unqualified and, as such, are not fairly or adequately representing the interests of the shareholders.

_____ 5. Who hires the auditor?
  (a) The firm that is audited.
  (b) The auditor's accounting firm.

(c) The Financial Accounting Standards Board.

(d) The Securities and Exchange Commission.

_____ 6. What subject(s) should the management discussion and analysis section discuss?

(a) Liquidity.

(b) Commitments for capital expenditures.

(c) A breakdown of sales increases into price and volume components.

(d) All of the above.

_____ 7. What is the allocation of the cost of fixed assets called?

(a) Fixed cost allocation.

(b) Depreciation.

(c) Salvage value.

(d) Matching revenues and expenses.

_____ 8. Why could depreciation expense be considered a discretionary item?

(a) Management must estimate the useful life of the asset.

(b) A salvage value must be estimated.

(c) Management must select a method of depreciation.

(d) All of the above.

_____ 9. What do the choices and estimates relating to depreciation affect?

(a) Gross fixed assets on the balance sheet and depreciation expense on the income statement.

(b) Accumulated depreciation on the income statement and depreciation expense on the balance sheet.

(c) Net fixed assets on the balance sheet and depreciation expense on the income statement.

(d) Only net fixed assets on the balance sheet.

_____ 10. Which of the following statements is true?

(a) Published financial statements are prepared according to the cash basis of accounting.

(b) Published financial statements are prepared according to the accrual basis of accounting.

(c) Published financial statements may be prepared according to either the accrual or cash basis of accounting.

(d) Published financial statements must be prepared according to both the accrual and cash basis.

_____ 11. Why do some firms present two figures for earnings per share—basic and fully diluted?

(a) The auditor may believe that as a result of poor management, future earnings potential has been diluted, and, therefore, the firm should adjust current earnings per share to reflect this.

(b) The financial statements contain many accounting changes that affect income in the current year but not future earnings potential or cash flow. Therefore, net income is adjusted for these items and referred to as fully diluted.

(c) The firm has a complex capital structure with convertible securities, stock options, and warrants, which may represent potential "dilution" of earnings per share.

(d) The firm expects to issue more stock within the next year that will lower earnings per share.

_____ 12. Which balance sheet account is used to reconcile the differences that arise because of temporary differences in tax actually paid to the IRS and income tax expense reported in the income statement?
  (a) Taxes payable.
  (b) Deferred taxes.
  (c) Taxes receivable.
  (d) Tax adjustment liability.

_____ 13. Why might the use of accelerated depreciation rather than straight-line depreciation produce earnings of higher quality?
  (a) Accelerated depreciation more accurately reflects financial reality because higher depreciation expense would be taken in the early years of its productive period.
  (b) During inflationary periods, rising prices increase replacement costs of most assets, resulting in an understatement of depreciation based on historical cost.
  (c) Both (a) and (b).
  (d) None of the above.

_____ 14. Which of the following are methods by which management can manipulate earnings and possibly lower the quality of reported earnings?
  (a) Changing an accounting policy to increase earnings.
  (b) Refusing to take a loss on inventory in an accounting period when the inventory is known to be obsolete.
  (c) Decreasing discretionary expenses.
  (d) All of the above.

_____ 15. Which of these statements is true during periods of inflation?
  (a) Depreciation expense tends to be understated.
  (b) Depreciation expense tends to be overstated.
  (c) The firm should change the method it uses to account for depreciation.
  (d) Gross fixed assets are overstated.

_____ 16. Which section or pieces of information can be ignored when analyzing financial statements?
  (a) Auditor's report.
  (b) Management discussion and analysis.
  (c) The statement of cash flows.
  (d) None of the above.

17. Where would you find the following information?
_____   (1) An attestation to the fairness of financial statements.
_____   (2) Summary of significant accounting policies.
_____   (3) Cash flow from operating, financing, and investing activities.
_____   (4) A qualified opinion.
_____   (5) Information about principal, interest, and maturity of long-term debt.
_____   (6) Financial position on a particular date.
_____   (7) Discussion of the company's results of operations.
_____   (8) Description of pension plans.
_____   (9) Anticipated commitments for capital expenditures.
_____   (10) Reconciliation of beginning and ending balances of equity accounts.
        (a) Financial statements.
        (b) Notes to the financial statements.

    (c) Auditor's report.

    (d) Management discussion and analysis.

STUDY QUESTIONS AND PROBLEMS

1.1 What is the difference between an annual report and a 10-K report?

1.2 What are the particular items an analyst should review and study in an annual report, and what material should be avoided?

1.3 What causes an auditor's report to be qualified? adverse? a disclaimer of opinion? unqualified with explanatory language?

1.4 Why is depreciation expense not a precise measure of the annual outflow associated with capital assets?

1.5 What is meant by keeping "two sets of books," and what is the significance to the financial statement analyst?

1.6 How has inflation caused distortion of financial statements?

1.7 What are the intangible factors that are important in evaluating a company's financial position and performance but are not available in the annual report?

1.8 Timber Products recently purchased new machinery at a cost of $450,000. Management estimates that the equipment will have a useful life of 15 years and no salvage value at the end of the period. If the straight-line depreciation method is used for financial reporting, calculate:

    (a) Annual depreciation expense.

    (b) Accumulated depreciation at the end of year 1 and year 2.

    (c) The balance sheet account: fixed assets (net), at the end of year 1 and year 2.

    Assume depreciation expense for tax purposes in year 1 is $45,000 and that the firm's tax rate is 30%.

    (d) By how much will depreciation expense reported for tax purposes in year 1 exceed depreciation expense reported in the financial statements in year 1?

    (e) What is the difference between taxes actually paid in year 1 and tax expense reported in the financial statements in year 1?

1.9 R-M Corp.—An earnings quality problem.

C. Stern, chief financial officer of R-M Corp., has just reviewed the current year's third-quarter financial results with company president R. Macon. R-M Corp. sets an annual target for earnings growth of 12%. It now appears likely that the company will fall short of that goal and achieve only a 9% increase in earnings. This would have a potentially detrimental impact of the firm's stock price. Macon has directed Stern to develop alternative plans to stimulate earnings during the last quarter in order to reach the 12% target.

Stern has approached you, a recent finance graduate of a well-known southwestern business school, to make recommendations for meeting the firm's earnings growth objective during the current year.

Discuss techniques that could be used to increase earnings. Differentiate between those that would

    (a) Increase earnings but lower quality of reported earnings.

    (b) Increase earnings and also have a positive "real" impact on the firm's financial position.

1.10 Writing Skills Problem

Staff members from the marketing department of your firm are doing a splendid job selling products to customers. Many of the customers are so pleased, in fact, they are also buying shares in the company's stock, which means that they receive a copy of the firm's annual report. Unfortunately, questions sometimes arise that the marketing staff members are woefully inadequate at answering. Technical questions about the firm's financial condition and performance are referred to the chief financial officer, but the director of marketing has asked you to write a memo in which you explain the key elements in an annual report so that marketing representatives are better prepared to respond to questions of a more general nature.

Required: Write a memo no longer than one page (single-spaced, double-spaced between paragraphs) in which you describe the contents of an annual report so that marketing personnel can understand the basic requirements. The memo should be dated and addressed to B. R. Neal, Director of Marketing, from you; the subject is "Contents of an Annual Report."

To the Student: In business writing, the primary elements are *clarity* and *conciseness*. You must keep in mind the audience you are addressing and the objective of the communication.

1.11 Internet Problem

Arthur Levitt, Chairman of the SEC, gave a speech entitled "The Numbers Game" on September 28, 1998, at the New York University Center for Law and Business. The complete text of the Levitt speech is available at (www.prenhall.com/fraser). Read the speech and then answer the following questions:

(a) What is earnings management?

(b) Why do companies employ earnings management techniques?

(c) Describe five popular techniques used by companies that Levitt believes are illusions. Do you know of companies that have used these techniques?

(d) What recommendations does Levitt propose to address the problems created by earnings management?

(e) What concerns does Levitt have with regard to the auditing process? What remedies to this problem does he suggest? Do you believe these remedies will be effective? Why or why not?

1.12 Annual Report Problem

The 1998 PETsMART Annual Report can be found at the following Web site: www.prenhall.com/fraser

Using the annual report, answer the following questions:

(a) Describe the type of business in which PETsMART operates. Discuss the competition that exists in this industry and identify any companies that might be competitors of PETsMART.

(b) What type of audit opinion was given for the financial statements of PETsMART? Explain the key items discussed in the audit report.

(c) Read the Management Discussion and Analysis (MD&A). Discuss whether the items that should be discussed in the MD&A are included. Support your answer with examples from the PETsMART MD&A.

(d) After reading the MD&A, discuss the future prospects of PETsMART. Do you have any concerns? If so, describe those concerns.

La-Z-Boy Mini-Case

La-Z-Boy is the nation's leading manufacturer of upholstered seating, and the third largest manufacturer of residential furniture overall. Most La-Z-Boy furniture retails in a broad middle-price range. La-Z-Boy operates 24 plants in the United States and Canada. Excerpts from the 1994 and 1995 Management Discussion and Analysis are on pages 38–42.

REQUIRED:

1. Discuss the future outlook and the goals La-Z-Boy has set for itself in the 1994 Management Discussion and Analysis.
2. Compare the 1995 Management Discussion and Analysis to the 1994 outlook. Has La-Z-Boy achieved the goals it set forth in 1994? Explain.
3. Discuss the quality of the La-Z-Boy Management Discussion and Analysis for 1994 and 1995.

1994—MANAGEMENT DISCUSSION AND ANALYSIS

La-Z-Boy's market share of all U.S. upholstery furniture products is above 8%.

On the basis of available market share data (in dollars), La-Z-Boy has 30–35% of the U.S. single-seat recliner market and is the world's largest recliner manufacturer. (The next largest U.S. competitor holds roughly 20% of the U.S. market.) La-Z-Boy's sleep sofa current market share, approximately 12%, has been growing over the last three years.

Market share data by individual product lines other than recliners and sleepers (e.g., sofas, reclining sofas, wood bedroom and dining room, wood occasional, etc.) indicate that, although La-Z-Boy does not have a market share above 10% in any one line, the Company's market share has been growing over the last three years in most lines.

Outlook

La-Z-Boy's 1995 fiscal year to end April 29, 1995 will include 52 weeks compared to fiscal year 1994, which included 53 weeks. This is approximately a 2% reduction in the length of the year which will affect sales and other financial comparisons from year to year.

The Company expects the economic recovery to continue through calendar year 1994. Sales in fiscal year 1995 are expected to exceed the 1994 results but due to the stronger than expected year in 1994, the double-digit sales increase experienced in 1994 is not expected to repeat.

One of La-Z-Boy's financial objectives is to achieve sales increases of 10% per year or increases at least greater than that of the furniture industry. Some furniture industry forecasts for calendar year 1994 over 1993 are in the 5–7% range. For 1994, La-Z-Boy sales increased 18% over 1993.

The Company's major residential efforts and opportunities for sales growth greater than industry averages are focused outside the recliner market segment; e.g., stationary upholstery (single and multi-seat), reclining sofas and modulars, wood occasional and wall units and wood bedroom and dining room.

The newly formed La-Z-Boy Contract Furniture Group sales growth rate in the next few years is expected to exceed the average of the other divisions. Today, this division is not generating a profit and profits are not expected to improve in 1995 due to large research and development expenditures, reorganization costs and startup costs associated with the recent merger of the two formerly separate contract divisions. Eventually, profit margins comparable to the Company's average rates are believed to be able to be achieved. Profitability at this level would help the Company reach the financial goals described below even though this division is not large enough to dramatically affect the results.

A second financial goal is to improve operating profit as a percent of sales in 1995 compared to 1994. For 1994, the operating profit margin was 7.5% of sales.

A third goal is to achieve operating profit, interest income and other income (return) as a percent of beginning of the year capital of 20%. For 1994, return on capital was 19.4%.

La-Z-Boy has an opportunity to improve its margin through increases in efficiency, improvements in the utilization of equipment and facilities and increases in sales volumes, even though product line growth may be in lines with lower gross margins.

Capital expenditures are forecast to be approximately $19 to $24 million in 1995 compared to $17.5 million in 1994. The 1995 forecast includes the construction of a new upholstery factory in Arkansas. The 396,000 square foot plant is being constructed to replace an existing older 200,000 square foot plant. Long term financing of the expected $7 million cost is planned to be through the use of industrial revenue bonds.

The effect of environmental costs on future financial results is not subject to reasonable estimation. However, management does not anticipate that they will have a material adverse effect.

Analysis of Operations
Year Ended April 29, 1995
(1995 compared with 1994)

La-Z-Boy's sales increased 6% in fiscal 1995 over 1994. However, on a comparable per-week basis, the increase was 8% due to 1995 containing 52 weeks compared to 53 weeks in 1994. La-Z-Boy believes the increase was primarily the result of the general economic recovery. Selling price increases were generally in the 2–3% range with the remainder of the sales increase due to volume. Major product lines that experienced growth above the Company average were the lower-end recliners, modulars, tables and wall units (wood and other), and sofas.

All sales growth over the past seven years has been internally generated. The 1995 sales on a per-week basis increased over 1994 at all five operating divisions with particular strength at Hammary.

The 1995 gross margin (gross profit dollars as a percent of sales) of 26.0% declined from the 26.2% gross margin in 1994. The favorable impacts of selling price increases and improved plant efficiency at most plants were offset by cost increases relating to leather, fabric, cartoning and premium (not frame stock) lumber. Product line mix changes toward products with lower gross margins also continued in 1995. In addition, the gross margins for the contract and Canadian divisions were below the prior year.

The contract decline was largely due to incentives and costs associated with the introduction of new products. The Canadian decline was primarily due to the unfavorable Canadian/U.S. dollar exchange rate along with product line mix changes toward products with lower gross margins.

The 1995 S, G & A expense of 18.6% was down slightly from 18.8% in 1994. Advertising expense increased in 1995 primarily due to the launch of a national television advertising program. A reduction in bad debt expense in 1995 partially offset the advertising increase.

As expected, the La-Z-Boy Contract Furniture Group did not generate a profit in 1995. This division was formed in 1994 through the merger of two former divisions. In addition to the gross margin effects discussed above, the division incurred increased research and development expenditures, reorganization costs and startup costs associated with the merger.

Income tax expense as a percent of pretax income increased to 41.5% in 1995 from 40.3% in 1994. The increase was primarily due to changes in profitability among divisions which were partially offset by some favorable adjustments relating to the 1994 change in accounting for income taxes.

Liquidity and Financial Condition

Effective April 29, 1995, La-Z-Boy acquired England/Corsair Inc., a manufacturer of upholstered furniture. Payment was in the form of La-Z-Boy common stock, cash and notes, with additional incentives available during each of the next two years if England/Corsair exceeds certain profit targets. England/Corsair employs approximately 1,500 employees at its six manufacturing facilities and generates annual sales in excess of $100 million.

Cash flows from operations amounted to $40 million in 1995, $28 million in 1994 and $35 million in 1993 and have usually been adequate for day-to-day expenditures, dividends to shareholders and capital expenditures.

Capital expenditures were $19.0 million in 1995 compared to $17.5 million in 1994 and $12.2 million in 1993. Some capacity expansions occurred in 1995 and 1994 while 1993 did not require expansions. Capacity utilization was approximately 70% at the end of 1995 and 1994.

In 1995, La-Z-Boy obtained $7.5 million through the sale of an industrial revenue bond. The proceeds were used to construct a new plant in Siloam Springs, Arkansas. Retirements of debt totaled between $1 million and $7 million for each of the last three years and were primarily related to paying down the $53 million debt incurred in 1987 to acquire an operating division.

To acquire England/Corsair, La-Z-Boy issued $10.0 million of notes to the former shareholders payable in annual installments over the next four years. England/Corsair's debt of $7.4 million and capital lease obligations of $7.0 million were assumed by La-Z-Boy as of April 29, 1995.

La-Z-Boy is subject to contingencies pursuant to environmental laws and regulations. La-Z-Boy accrues for certain environmental remediation activities related to past operations including Superfund clean-up and Resource Conservation and Recovery Act (RCRA) compliance activities, for which commitments have been made and reasonable cost estimates are possible. La-Z-Boy has been identified as a

Potentially Responsible Party (PRP) at two clean-up sites: Organic Chemical and Seaboard Chemical Company. At each site, La-Z-Boy has been identified as a de minimus contributor and volumetric assessments indicate that La-Z-Boy's contributions to each site have been less than 0.1% of the total. Each site has either completed or has begun the first phase of clean-up. The total clean-up costs expected to be incurred at each site have not yet been accurately estimated, and await the results of the currently ongoing remedial investigation/feasibility studies. La-Z-Boy is also participating with a number of other companies in the voluntary RCRA closure of the Caldwell Systems site. La-Z-Boy's volumetric assessment at this site is in the 1% range. The Steering Committee responsible for negotiating the clean-up plan with the EPA has recently reinitiated its negotiations in anticipation of clean-up activities. Estimates of the clean-up costs at the Caldwell site are being developed. The number of PRP's and voluntary participants at the three sites range from 182 to in excess of 1,750. Based on a review of the number, composition and financial stability of the PRP's and voluntary participants at each site, along with clean-up costs already expended and the preliminary estimates currently available, management does not believe that any significant risk exists that La-Z-Boy will be required to incur total costs in excess of $100,000 at any of the sites. At April 29, 1995, a total of $300,000 has been accrued with respect to these three sites. La-Z-Boy is also conducting voluntary compliance audits at La-Z-Boy owned facilities.

Outlook

England/Corsair results will be included in the 1996 Consolidated Statement of Income. The combination of England/Corsair sales with anticipated growth in the other divisions is expected to push 1996 sales over the $1 billion level.

One of La-Z-Boy's financial goals is to achieve sales increases of 10% per year or increases at least greater than that of the furniture industry. Some furniture industry forecasts for calendar year 1995 over 1994 are in the 2–3% range. For 1995, La-Z-Boy sales increased 8% over 1994 on a comparable per-week basis while the industry may have increased approximately 6–9%.

The Company's major residential efforts and opportunities for sales growth greater than industry averages are focused outside the recliner market segment, e.g., stationary upholstery (single and multi-seat), reclining sofas and modulars, wood occasional and wall units and wood bedroom and dining room.

The number of proprietary stores is expected to increase in 1996 for all divisions and is a major contributor to La-Z-Boy's ability to achieve its sales goal.

During the fourth quarter of 1995, the Company began to experience a reduction in the backlog of orders compared to the prior year. As a result, sales in the first quarter of 1996 may be flat or below 1995's first quarter sales on a comparable basis excluding England/Corsair.

The La-Z-Boy Contract Furniture Group sales growth rate in the next few years is expected to exceed the average of the other divisions.

A second financial goal is to improve operating profit as a percent of sales in 1996 compared to 1995. For 1995, the operating profit margin was 7.4% of sales which matched the prior year. Achieving this goal in 1996 may be difficult partly due to the inclusion of England/Corsair which in recent years has had an operating profit margin below the Company average, but above 4.0% and a company wide projected slowing of sales growth.

A third goal is to achieve a 20% return on capital (operating profit, interest income and other income as a percent of beginning of the year capital) in 1996. For 1995, return on capital was 18.9% which was a decline from the 1994 return of 19.1%. This goal has been in place for several years and will be more difficult to achieve in the future partly due to the recent addition of capital relating to the England/Corsair acquisition.

La-Z-Boy has an opportunity to improve its margins through increases in efficiency, improvements in the utilization of equipment and facilities and increases in sales volumes, even though sales growth may be in product lines with lower gross margins and advertising expenses are expected to increase.

Capital expenditures are forecast to be approximately $18 to $22 million in 1996 compared to $19 million in 1995.

For a number of years, the La-Z-Boy Contract Furniture Group has not generated an operating profit. Management feels the division must simplify the product mix and reduce SKU's to improve service, quality and delivery lead time. Eventually, profit margins comparable to the Company's average rates are believed to be achievable. Profitability at this level would help the Company reach the financial goals described previously even though this division is not large enough to dramatically affect the consolidated results. Given no recession, no major competitive environment changes, no major strategic changes and other similar assumptions, the La-Z-Boy Contract Furniture Group's profitability is expected to improve in 1996 and the division is expected to begin generating an operating profit between 1997 and 1998.

Chambers Development Company Mini-Case

Chambers Development Company is a provider of integrated solid waste management services in the United States. The following excerpts are provided from the Chambers Development Company's 1989 and 1991 annual reports.

1989—MANAGEMENT DISCUSSION AND ANALYSIS

Financial Overview

The company continued its record of strong performance and growth in 1989 as net sales increased 32.7% over the prior year, following a 133.1% increase in 1988 over 1987. Net income in 1989 was $27.1 million, up from $20.7 million in 1988 and $10 million in 1987. Similar achievements were reflected in the company's fully diluted earnings per share, which increased from $ .44 in 1987 to $ .86 in 1988 to $1.03 in 1989.

Additionally, the company has enhanced its financial position in recent years with a number of debt and equity transactions.

Results of Operations

Net sales increased to $181.9 million in 1989, up from $137 million in 1988 and $58.8 million in 1987. Waste services continued to represent an increasing percentage of the company's net sales, providing 65.0%, 87.1%, and 89.7% of total net sales in 1987, 1988, and 1989, respectively. Net sales from the waste services segment reached a record level of $163.1 million in 1989, an increase of 36.7% over 1988, following a 212.2% increase in 1988 over 1987. Security services sales rebounded from a 14.0% decrease from 1987 to 1988, to increase by 6.3% to $18.8 million in 1989.

The increases in waste services net sales reflect a number of positive factors. The largest single factor in 1988 was the commencement of operations at two transfer stations in Morris County, New Jersey. These transfer stations opened in January 1988, and produced $44.9 million in net sales during the year. Full year operations under the company's waste disposal contracts entered into in late 1987 relating to Passaic, Essex and Union Counties in New Jersey, together with transportation revenues from Union and Essex Counties, constituted an additional $22.3 million of the 1988 increase in net sales. To a lesser degree, acquisitions, other new contracts, and price increases under existing commercial and residential contracts and at the company's landfills also contributed to the increase.

During 1989, volume growth accounted for a 16.8% increase in waste services net sales over the prior year, with price increases and acquisitions accounting for 10.9% and 9.0%, respectively. The company's contract to transport waste from Essex County, New Jersey, which began in December 1988, was the largest contributor to the volume growth. Net sales from the disposal contract with Passaic County, New Jersey also contributed to the volume increase. Combined net sales generated from both the Morris County transfer stations and the New Jersey contracts described above totaled $86.7 million in 1989. These contracts, although of limited duration, should provide the company with significant sales for the next several years. The company was informed, however, that the planned waste-to-energy facility in Essex County may commence operation in late 1990; when that facility opens, the company's contracts in Essex County are expected to terminate. Other factors contributing to the Company's internal growth were new collection, transportation, and disposal service contracts with commercial and municipal entities and increased utilization of the company's landfill capacities.

The increase in waste services net sales in 1989 due to acquisitions reflects 14 new collection, hauling, and recycling businesses. The company's corporate development activities continue to focus on prudent expansion into new market territories, the improvement of market share in existing areas, and the enhancement of complementary landfill and hauling activities. The impact of price increases on waste services net sales in 1989 primarily reflects the passing through to the customer of higher disposal costs (as discussed more fully below) and scheduled contractual price increases.

In a significant event affecting future net sales, during 1989, the company and Morris County, New Jersey executed an agreement concerning the settlement of the proceedings before the New Jersey Office of Administrative Law establishing rates for the company's services at its two transfer stations in Morris County. Under the terms of the agreement, the company will provide a rate reduction from $122 to $118 per ton of municipal solid waste beginning in 1990; the rate will be increased to $125 per ton in 1991 and $132 per ton in 1992. Under the settlement, which is subject to certain regulatory approvals, the company will continue to operate the transfer stations through 1994, an extension of two years over the original contract, unless the County's planned resource recovery facility has commenced operations. The extension of these operations allows the company to recover certain costs associated with the transfer stations over an extended life. If the regulatory approvals are not received, the company will be entitled to resume the rate establishment proceedings.

The increase in security services sales in 1989 is due primarily to the acquisition of seven security services companies during the year and the company's emphasis on an improved marketing program. The acquisitions accounted for an 18.4% increase in security net sales, which more than offset the 9.6% decrease due to the decline in nuclear security services. Nuclear security net sales decreased from 1987 to 1988 and again in 1989 due to a reduction in services provided to Duquesne Light Company resulting from the winding down of construction, and final completion during 1988, at its Beaver Valley Nuclear Power Station #2.

Operating expenses increased 28.9% in 1989 over 1988, following a 167.8% increase over 1987. The increases in both 1988 and 1989 primarily resulted from operations at the two transfer stations in Morris County, New Jersey. Operating expenses at these transfer stations exceed those at most of the company's facilities, largely due to higher disposal costs paid to third parties. Additionally, increased volume in 1989 from the Passaic and Union County disposal contracts and the temporary disposal of certain waste at third-party landfills contributed to the overall increase in operating expenses. The company believes that disposal cost increases are likely to continue in future years, largely attributable to the increasing scarcity of landfill airspace, the higher costs associated with environmental compliance, and landfill closure and post-closure requirements. The company believes that these increased costs can be recovered through increased prices and a continued strategy of developing and operating regional sanitary landfills.

Selling, general, and administrative expenses as a percentage of net sales decreased to 11.7% in 1989 from 13.1% in 1988 and 17.0% in 1987, due largely to the increase in net sales associated with the New Jersey waste disposal and transportation operations, which required proportionately lower levels of indirect and overhead costs. Additionally, volume and price increases permitted certain fixed components of selling, general, and administrative expenses to be spread over an expanded revenue base.

Depreciation and amortization expense has remained relatively constant as a percentage of sales; while increasing in dollar amount by 42.7% in 1989 and 121.4% in 1988. Due to continuing changes in environmental regulations, the costs to develop environmentally safe landfills have risen dramatically. These increased costs are reflected in the company's significant investment in the construction and expansion of its sanitary landfills and the resulting depreciation.

As a result of the factors discussed above, earnings from operations increased by $13 million, or 51.3%, from 1988 to 1989, and by $12.4 million, or 96.0%, from 1987 to 1988.

Interest expense, primarily attributable to the waste services segment, increased 54.9% from $0.5 million in 1987 to $0.7 million in 1988, and increased 86.0% to $1.3 million in 1989. The increase in 1989 was due to the issuance of the 6 3/4% Debentures. The level of interest expense for each year was substantially less than actual interest charges as a result of interest capitalization related to the company's development of its sanitary landfills. The increase in total interest charges as a result of higher levels of long-term obligations reflects the company's acquisition strategy and expansion into new geographical areas, the upgrading and additional purchases of equipment used in collection, hauling and recycling services, and the substantial investment in developing existing and newly acquired landfills.

LIQUIDITY AND CAPITAL RESOURCES

The company continually evaluates the cash flows necessary to develop existing and proposed sanitary landfills, to acquire additional solid waste and security businesses, and to fund property, equipment and associated needs for internal expansion. Based on its evaluation, in April 1989, the company completed a public offering of 2,750,000 shares of its Class A Common Stock, which provided $64.9 million in net proceeds to the company. Part of the proceeds were used to retire $35 million in outstanding indebtedness under the company's revolving credit agreement. The balance was added to working capital to be used for general corporate purposes and capital expenditures, including acquisitions.

On September 28, 1989, the company issued $110 million of 6 3/4% Debentures, which are convertible into shares of Class A Common Stock at a conversion price of $42.25 per share.

During 1989, the net proceeds of the financing activities described above and the net cash provided by operations totaled $220.2 million, which more than offset the $145.8 million utilized for net capital expenditures, acquisitions of businesses and other investing activities. During 1989, the company expended $62.8 million for the continuing development of its sanitary landfills and $10 million to obtain hauling, collection, and recycling vehicles and equipment.

The company currently anticipates expending $120 to $140 million in 1990 for the development of its existing and proposed sanitary landfills and in connection with the acquisition of solid waste and security businesses and other property and equipment. The company's anticipated capital expenditures for landfill development and related environmental matters, are however, for several reasons, extremely difficult to quantify. A number of uncertainties are inherent in the waste management industry, including such matters as changing laws and regulations which may require upgrading or corrective actions at landfills, competitive bidding processes for major contracts, possible delays or difficulties in permitting existing and proposed facilities, potential local opposition to siting of waste disposal facilities, and difficulties in predicting the outcome of acquisition negotiations.

With continuing changes in environmental regulations, the costs to develop environmentally safe landfills have increased dramatically and are expected to continue increasing as more states enact or revise such regulations. The company, like others in the industry, cannot predict with certainty whether particular proposed projects will result in revenue-producing operations, despite substantial expenditures in developing such projects. The permitting process for landfills is often lengthy and subject to intense public and regulatory scrutiny, thereby placing a premium on financial flexibility to enable the company to develop those projects which become viable.

In order to maintain that flexibility, the company is continually evaluating its anticipated cash flow needs. In both 1988 and 1989, the company completed several substantial debt and equity financings in both public and private markets, as discussed in the preceding paragraphs, to enable it to continue its growth. The company's long-range capital requirements are expected to be met by a combination of debt and equity placements, together with utilization of existing credit facilities and cash provided by operating activities.

1991—REPORT OF INDEPENDENT AUDITORS

To the Board of Directors and Stockholders of Chambers Development Company, Inc.:

We have audited the accompanying consolidated balance sheets of Chambers Development Company, Inc. and subsidiaries as of December 31, 1991 and 1990, and the related consolidated statements of operations, stockholders' equity and cash flows for each of the three years in the period ended December 31, 1991. These financial statements are the responsibility of the Company's management. Our responsibility is to express an opinion on these financial statements based on our audits.

We conducted our audits in accordance with generally accepted auditing standards. Those standards require that we plan and perform the audit to obtain reasonable assurance about whether the financial statements are free of material misstatement. An audit includes examining, on a test basis, evidence supporting the amounts and disclosures in the financial statements. An audit also includes assessing the accounting principles used and significant estimates made by management, as well as evaluating the overall financial statement presentation. We believe that our audits provide a reasonable basis for our opinion.

In our opinion, such consolidated financial statements present fairly, in all material respects, the financial position of Chambers Development Company, Inc. and subsidiaries as of December 31, 1991 and 1990 and the results of their operations and their cash flows for each of the three years in the period ended December 31, 1991 in conformity with generally accepted accounting principles.

As discussed in Note B to the consolidated financial statements, the accompanying consolidated financial statements for 1990 and 1989 have been restated.

As discussed in Note P to the consolidated financial statements, certain actions have been brought under federal and state securities laws against the Company, certain of its present and former officers and directors, and others alleging, among other things, misrepresentation by the Company of its earnings and financial condition. The outcome of these actions is not presently determinable. Accordingly, no provision for any liability that may result from these actions has been made in the accompanying consolidated financial statements.

Deloitte & Touche
Pittsburgh, Pennsylvania
December 23, 1992

1991—INTRODUCTION TO ANNUAL REPORT

On February 5, 1992, Chambers Development Company, Inc. (the "Company"), originally announced its financial results for the year ended December 31, 1991. On March 17, 1992, the Company announced a change in its accounting method with respect to capitalization of certain costs and expenses which resulted in a revision of previously-announced financial results for the year ended December 31, 1991. On April 15, 1992, the Company dismissed its then current auditors, Grant Thornton, and retained Deloitte & Touche to audit its consolidated financial statements for the year ended December 31, 1991 and in July, 1992, engaged Deloitte & Touche to audit the Company's consolidated financial statements for the years ended December 31, 1990 and 1989. On October 20, 1992, the Company announced a restatement of its previously reported financial results for 1991 and prior years, and a reduction of $362 million in both earnings originally reported since its inception and retained earnings at December 31, 1991. Deloitte & Touche has now completed its audits of the Company's consolidated financial statements for the years ended December 31, 1991, 1990 and 1989, thus enabling the Company to file this report on Form 10-K with the Securities and Exchange Commission.

As a result of certain of the events referred to in the preceding paragraph, the Company was not in compliance with certain covenants of its various long-term borrowing agreements. The Company has obtained interim waivers of the defaults and is negotiating with the lenders for a comprehensive amendment of the agreements. While the Company is making every effort to negotiate a longer-term transaction, and management of the Company believes that a satisfactory agreement will be reached, there is no assurance that such a resolution will be achieved. In the absence of such an agreement, or in the alternate, a restructuring or refinancing of its principal borrowing agreements, the liquidity and business of the Company would be materially adversely affected. The Company has also become a defendant in litigation arising out of certain of the events described in the preceding paragraph. An unfavorable result in that litigation could have a material adverse effect on the Company.

1991—SUMMARY OF RESTATEMENT

A summary of the cumulative effect on retained earnings through December 31, 1991 and 1990 of these revisions is as follows (in millions):

	1991	*1990*
Reduction in property and equipment	$362	$230
Reduction in intangible assets	43	26
Reduction in deferred costs	28	22
Reduction in provision for income taxes	(76)	(45)
Other, principally increase in accrued closure and postclosure costs	5	7
Cumulative reduction in retained earnings	$362	$240

Details of the Restatement

Certain of the aforementioned capitalized amounts were originally recorded as assets on the basis that they resulted from, or were indirectly related to, permitting and construction activities at the Company's landfills. In particular, the Company had capitalized certain operating costs which were incurred between 1988 and 1991 when various Pennsylvania sites, due to repermitting and construction activities, had their operations substantially reduced in terms of service capacity to the Company's collection and hauling operations and the Company's long-term disposal agreements with third parties. During the period of repermitting, the Company was required, pursuant to the 1988 Pennsylvania regulations, to cease or substantially alter its operations at existing Pennsylvania facilities to implement new construction standards, to add additional monitoring for methane gas, and to implement the new leachate treatment and disposal provisions. These actions also required costly nonrecurring expenditures in the Company's collection and hauling operations, as certain of the vehicles and waste streams of the Company were redirected and rerouted to alternate landfill sites, both Company-owned and external. It is the view of the Company that, but for the repermitting and construction activities on the Pennsylvania sites which were necessary to continue the operations of such sites into future periods, the operating costs and expenses would not have been incurred.

The Pennsylvania sites have now been fully repermitted and are operational, and the Company does not anticipate the incurrence of similar costs in the future.

Other amounts originally capitalized or deferred that have been retroactively charged to costs and expenses included interest on the aforementioned amounts capitalized as property, that have been restated as charges to costs and expenses, as well as interest on property during periods when it was ready for its intended use, although not placed in service at utilization levels consistent with full design capacity.

The retroactive charges to costs and expenses also include compensation and related costs of certain regional and corporate office personnel, including engineering, legal, executive and development personnel, whose activities pertained, in part, to the permitting and construction of landfills and to the development of new businesses. During the audits recently completed, the Company determined that there were not sufficient contemporaneously prepared documents that would enable the Company to determine accurately the amounts appropriate to capitalize or defer. If adequate records were available to support the capitalization or deferral of the costs that were related to construction and other activities of these personnel, the amounts so supported would have been included on the consolidated balance sheets in accordance with generally accepted accounting principles.

REQUIRED:

1. Why is the Management Discussion and Analysis section of the annual report useful to the financial analyst? What types of information can be found in this section?
2. Using the excerpts from the 1989 Management Discussion and Analysis section of the Chambers Development Company annual report, evaluate the presentation provided. Has the company discussed the types of information that should

be found in this section? Based on this section only, what is your assessment of the prospects for this company?

3. Is the opinion in the 1991 auditor's report unqualified, qualified, adverse or a disclaimer of opinion? Explain.

4. Based on the material provided from the 1991 annual report, discuss the quality of financial reporting for Chambers Development Company. Which items might concern a prospective investor?

CHAPTER

2

The Balance Sheet

Old accountants never die;
they just lose their balance.

—ANONYMOUS

A balance sheet, also called the statement of condition or statement of financial position, provides a wealth of valuable information about a business firm, particularly when examined over a period of several years and evaluated in relation to the other financial statements. A prerequisite to learning what the balance sheet can teach us, however, is a fundamental understanding of the accounts in the statement and the relationship of each account to the financial statements as a whole.

Consider, for example, the balance sheet *inventory* account. Inventory is an important component of liquidity analysis, which considers the ability of a firm to meet cash needs as they arise. (Liquidity analysis will be discussed in chapter 5.) Any measure of liquidity that includes inventory as a component would be meaningless without a general understanding of how the balance sheet inventory amount is derived. This chapter will thus cover such issues as what inventories are, how the inventory balance is affected by accounting policies, why companies choose and sometimes change methods of inventory valuation, where to find disclosures regarding inventory accounting, and how this one account contributes to the overall measurement of a company's financial condition and operating performance. This step-by-step descriptive treatment of inventories and other balance sheet accounts will provide the background necessary to analyze and interpret balance sheet information.

Financial Condition

The balance sheet shows the financial condition or financial position of a company *on a particular date*. The statement is a summary of what the firm *owns* (assets) and what the firm *owes* to outsiders (liabilities) and to internal owners (stockholders' equity). By definition, the account balances on a balance sheet must balance; that is, the total of all assets must equal the sum of liabilities and stockholders' equity. The balancing equation is expressed as:

$$\text{Assets} = \text{Liabilities} + \text{Stockholders' equity}$$

This chapter will cover account by account the consolidated balance sheet of Recreational Equipment and Clothing, Inc. (R.E.C. Inc.) (Exhibit 2.1.).

This particular firm sells recreational products through retail outlets, some owned and some leased, in cities located throughout the southwestern United States. Although the accounts on a balance sheet will vary somewhat by firm and by industry, those described in this chapter will be common to most companies.

CONSOLIDATION

Note first that the statements are "consolidated" for R.E.C. Inc. and subsidiaries. When a parent owns more than 50% of the voting stock of a subsidiary, the financial statements are combined for the companies in spite of the fact that they are separate legal entities. The statements are consolidated because the companies are *in substance* one company, given the proportion of control by the parent. In the case of R.E.C. Inc., the subsidiaries are wholly owned, which means that the parent controls 100% of the voting shares of the subsidiaries. Where less than 100% ownership exists, there are accounts in the consolidated balance sheet and income statement to reflect the minority interest in net assets and income.

BALANCE SHEET DATE

The balance sheet is prepared at a point in time at the end of an accounting period, a year, or a quarter. Most companies, like R.E.C. Inc., use the calendar year with the accounting period ending on December 31. Interim statements would be prepared for each quarter, ending March 31, June 30, and September 30. Some companies adopt a fiscal year ending on a date other than December 31.

The fact that the balance sheet is prepared on a particular date is significant. For example, cash is the first account listed on the balance sheet and represents the amount of cash on December 31; the amount could be materially different on December 30 or January 2.

EXHIBIT 2.1

R.E.C. INC.
CONSOLIDATED BALANCE SHEETS AT DECEMBER 31, 2002 AND 2001
(IN THOUSANDS)

	2002	*2001*
Assets		
Current Assets		
Cash	$ 4,061	$ 2,382
Marketable securities (Note A)	5,272	8,004
Accounts receivable, less allowance for doubtful accounts of $448 in 2002 and $417 in 2001	8,960	8,350
Inventories (Note A)	47,041	36,769
Prepaid expenses	512	759
Total current assets	65,846	56,264
Property, Plant, and Equipment (Notes A, C, and E)		
Land	811	811
Buildings and leasehold improvements	18,273	11,928
Equipment	21,523	13,768
	40,607	26,507
Less accumulated depreciation and amortization	11,528	7,530
Net property, plant, and equipment	29,079	18,977
Other Assets (Note A)	373	668
Total Assets	$95,298	$75,909
Liabilities and Stockholders' Equity		
Current Liabilities		
Accounts payable	$14,294	$7,591
Notes payable—banks (Note B)	5,614	6,012
Current maturities of long-term debt (Note C)	1,884	1,516
Accrued liabilities	5,669	5,313
Total current liabilities	27,461	20,432
Deferred Federal Income Taxes (Notes A and D)	843	635
Long-Term Debt (Note C)	21,059	16,975
Commitments (Note E)		
Total liabilities	49,363	38,042
Stockholder's Equity		
Common stock, par value $1, authorized, 10,000,000 shares; issued, 4,803,000 shares in 2002 and 4,594,000 shares in 2001 (Note F)	4,803	4,594
Additional paid-in capital	957	910
Retained earnings	40,175	32,363
Total stockholders' equity	45,935	37,867
Total Liabilities and Stockholders' Equity	$95,298	$ 75,909

The accompanying notes are an integral part of these statements.

COMPARATIVE DATA

Financial statements for only one accounting period would be of limited value because there would be no reference point for determining changes in a company's financial record over time. As part of an integrated disclosure system required by the SEC, the information presented in annual reports to shareholders includes two-year audited balance sheets and three-year audited statements of income and cash flows. The balance sheet for R.E.C. Inc. thus shows the condition of the company at December 31, 2002 and 2001.

Assets

CURRENT ASSETS

Assets are segregated on a balance sheet according to how they are utilized (Exhibit 2.2). Current assets include cash or those assets expected to be converted into cash within one year or one operating cycle, whichever is longer. The *operating cycle* is the time required to purchase or manufacture inventory, sell the product, and collect the cash. For most companies, the operating cycle is less than one year, but in some industries—such as tobacco and wine—it is longer. The designation "current" refers

EXHIBIT 2.2

R.E.C. INC.
CONSOLIDATED BALANCE SHEETS AT DECEMBER 31, 2002 AND 2001
(IN THOUSANDS)

	2002	2001
Assets		
Current Assets		
Cash	$ 4,061	$ 2,382
Marketable securities (Note A)	5,272	8,004
Accounts receivable, less allowance for doubtful accounts of $448 in 2002 and $417 in 2001	8,960	8,350
Inventories (Note A)	47,041	36,769
Prepaid expenses	512	759
Total current assets	65,846	56,264
Property, Plant, and Equipment (Notes A, C, and E)		
Land	811	811
Buildings and leasehold improvements	18,273	11,928
Equipment	21,523	13,768
	40,607	26,507
Less accumulated depreciation and amortization	11,528	7,530
Net property, plant, and equipment	29,079	18,977
Other Assets (Note A)	373	668
Total Assets	$95,298	$75,909

essentially to those assets that are continually used up and replenished in the ongo-ing operations of the business. The term *working capital* or *net working capital* is used to designate the amount by which current assets exceed current liabilities (cur-rent assets less current liabilities).

CASH AND MARKETABLE SECURITIES

These two accounts, shown separately for R.E.C. Inc. in Exhibit 2.2, are often com-bined as "cash and cash equivalents." The cash account is exactly that, cash in any form—cash awaiting deposit or in a bank account. Marketable securities (also referred to as short-term investments) are cash substitutes, cash that is not needed immediately in the business and is temporarily invested to earn a return. These investments are in instruments with short-term maturities (less than one year) to minimize the risk of interest rate fluctuations. They must be relatively riskless securities and highly liquid so that funds can be readily withdrawn as needed. Instruments used for such purposes include U.S. Treasury bills, certificates, notes, and bonds; negotiable certificates of deposit at financial institutions; and commercial paper (unsecured promissory notes of large business firms).

Under an accounting rule issued in 1993, the valuation of marketable securities on the balance sheet as well as other investments in debt and equity securities depends upon the intent of the investment. Statement of Financial Accounting Standards No. 115, "Accounting for Certain Investments in Debt and Equity Securities,"[1] effective for fiscal years beginning after December 15, 1993, requires the separation of invest-ment securities into three categories:

1. *Held to maturity* applies to those debt securities that the firm has the positive intent and ability to hold to maturity; these securities are reported at amortized *cost.*
2. *Trading securities* are debt and equity securities that are held for resale in the short-term, as opposed to being held to realize longer-term gains from capital appreciation. These securities are reported at *fair value* with unrealized gains and losses included in earnings.
3. *Securities available for sale* are debt and equity securities that are not classified as one of the other two categories, either held to maturity or trading securities. Securities available for sale are reported at *fair value* with unrealized gains and losses included in comprehensive income. The cumulative net unrealized gains or losses are reported in the accumulated other comprehensive income section of stockholders' equity.

---

[1] Some terms that may be helpful to the reader are the following: *Debt securities* are securities representing a creditor relationship, including U.S. Treasury securities, municipal securities, corporate bonds, convertible debt, and commercial paper. *Equity securities* represent an ownership interest in an entity, including common and pre-ferred stock. *Fair value* is the amount at which a financial instrument could be exchanged in a current transaction between willing parties; if a quoted market price is available, the fair value is the number of trading units multi-plied by the market price. *Amortized cost* refers to the fact that bonds (a debt security) may sell at a premium or discount because the stated rate of interest on the bonds is different from market rate of interest; the premium or discount is "amortized" over the life of the bonds so that at maturity the cost equals the face amount.

For more reading about FASB Statement No. 115, see J. T. Parks, "FASB 115: It's Back to the Future for Market Value Accounting," *Journal of Accountancy,* September 1993.

FASB Statement No. 115 does not apply to investments in consolidated subsidiaries nor to investments in equity securities accounted for under the equity method (discussed in chapter 3).

This accounting requirement most significantly affects financial institutions and insurance companies, which trade heavily in securities as part of their operating activities. The kinds of securities held by companies such as R.E.C. Inc. under the category "marketable securities" or "cash equivalents" are selected for ready conversion into cash, and they have market values that are equal to or very close to cost, as reported in Note A (see Exhibit 1.2) to the R.E.C. Inc. financial statements. ("Marketable securities consist of short-term, interest-bearing securities stated at cost, which approximates market.") Should values be different from cost, however, then the company would have to determine which category of investment applies. For example, if these kinds of securities were considered to be "available for sale," they would be marked to current value, and cumulative unrealized gains and losses would be carried as a component of stockholders' equity in the balance sheet.

ACCOUNTS RECEIVABLE

Accounts receivable are customer balances outstanding on credit sales and are reported on the balance sheet at their net realizable value, that is, the actual amount of the account less an *allowance for doubtful accounts*. Management must estimate— based on such factors as past experience, knowledge of customer quality, the state of the economy, the firm's collection policies—the dollar amount of accounts they expect will be uncollectible during an accounting period. Actual losses are written off against the allowance account, which is adjusted at the end of each accounting period.

The allowance for doubtful accounts can be important in assessing earnings quality. If, for instance, a company expands sales by lowering its credit standards, there should be a corresponding percentage increase in the allowance account. The estimation of this account will affect both the valuation of accounts receivable on the balance sheet and the recognition of bad debt expense on the income statement. The analyst should be alert to changes in the allowance account—both relative to the level of sales and the amount of accounts receivable outstanding—and to the justification for any variations from past practices.

The allowance account for R.E.C. Inc. represents approximately 5% of total customer accounts receivable. To obtain the exact percentage figure, the amount of the allowance account must be added to the net accounts receivable balance shown on the face of the statement:

	2002	2001
$\dfrac{\text{Allowance for doubtful accounts}}{\text{Accounts receivable (net)} + \text{Allowance}}$	$\dfrac{448}{8{,}960 + 448} = 4.8\%$	$\dfrac{417}{8{,}350 + 417} = 4.8\%$

The allowance account, which is deducted from the balance sheet accounts receivable account, should reflect the volume of credit sales, the firm's past experience with customers, the customer base, the firm's credit policies, the firm's collection practices, economic conditions, and changes in any of these. There should be a consistent relationship between the rate of change in sales, accounts receivable, and the allowance for doubtful accounts. If the amounts are changing at significantly different rates or in different directions, for example, if sales and accounts receivable are increasing, but the allowance account is decreasing or is increasing at a much smaller rate, the analyst should be alert to the potential for manipulation using the allowance account. Of course, there could be a plausible reason for such a change.

The relevant items needed to relate sales growth with accounts receivable and the allowance for doubtful accounts are found on the income statement (sales) and balance sheet (accounts receivable and allowance for doubtful accounts). The following information is from the income statement and balance sheet of R.E.C. Inc.

(In thousands)	*2002*	*2001*	*% Change*
Net sales	$215,600	$153,000	40.9
Accounts receivable (total)	9,408	8,767	7.3
Allowance for doubtful accounts	448	417	7.4

Between 2002 and 2001, sales for R.E.C. Inc. increased substantially (40.9%), and accounts receivable and the allowance account increased slightly (7.3% and 7.4%). It appears that the increase in sales in 2002 was not a result of a loosening of credit, which is a good sign. Another positive sign is that the allowance account has increased as accounts receivable has increased. Had the allowance account decreased there would be concern that management may be manipulating the numbers in order to increase the earnings number. Further analysis of accounts receivable and its quality is covered in chapter 5.

INVENTORIES

Inventories are items held for sale or used in the manufacture of products that will be sold. A retail company, such as R.E.C. Inc., lists only one type of inventory on the balance sheet: merchandise inventories purchased for resale to the public. A manufacturing firm, in contrast, would carry three different types of inventories: raw materials or supplies, work-in process, and finished goods. For most firms, inventories are the firm's major revenue producer. Exceptions would be service-oriented companies that carry little or no inventory. Exhibit 2.3 illustrates the proportion of inventories at the manufacturing, wholesale, and retail levels. For these industries—drugs, household appliances, and sporting goods—the percentage of inventories to total assets ranges from 23% to 36.5% at the manufacturing stage to about 45% to 64% for retail firms. The balance sheet for R.E.C. Inc. reveals that inventories comprise slightly under 50% of total assets.

	2002	*2001*
Inventories/Total assets	47,041/95,298 = 49.4%	36,769/75,909 = 48.4%

Given the relative magnitude of inventory, the accounting method chosen to value inventory and the associated measurement of cost of goods sold have a considerable impact on a company's financial position and operating results. Understanding the fundamentals of inventory accounting and the effect various methods have on a company's financial statements is essential to the user of financial statement information.

EXHIBIT 2.3   Inventories as a Percentage of Total Assets

	%
Manufacturing	
Drug and medicine	23.0
Household electric appliances	26.2
Sporting and athletic goods	36.5
Wholesale	
Drugs	33.8
Electrical appliances	41.3
Sporting and recreational goods	46.2
Retail	
Drugs	45.2
Household appliances	46.0
Sporting good and bicycles	63.8

Source: Robert Morris Associates, *Annual Statement Studies,* Philadelphia, PA, 1998.

INVENTORY ACCOUNTING METHODS

The method chosen by a company to account for inventory determines the value of inventory on the balance sheet and the amount of expense recognized for cost of goods sold on the income statement. The significance of inventory accounting is underlined by the presence of inflation and by the implications for tax payments and cash flow. Inventory valuation is based on an *assumption* regarding the flow of goods and has nothing whatever to do with the *actual* order in which products are sold. The cost flow assumption is made in order to *match* the cost of products sold during an accounting period to the revenue generated from the sales and to assign a dollar value to the inventory remaining for sale at the end of the accounting period.

The three cost flow assumptions most frequently used by U.S. companies are *FIFO* (first in, first out), *LIFO* (last in, first out), and *average cost.* As the terms imply, the FIFO method assumes the first units purchased are the first units sold during an accounting period; LIFO assumes that the items bought last are sold first; and the average cost method uses an average purchase price to determine the cost of products sold. A simple example should highlight the differences in the three methods. A new company in its first year of operations purchases five products for sale in the order and at the prices shown:

Item	Purchase Price
#1	$5
#2	$7
#3	$8
#4	$9
#5	$11

The company sells three of these items, all at the end of the year. The cost flow assumptions would be:

Accounting Method	Goods Sold	Goods Remaining in Inventory
FIFO	#1, #2, #3	#4, #5
LIFO	#5, #4, #3	#2, #1
Average cost	[Total cost/5] × 3	[Total cost/5] × 2

The resulting effect on the income statement and balance sheet would be:

Accounting Method	Cost of Goods Sold (Income Statement)	Inventory Valuation (Balance Sheet)
FIFO	$20	$20
LIFO	$28	$12
Average cost	$24	$16

It can be clearly seen that during a period of inflation, with product prices increasing, the LIFO method produces the highest cost of goods sold expense ($28) and the lowest ending valuation of inventory ($12). Further, cost of goods sold under the LIFO method most closely approximates the current cost of inventory items since they are the most recent purchases. On the other hand, inventories on the balance sheet are undervalued with respect to replacement cost because they reflect the older costs when prices were lower. If a firm uses LIFO to value inventory, no restatement is required to adjust cost of goods sold for inflation because LIFO matches current costs to current sales. Inventory on the balance sheet, however, would have to be revalued upward to account for inflation. FIFO has the opposite effect; during a period of rising prices, balance sheet inventory is valued at current cost, but cost of goods sold on the income statement is understated.

In an annual survey of accounting practices followed by 600 industrial and merchandising corporations in the U.S. in the early 1970s, 146 companies surveyed reported using LIFO to account for all or part of inventory. By the 1990s, this number had increased to 326.[2] Why have so many companies switched to LIFO? The answer is taxes.

Referring back to the example, note that when prices are rising, LIFO produces the largest cost of goods sold expense. The greater the expense deduction, the lower is taxable income. Use of LIFO thus reduces a company's tax bill during inflation. Unlike the case for some accounting rules—where a firm is allowed to use one method for tax and another method for reporting purposes—a company that elects LIFO to figure taxable income must also use LIFO for reported income. The many companies that have switched to LIFO from other methods are apparently willing to trade lower reported earnings for the positive cash benefits resulting from LIFO's beneficial tax effect. There is evidence, however, that the trend toward LIFO is reversing and that the number of firms electing FIFO is gradually increasing. Reasons could include both a lower inflation rate and the desire to report higher accounting earnings.

In the earlier example, LIFO produced lower earnings than FIFO or average cost, but there can be exceptions. Obviously, in a *period of falling prices* the results would reverse. Also, some firms experience price movements that are counter to the general trend—the high technology industry, where prices on many products have declined, is

---

[2] *Accounting Trends and Techniques,* American Institute of Certified Public Accountants, 1971 and 1998.

a case in point. Another interesting phenomenon—a *base LIFO layer liquidation*—occurs with use of LIFO in a situation where the firm sells more goods than purchased during an accounting period. Continuing the previous example, the valuation of inventory at the end of year 1 was as follows:

Accounting Method	*Items*	*Inventory Valuation*
FIFO	#4, #5	$20
LIFO	#1, #2	$12
Average cost	[Total cost/5] × 2	$16

Suppose that during its second year of operations, the company bought two more items: #6 for $12 and #7 for $14. Further assume that the firm sold those newly purchased items plus the two items remaining in stock at the end of year 1. Cost of goods sold under the three assumptions would be:

Accounting Method	*Old + New Inventory*	*Cost of Goods Sold*
FIFO	$20 + $26	$46
LIFO	$12 + $26	$38
Average cost	$16 + $26	$42

In this situation the lowest cost of goods sold expense results from using LIFO because the older, less expensive items were sold. Usually companies maintain a base layer of LIFO inventory that remains fairly constant. Goods are bought during the year and sales are made from the more recent purchases (for purposes of cost allocation). It is only when stocks of inventory are substantially reduced that the base layer is affected, and LIFO earnings are higher. Base LIFO layer liquidations occur when companies are shrinking rather than increasing inventories. There is an actual reduction of inventory levels, but the earnings boost stems from the cost flow assumption: that the older and lower priced products are those being sold. The effects of LIFO reductions, which are disclosed in notes to the financial statements, can be substantial.[3]

Because the inventory cost flow assumption has a significant impact on financial statements—the amount of inventory reported on the balance sheet and the cost of goods sold expense in the income statement—it is important to know where to find its disclosure. The method used to value inventory will be shown either on the face of the balance sheet with the inventory account or, more commonly, in the note to the financial statements relating to inventory. R.E.C. Inc. has the following explanation in Note A: Inventories are carried at the lower of cost (LIFO) or market. This statement indicates that the LIFO method is used to determine cost. The fact that inventories are valued at the lower of cost or market reflects the accounting convention of conservatism. If the actual market value of inventory falls below cost, as determined by the cost flow assumption (LIFO for R.E.C. Inc.), then inventory will be written down to market price. Notice that the phrase is "lower" of cost or market. The carrying value of inventory would never be written up to market value; only down.

---

[3] To avoid the LIFO liquidation problem, some firms use the dollar-value LIFO method, which is applied to goods in designated pools and measures inventory changes in cost dollars—using a price index—rather than physical units.

The inventory note for R.E.C. Inc. also provides information regarding the value of inventory had FIFO been used, since the FIFO valuation would be higher than that recorded on the balance sheet and more closely approximates current value: "If the first in, first out (FIFO) method of inventory accounting had been used, inventories would have been approximately $2,681,000 and $2,096,000 higher than reported at December 31, 2002 and 2001."

PREPAID EXPENSES

Certain expenses, such as insurance, rent, property taxes, and utilities, are sometimes paid in advance. They are included in current assets if they will expire within one year or one operating cycle, whichever is longer. Generally, prepayments are not material to the balance sheet as a whole. For R.E.C. Inc., prepaid expenses represent less than 1% of total current assets in 2002.

PROPERTY, PLANT, AND EQUIPMENT

This category encompasses a company's fixed assets (also called tangible, long-lived, and capital assets)—those assets not used up in the ebb and flow of annual business operations. These assets produce economic benefits for more than one year, and they are considered "tangible" because they have a physical substance. Fixed assets other than land (which has a theoretically unlimited life span) are "depreciated" over the period of time they benefit the firm. The process of depreciation is a method of allocating the cost of long-lived assets. The original cost, less any estimated residual value at the end of the asset's life, is spread over the expected life of the asset. Cost is also considered to encompass any expenditures made to ready the asset for operating use. On any balance sheet date property, plant, and equipment is shown at book value, which is the difference between original cost and any accumulated depreciation to date.

Management has considerable discretion with respect to fixed assets, as was explained in chapter 1. Depreciation involves estimates of the economic life of the asset and any salvage value expected to be recoverable at the end of this life. Further, the amount of depreciation expense recognized each period is determined by the depreciation method chosen. Although the total amount of depreciation over the asset's life is the same regardless of method, the rate of depreciation varies. The straight-line method spreads the expense evenly by periods, and the accelerated methods yield higher depreciation expense in the early years of an asset's useful life, and lower depreciation expense in the later years. Another depreciation choice is the unit-of-production method, which bases depreciation expense for a given period on actual use. According to *Accounting Trends and Techniques,* the vast majority of companies use the straight-line method for financial reporting:[4]

Straight line	578
Accelerated	86
Units of production	39

Refer now to the property, plant, and equipment section of the R.E.C. Inc. balance sheet. First note that there are three categories listed separately: land, buildings and

---

[4] *Accounting Trends and Techniques,* American Institute of Certified Public Accountants, 1998.

leasehold improvements, and equipment. *Land,* as designated in the fixed asset section, refers to property used in the business; this would be land on which there are corporate offices and retail stores. Any land held for investment purposes would be segregated from property used in the business. (For R.E.C. Inc., see the "Other Assets" section.)

R.E.C. Inc. owns some of its retail outlets, and others are leased. *Buildings* would include those stores owned by the company as well as its corporate offices. *Leasehold improvements* are additions or improvements made to leased structures. Because leasehold improvements revert to the property owner when the lease term expires, they are amortized by the lessee over the economic life of the improvement or the life of the lease, whichever is shorter. [5]

Some companies may also have an account called construction in progress. These are the costs of constructing new buildings that are not yet complete. R.E.C. Inc. does not include this account on their balance sheet.

Equipment represents the original cost, including delivery and installation charges, of the machinery and equipment used in business operations. Included are a variety of items such as the centralized computer system; equipment and furnishings for offices, stores, and warehouses; and delivery trucks. The final two lines under the property, plant, and equipment section for R.E.C. Inc. show the amount of accumulated depreciation and amortization (for all items except land) and the amount of net property, plant, and equipment after the deduction of accumulated depreciation and amortization.

The relative proportion of fixed assets in a company's asset structure will largely be determined by the nature of the business. A firm that manufactures products would likely be more heavily invested in capital equipment than a retailer or wholesaler. Exhibit 2.4 shows the relative percentage of net fixed assets to total assets for the same three industries identified in Exhibit 2.3.

---

[5] *Amortization* is the term used to designate the cost allocation process for assets other than buildings, machinery, and equipment—such as leasehold improvements and intangible assets, discussed later in the chapter.

EXHIBIT 2.4 Net Fixed Assets as a Percent of Total Assets

	%
Manufacturing	
Drug and medicine	25.5
Household electric appliances	22.9
Sporting and athletic goods	19.4
Wholesale	
Drugs	10.4
Electrical appliances	10.5
Sporting and recreational goods	9.6
Retail	
Drugs	13.3
Household appliances	17.8
Sporting good and bicycles	14.8

Source: Robert Morris Associates, *Annual Statement Studies,* Philadelphia, PA, 1998.

Fixed assets are most prominent at the manufacturing level; retailers are next, probably because retailers require stores and buildings in which to sell products; and the wholesale segment requires the least investment in fixed assets.

For R.E.C. Inc., net fixed assets have increased in proportion to total assets between 2001 and 2002 from 25% to 30%:

	2002		*2001*	
$\dfrac{\text{Net property, plant, and equipment}}{\text{Total assets}}$	$\dfrac{29,079}{95,298}$	$= 30.5\%$	$\dfrac{18,977}{75,909}$	$= 25.0\%$

Chapter 5 covers the financial ratios used to measure the efficiency of managing these assets.

OTHER ASSETS

Other assets on a firm's balance sheet can include a multitude of other noncurrent items such as property held for sale, start-up costs in connection with a new business, the cash surrender value of life insurance policies, and long-term advance payments. For R.E.C. Inc., other assets represent minor holdings of property not used in business operations (as explained in Note A to the financial statements).

Additional categories of noncurrent assets frequently encountered (but not present for R.E.C. Inc.) are long-term investments[6] and intangible assets, such as goodwill recognized in business combination, patents, trademarks, copyrights, brand names, and franchises. Of the intangible assets, *goodwill* is the most important for analytical purposes because of its potential materiality on the balance sheet of firms heavily involved in acquisitions activity. Goodwill arises when one company acquires another company (in a business combination accounted for as a purchase) for a price in excess of the fair market value of the net identifiable assets (identifiable assets less liabilities assumed) acquired. This excess price is recorded on the books of the acquiring company as goodwill. The cost of goodwill is amortized over its estimated life, a period not to exceed 40 years. Information about goodwill and other intangible assets is disclosed in notes to the financial statements, such as the following:

> As a creator and distributor of branded information and entertainment copyrights, Time Warner has a significant and growing number of intangible assets, including goodwill, cable television and sports franchises, film and television libraries, music catalogues, contracts and copyrights, and other copyrighted products and trademarks.
>
> Time Warner amortizes goodwill and sports franchises over periods up to forty years using the straight-line method. Cable television franchises, film and television libraries, music catalogues, contracts and copyrights, and other intangible assets are amortized over periods up to twenty years using the straight-line method. Amortization of intangible assets amounted to $800

---

[6] Reporting requirements for investments in debt and equity securities must follow the provisions of FASB Statement No. 115, presented earlier in the chapter. A more extensive discussion of investments in unconsolidated subsidiaries is provided in chapter 3. As noted earlier in the chapter, FASB Statement No. 115 does not apply to investments in consolidated subsidiaries nor to investments in equity securities accounted for by the equity method.

million in 1998, $912 million in 1997 and $681 million in 1996. Accumulated amortization of intangible assets at December 31, 1998 and 1997 amounted to $3.9 billion and $3.181 billion, respectively.[7]

In 1998, Time Warner had $11.9 billion of goodwill and $3.7 billion of other intangible assets. Together these accounts represented more than 49% of Time Warner's total assets.

Liabilities

CURRENT LIABILITIES

Liabilities represent claims against assets, and current liabilities are those that must be satisfied in one year or one operating cycle, whichever is longer. Current liabilities

---

[7] Time Warner Inc., *1998 Annual Report,* p. 67.

EXHIBIT 2.5

R.E.C. INC.
CONSOLIDATED BALANCE SHEETS AT DECEMBER 31, 2002 AND 2001
(IN THOUSANDS)

	2002	2001
Liabilities and Stockholders' Equity		
Current Liabilities		
Accounts payable	$14,294	$ 7,591
Notes payable—banks (Note B)	5,614	6,012
Current maturities of long-term debt (Note C)	1,884	1,516
Accrued liabilities	5,669	5,313
Total current liabilities	27,461	20,432
Deferred Federal Income Taxes (Notes A and D)	843	635
Long-term Debt (Note C)	21,059	16,975
Commitments (Note E)		
Total liabilities	49,363	38,042
Stockholders' Equity		
Common stock, par value $1, authorized, 10,000,000 shares; issued, 4,803,000 shares in 2002 and 4,594,000 shares in 2001 (Note F)	4,803	4,594
Additional paid-in capital	957	910
Retained earnings	40,175	32,363
Total stockholders' equity	45,935	37,867
Total Liabilities and Stockholders' Equity	$95,298	$75,909

The accompanying notes are an integral part of these statements.

include accounts and notes payable, the current portion of long-term debt, accrued liabilities, and deferred taxes.

ACCOUNTS PAYABLE

Accounts payable are short-term obligations that arise from credit extended by suppliers for the purchase of goods and services. For example, when R.E.C. Inc. buys products on credit from a wholesaler for eventual sale to its own customers, the transaction creates an account payable.

This account is eliminated when the bill is satisfied. The ongoing process of operating a business results in the spontaneous generation of accounts payable, which increase and decrease depending on the credit policies available to the firm from its suppliers, economic conditions, and the cyclical nature of the firm's own business operations. Note that R.E.C. Inc. has almost doubled the amount of accounts payable between 2001 and 2002 (Exhibit 2.5). Part of the balance sheet analysis should include an exploration of the causes for this increase. To jump briefly ahead, the reader might also note that the income statement reveals a significant sales increase in 2002. Perhaps the increase in accounts payable is at least partially explained by this sales growth.

NOTES PAYABLE

Notes payable are short-term obligations in the form of promissory notes to suppliers or financial institutions. For R.E.C. Inc. these notes (explained in Note B to the financial statements) are payable to a bank and reflect the amount extended under a line of credit. A line of credit permits borrowing from a financial institution up to a maximum amount. The total amount that can be borrowed under R.E.C. Inc.'s line of credit is $10 million, of which about half ($5,614,000) was outstanding debt at the end of 2002.

CURRENT MATURITIES OF LONG-TERM DEBT

When a firm has bonds, mortgages, or other forms of long-term debt outstanding, the portion of the principal that will be repaid during the upcoming year is classified as a current liability. The currently maturing debt for R.E.C. Inc. occurs as the result of several long-term obligations, described in Note C to the financial statements. The note lists the amount of long-term debt outstanding, less the portion due currently, and also provides the schedule of current maturities for the next five years.

ACCRUED LIABILITIES

Like most large corporations, R.E.C. Inc. uses the accrual rather than the cash basis of accounting: revenue is recognized when it is earned, and expenses are recorded when they are incurred, regardless of when the cash is received or paid. Accrued liabilities result from the recognition of an expense in the accounting records prior to the actual payment of cash. Thus, they are liabilities because there will be an eventual cash outflow to satisfy the obligations.

Assume that a company has a $100,000 note outstanding, with 12% annual interest due in semiannual installments on March 31 and September 30. For a balance sheet prepared on December 31, interest will be accrued for three months (October, November, and December):

$100,000 \times .12 = \$12,000$ annual interest;

$\$12,000/12 = \$1,000$ monthly interest;

$\$1,000 \times 3 = \$3,000$ accrued interest for three months.

The December 31 balance sheet would include an accrued liability of $3,000. Accruals also arise from salaries, rent, insurance, taxes, and other expenses.

UNEARNED REVENUE OR DEFERRED CREDITS

Companies that are paid in advance for services or products record a liability upon the receipt of cash. The liability account is referred to as *unearned revenue* or *deferred credits*. The amounts in this account will be transferred to a revenue account when the service is performed or the product delivered as required by the matching concept of accounting. R.E.C. Inc. does not have unearned revenue because it is a retail company that does not generally receive payment in advance of selling its products. However, companies in high technology, publishing, or manufacturing industries are apt to have unearned revenue accounts on their balance sheets. For example, Intel Corporation shows $304 million on its 1995 balance sheet for "Deferred income on shipments to distributors." In the footnotes to the financial statements, this account is explained as follows: "Certain of the Company's sales are made to distributors under agreements allowing price protection and/or right of return on merchandise unsold by the distributors. Because of frequent sales price reductions and rapid technological obsolescence in the industry, Intel defers recognition of such sales until the merchandise is sold by the distributors."[8]

DEFERRED FEDERAL INCOME TAXES

Deferred taxes are the result of temporary differences in the recognition of revenue and expense for taxable income relative to reported income. The accounting principles for recording and reporting deferred taxes are specified in Statement of Financial Accounting Standards No. 109, "Accounting for Income Taxes," which superseded Statement of Financial Accounting Standards Number 96 and is effective for fiscal years beginning after December 15, 1992. Most large companies use one set of rules for calculating income tax expense, paid to the IRS, and another set for figuring income reported in the financial statements. The objective is to take advantage of all available tax deferrals in order to reduce actual tax payments, while showing the highest possible amount of reported net income. There are many areas in which firms are permitted to use different procedures for tax and reporting purposes. One such example, based on depreciation methods, was discussed in chapter 1. Most firms use an accelerated method (the Modified Accelerated Cost Recovery System) to figure taxable income and the straight-line method for reporting purposes. The effect is to recognize more depreciation expense in the early years of an asset's useful life for tax calculations.

Although depreciation methods are the most common source, other temporary differences arise from the methods used to account for installment sales, long-term contracts, leases, warranties and service contracts, pensions and other employee benefits,

---

[8] Intel, *1995 Annual Report,* pp. 18–19

and subsidiary investment earnings. They are called *temporary differences* (or timing differences) because, in theory, the total amount of expense and revenue recognized will eventually be the same for tax and reporting purposes. There are also *permanent differences* in income tax accounting. Municipal bond revenue, for example, is recognized as income for reporting purposes but not for tax purposes; life insurance premiums on officers are recognized as expense for financial reporting purposes but are not deductible for income tax purposes. These permanent differences do not affect deferred taxes because a tax will never be paid on the income.

The deferred tax account reconciles the temporary differences in expense and revenue recognition for any accounting period. Under FASB Statement No. 109,[9] business firms recognize deferred tax liabilities for all temporary differences, that is, when the item causes financial income to exceed taxable income with an expectation that the difference will be offset in future accounting periods. Deferred tax assets are reported for deductible temporary differences and operating loss and tax credit carryforwards. A deductible temporary difference is one that causes taxable income to exceed financial income, with the expectation that the difference will be offset in the future. Measurement of tax liabilities and assets is based on provisions of the enacted tax law; effects of future anticipated changes in tax law are not considered. A *valuation allowance* is used to reduce deferred tax assets to expected realizable amounts when it is determined that is more likely than not that some of the deferred tax assets will not be realized.

To illustrate the accounting for deferred taxes, assume that a company has a total annual revenue of $500,000; expenses other than depreciation are $250,000; and depreciation expense is $100,000 for tax accounting and $50,000 for financial reporting (eventually this difference would reverse and the reported depreciation expense in later years would be greater than the tax depreciation expense). The income for tax and reporting purposes would be computed two ways, assuming a 34% tax rate:

	Tax	*Reporting*
Revenue	$500,000	$500,000
Expenses	(350,000)	(300,000)
Earnings before tax	$150,000	$200,000
Tax expense (× .34)	(51,000)	(68,000)
Net income	$ 99,000	$132,000

Taxes actually paid ($51,000) are less than the tax expense ($68,000) reported in the financial statements. To reconcile the $17,000 difference between the expense recorded and the cash outflow, there is a deferred tax liability of $17,000:

Reported tax expense	$68,000
Cash paid for taxes	51,000
Deferred tax liability	$17,000

Deferred taxes are classified as current or noncurrent on the balance sheet, corresponding to the classification of related assets and liabilities underlying the temporary

---

[9] For more reading about FASB 109, its application and implementation, see W. J. Read and A. J. Bartsch, "Accounting for Deferred Taxes Under FASB 109"; and G. J. Gregory, T. R. Petree, and R. J. Vitray, "FASB 109: Planning for Implementation and Beyond," *Journal of Accountancy,* December 1992.

difference. For example, a deferred tax asset arising from accounting for 90-day warranties would be considered current. On the other hand, a temporary difference based on five-year warranties would be noncurrent; depreciation accounting would also result in a noncurrent deferred tax because of the noncurrent classification of the underlying plant and equipment account. A deferred tax asset or liability that is not related to an asset or liability for financial reporting, including deferred tax assets related to carryforwards, is classified according to anticipated reversal or benefit. At the end of the accounting period, the firm will report one net current amount and one net noncurrent amount unless the liabilities and assets are attributable to different tax-paying components of the enterprise or to different tax jurisdictions. Thus, the deferred tax account can conceivably appear on the balance sheet as a current asset, current liability, noncurrent asset, or noncurrent liability.

R.E.C. Inc. reports deferred Federal income taxes as a noncurrent liability. The temporary differences are based on depreciation methods and long-term installment sales.

An illustration of the disclosures related to deferred income taxes follows. Exhibit 2.6 shows an excerpt from Maytag Corporation's 1998 footnote on income taxes. The seven temporary differences that have created the net deferred tax asset are listed at the top of the exhibit. Two items, "Book/tax basis differences" and

EXHIBIT 2.6   Income Taxes—Maytag Corporation

Deferred income taxes reflect the expected future tax consequences of temporary differences between the book carrying amounts and the tax basis of assets and liabilities. Deferred tax assets and liabilities consisted of the following:

		December 31
In thousands	1998	1997
Deferred tax assets (liabilities)		
Book/tax basis differences	$ (63,940)	$ (54,301)
Postretirement benefit liability	180,349	177,823
Product warranty/liability accruals	30,092	23,715
Pensions and other employee benefits	20,879	13,567
Advertising and sales promotion accruals	9,868	11,400
Interest rate swaps	11,620	13,838
Other—net	(4,805)	1,072
	184,063	187,114
Less valuation allowance for deferred tax assets	45,967	45,776
Net deferred tax assets	$ 138,096	$ 141,338
Recognized in consolidated balance sheets		
Deferred tax assets—current	$ 39,014	$ 46,073
Deferred tax assets—noncurrent	120,273	118,931
Deferred tax liabilities—noncurrent	(21,191)	(23,666)
Net deferred tax assets	$ 138,096	$ 141,338

"Other—net" have resulted in deferred tax liabilities. This means that Maytag has taken greater deductions on their tax return for these items than was recorded on their income statement. The other five items have resulted in deferred tax assets. In this case, the company has deducted more items on the income statement compared to the deductions taken on the tax return. The overall net deferred tax asset of $138,096 indicates that in the future, Maytag should pay $138,096 less in taxes when these temporary differences reverse. The main reason for the net deferred tax asset is the "Postretirement benefit liability." Companies record expenses for postretirement benefits when earned by the employee, but are not allowed to deduct these expenses for tax purposes until the amounts are actually paid in cash. The valuation allowance of $45,967 is the amount that Maytag projects will not be realized in the future. Notice that Maytag recognizes deferred tax items in three classifications on the balance sheet: current assets, noncurrent assets, and noncurrent liabilities. The largest amount, $120,273, can probably be attributed to the deferred tax asset created by the postretirement benefit liability temporary difference. The majority of postretirement benefits are noncurrent.

LONG-TERM DEBT

Obligations with maturities beyond one year are designated on the balance sheet as noncurrent liabilities. This category can include bonded indebtedness, long-term notes payable, mortgages, obligations under leases, pension liabilities, and long-term warranties. In Note C to the financial statements, R.E.C. Inc. specifies the nature, maturity, and interest rate of each long-term obligation.

OTHER LIABILITIES

Other liability accounts (not present for R.E.C. Inc.), such as pension and lease obligations, can appear under the liability section of the balance sheet.[10] Statement of Financial Accounting Standards No. 106, "Employers' Accounting for Postretirement Benefits Other Than Pensions," adopted by the Financial Accounting Standards Board in 1990, has had a significant impact on many corporate balance sheets. This statement requires companies to disclose as a balance sheet liability the obligation for paying medical bills of retired employees and spouses—in accordance with the accrual method of accounting—by accruing promised future benefits as a form of deferred compensation. Most companies previously deducted medical expenses in the year paid. This accounting rule also impacts profitability for many firms by substantially increasing the recognition of annual postretirement benefit expense. Statement of Financial Accounting Standards No. 112, "Employers' Accounting for Postemployment Benefits," established accounting standards for benefits provided to former or inactive employees, their dependents, and beneficiaries and is effective for fiscal years beginning after December 15, 1993.

Adopting new accounting requirements has a major impact on the financial statements of some companies. DuPont, for example, reported charges to earnings in 1992 of about $5 billion for adopting the accounting requirements relating to deferred taxes and postretirement benefits:

---

[10] The disclosures relating to pension obligations and lease accounting are discussed in appendix A.

In the fourth quarter of 1992, the company adopted Statement of Financial Accounting Standards (SFAS) No. 106, 'Employers' Accounting for Post Retirement Benefits Other Than Pensions'; and SFAS No. 109 'Accounting for Income Taxes,' both retroactive to January 1, 1992. The company recorded charges to net income of $3,788 million ($5.63 per share) and $1,045 million ($1.55 per share), respectively, as of January 1, 1992 for the effects of transition to these two new standards.[11]

Many companies will list an account titled "Commitments and Contingencies" on the balance sheet even though no dollar amount will appear. This disclosure is intended to draw attention to the fact that required disclosures can be found in the notes to the financial statements. *Commitments* refer to contractual agreements that will have a significant financial impact on the company in the future. R.E.C. Inc. reports commitments in Note E that describe the company's operating leases. *Contingencies* refer to potential liabilities of the firm such as possible damage awards assessed in lawsuits. Generally, the firm cannot reasonably predict the outcome and/or the amount of the future liability; however, information about the contingency must be disclosed in the notes to the financial statements.

Stockholders' Equity

The ownership interests in the company are represented in the final section of the balance sheet, stockholders' equity or sharcholders' equity. Ownership equity is the residual interest in assets that remains after deducting liabilities. The owners bear the greatest risk because their claims are subordinate to creditors in the event of liquidation, but owners also benefit from the rewards of a successful enterprise. The relationship between the amount of debt and equity in a firm's capital structure and the concept of financial leverage, by which shareholder returns are magnified, is explored in chapter 5.

COMMON STOCK

R.E.C. Inc. has only common stock shares outstanding. Common shareholders do not ordinarily receive a fixed return but do have voting privileges in proportion to ownership interest. Dividends on common stock are declared at the discretion of a company's board of directors. Further, common shareholders can benefit from stock ownership through potential price appreciation (or the reverse can occur if the share price declines).

The amount listed under the common stock account is based on the par or stated value of the shares issued. The par or stated value usually bears no relationship to actual market price but rather is a floor price below which the stock cannot be sold initially. At year-end 2002, R.E.C. Inc. had 4,803,000 shares outstanding of $1 par value stock, rendering a total of $4,803,000 in the common stock account.

ADDITIONAL PAID-IN CAPITAL

This account reflects the amount by which the original sales price of the stock shares exceeded par value. If, for example, a company sold 1,000 shares of $1 par value stock

---

[11] DuPont, *1992 Annual Report*, p. 26.

for $3 per share, the common stock account would be $1,000, and additional paid-in capital would total $2,000.

Reference to the additional paid-in capital account for R.E.C. Inc. reveals that the firm's common stock initially sold at a price slightly higher than the $1 par value. The additional paid-in capital account is not affected by the price changes resulting from stock trading subsequent to its original issue.[12]

RETAINED EARNINGS

The retained earnings account is the sum of every dollar a company has earned since its inception, less any payments made to shareholders in the form of cash or stock dividends. Retained earnings do not represent a pile of unused cash stashed away in corporate vaults; retained earnings are funds a company has elected to reinvest in the operations of the business rather than pay out to stockholders in dividends. Retained earnings should not be confused with cash or other financial resources currently or prospectively available to satisfy financial obligations. Rather, the retained earnings account is the measurement of all undistributed earnings.

OTHER EQUITY ACCOUNTS

In addition to the stockholders' equity accounts shown on the R.E.C. Inc. balance sheet, there are other accounts that can appear in the equity section. These include preferred stock, accumulated other comprehensive income, and treasury stock. Exhibit 2.7 illustrates these additional items for Pfizer Inc.

Preferred stock usually carries a fixed annual dividend payment but no voting rights. Although Pfizer Inc. has authorized preferred stock, no shares have been issued to date.

Beginning in 1998, companies must report comprehensive income or loss for the accounting period. Prior to the issuance of FASB Statement No. 130, "Reporting

---

[12] The paid-in capital account can be affected by treasury stock transactions, preferred stock, retirement of stock, stock dividends and warrants and by the conversion of debt into stock.

EXHIBIT 2.7   Pfizer Inc. Shareholders' Equity at December 31 (in Millions)

	1998	1997	1996
Shareholders' Equity			
Preferred stock, without par value; 12 shares authorized, none issued	—	—	—
Common stock, $.05 par value; 3,000 shares authorized; issued: 1998—1,407; 1997—1,388; 1996—1,378	70	69	69
Additional paid-in capital	5,646	3,239	1,693
Retained earnings	11,439	9,349	8,017
Accumulated other comprehensive income/(expense)	(234)	(85)	145
Employee benefit trusts	(4,200)	(2,646)	(1,488)
Treasury stock, at cost: 1998—113; 1997—94; 1996—87	(3,911)	(1,993)	(1,482)
Total shareholders' equity	8,810	7,933	6,954

Comprehensive Income," several comprehensive income items bypassed the income statement and were reported as components of equity. Comprehensive income consists of two parts, net income and other comprehensive income. Other comprehensive income is reported in a separate equity account on the balance sheet generally referred to as *accumulated other comprehensive income/(expense)*. This account includes up to four items: (1) unrealized gains or losses in the market value of investments in available-for-sale securities, (2) any change in the excess of additional pension liability over unrecognized prior service cost, (3) certain gains and losses on derivative financial instruments, and (4) foreign currency translation adjustments resulting from converting financial statements from a foreign currency into U.S. dollars. (Comprehensive income and the four items noted above are discussed in chapter 3 and appendix A.)

Firms often repurchase shares of their own stock for a variety of reasons that include meeting requirements for employee stock option and retirement plans, building shareholdings for potential merger needs, increasing earnings per share by reducing the number of shares outstanding, preventing takeover attempts by reducing the number of shareholders, and as an investment use of excess cash holdings. If the repurchased shares are not retired, they are designated as *treasury stock* and are shown as an offsetting account in the stockholders' equity section of the balance sheet. Pfizer Inc. held 113 million shares of treasury stock at the end of 1998. The cost of the shares is shown as a reduction of stockholders' equity.[13]

Employee benefit trusts, an account shown in the Pfizer Inc. shareholders' equity section, is explained as follows:

> In 1993, we sold 40 million shares of treasury stock to the Pfizer, Inc. Grantor Trust in exchange for a $600 million note. The Trust is used primarily to fund our benefit plans including the stock option plan. The Balance Sheet reflects the fair value of shares owned by the Trust as a reduction of *Shareholders' Equity,* representing unearned benefit costs. This amount is reduced as benefits are satisfied.[14]

OTHER BALANCE SHEET ITEMS

Corporate balance sheets are not limited to the accounts described in this chapter for R.E.C. Inc. and other companies. The reader of annual reports will encounter additional accounts and will also find many of the same accounts listed under a variety of different titles. Those discussed in this chapter, however, should be generally sufficient for understanding the basics of most balance sheet presentations in a set of published financial statements. The balance sheet will recur through the remaining chapters of this book due to the interrelationship among the financial statements and because of its important role in the analysis of financial data.

---

[13] The two methods used to account for treasury stock transactions are the cost method (deducting the cost of the purchased shares from equity) and the par value method (deducting the par or stated value of the shares from equity). Most companies use the cost method.

[14] Pfizer, Inc., *1998 Annual Report,* p. 53.

SELF-TEST

Solutions are provided in appendix D.

____ 1. What does the balance sheet summarize for a business enterprise?
   (a) Operating results for a period.
   (b) Financial position at a point in time.
   (c) Financing and investment activities for a period.
   (d) Profit or loss at a point in time.

____ 2. What is the balancing equation for the balance sheet?
   (a) Assets = Liabilities + Stockholders' equity.
   (b) Assets + Stockholders' equity = Liability.
   (c) Assets + Liabilities = Stockholders' equity.
   (d) Revenues − Expenses = Net income.

____ 3. Why do annual reports include more than one year of the balance sheet and statements of income and cash flows?
   (a) The SEC requires only one year's data.
   (b) Financial statements for only one year would have no reference point for determining changes in a company's financial record over time.
   (c) The income statement is for a period of time, whereas the balance sheet is for a particular date.
   (d) The information is required as part of an integrated disclosure system adopted by shareholders.

____ 4. What does the cash account include?
   (a) Cash awaiting deposit.
   (b) Cash in bank accounts.
   (c) Both (a) and (b).
   (d) None of the above.

____ 5. Which of the following securities would be classified as marketable securities in the current asset section of the balance sheet?
   (a) Commercial paper, U.S. Treasury bills, land held for investment.
   (b) Commercial paper, U.S. Treasury bills, negotiable certificates of deposit.
   (c) Commercial paper, land held for investment, bonds with maturities in ten years.
   (d) U.S. Treasury bills, long-term stock investment, bonds with maturities in ten years.

____ 6. What type of firm generally has the highest proportion of inventory to total assets?
   (a) Retailers.
   (b) Wholesalers.
   (c) Manufacturers.
   (d) Service-oriented firms.

____ 7. Why is the method of valuing inventory important?
   (a) Inventory valuation is based on the actual flow of goods.
   (b) Inventories always account for more than 50% of total assets and therefore have a considerable impact on a company's financial position.
   (c) Companies desire to use the inventory valuation method, which minimizes the cost of goods sold expense.
   (d) The inventory valuation method chosen determines the value of inventory on the balance sheet and the cost of goods sold expense on the income state-

ment, two items having considerable impact on the financial position of a company.

_____ 8. What are three major cost flow assumptions used by U.S. companies in valuing inventory?
(a) LIFO, FIFO, average market.
(b) LIFO, FIFO, actual cost.
(c) LIFO, FIFO, average cost.
(d) LIFO, FIFO, double-declining balance.

_____ 9. Assuming a period of inflation, which statement is true?
(a) The FIFO method understates balance sheet inventory.
(b) The FIFO method understates cost of goods sold on the income statement.
(c) The LIFO method overstates balance sheet inventory.
(d) The LIFO method understates cost of goods sold on the income statement.

_____ 10. Why would a company switch to the LIFO method of inventory valuation?
(a) By switching to LIFO, reported earnings will be higher.
(b) A new tax law requires companies using LIFO for reported purposes also to use LIFO for figuring taxable income.
(c) LIFO produces the largest cost of goods sold expense in a period of inflation and thereby lowers taxable income and taxes.
(d) A survey by *Accounting Trends and Techniques* revealed that the switch to LIFO is a current accounting "fad."

_____ 11. Where can one most typically find the cost flow assumption used for inventory valuation for a specific company?
(a) In Robert Morris Associates, *Annual Statement Studies.*
(b) In the statement of retained earnings.
(c) On the face of the balance sheet with the total current asset amount.
(d) In the notes to the financial statements.

_____ 12. What type of firm generally has the highest proportion of fixed assets to total assets?
(a) Manufacturers.
(b) Retailers.
(c) Wholesalers.
(d) Retailers and wholesalers.

_____ 13. Companies A, B, and C:

	A	B	C
Inventory	$ 90,000	$120,000	$180,000
Property, plant, and equipment	$ 75,000	$ 30,000	$ 45,000
Total assets	$300,000	$300,000	$300,000

Which company is most likely a retailer? a wholesaler? a manufacturer?
(a) Company A, retailer; Company B, wholesaler; Company C, manufacturer.
(b) Company A, wholesaler; Company B, manufacturer; Company C, retailer.
(c) Company A, manufacturer; Company B, wholesaler; Company C, retailer.
(d) Company A, manufacturer; Company B, retailer; Company C, wholesaler.

_____ 14. Which group of items would most likely be included in the other assets account on the balance sheet?
(a) Inventories, marketable securities, bonds.
(b) Land held for investment purposes, start-up costs, long-term prepayments.

    (c) One-year prepaid insurance policy, stock investments, copyrights.

    (d) Inventories, franchises, patents.

_____ 15. What do current liabilities and current assets have in common?

    (a) Current assets are claims against current liabilities.

    (b) If current assets increase, then there will be a corresponding increase in current liabilities.

    (c) Current liabilities and current assets are converted into cash.

    (d) Current liabilities and current assets are those items that will be satisfied and converted into cash, respectively, in one year or one opening cycle, whichever is longer.

_____ 16. What is the difference between notes payable—banks and current maturities of long-term debt?

    (a) Notes payable—banks are short-term obligations, and current maturities of long-term are the portion of long-term debt that will be repaid during the upcoming year.

    (b) There is no difference.

    (c) Notes payable—banks are usually included under current liabilities, and current maturities of long-term debt are included under long-term debt.

    (d) Notes payable—banks are long-term liabilities, and current maturities of long-term debt are current liabilities.

_____ 17. Which of the following items could cause the recognition of accrued liabilities?

    (a) Sales, interest expense, rent.

    (b) Sales, taxes, interest income.

    (c) Salaries, rent, insurance.

    (d) Salaries, interest expense, interest income.

_____ 18. Which statement is false?

    (a) Deferred taxes are the product of temporary differences in the recognition of revenue and expense for taxable income relative to reported income.

    (b) Deferred taxes arise from the use of the same method of depreciation for tax and reporting purposes.

    (c) Deferred taxes arise when taxes actually paid are less than tax expense reported in the financial statements.

    (d) Temporary differences causing the recognition of deferred taxes may arise from the methods used to account for items such as depreciation, installment sales, leases, and pensions.

_____ 19. Which of the following would be classified as long-term debt?

    (a) Mortgages, current maturities of long-term debt, bonds.

    (b) Mortgages, long-term notes payable, bonds due in ten years.

    (c) Accounts payable, bonds, obligations under leases.

    (d) Accounts payable, long-term notes payable, long-term warranties.

_____ 20. What accounts are most likely to be found in the stockholders' equity section of the balance sheet?

    (a) Common stock, long-term debt, preferred stock.

    (b) Common stock, additional paid-in capital, liabilities.

    (c) Common stock, retained earnings, dividends payable.

    (d) Common stock, additional paid-in capital, retained earnings.

____ 21. What does the additional paid-in capital account represent?
     (a) The difference between the par and the stated value of common stock.
     (b) The price changes that result for stock trading subsequent to its original issue.
     (c) The market price of all common stock issued.
     (d) The amount by which the original sales price of stock exceeds the par value.

____ 22. What does the retained earnings account measure?
     (a) Cash held by the company since its interception.
     (b) Payments made to shareholders in the form of cash or stock dividends.
     (c) All undistributed earnings.
     (d) Financial resources currently available to satisfy financial obligations.

23. Listed below are balance sheet accounts for Elf's Gift Shop. Mark current accounts with "C" and noncurrent accounts with "NC."
____ (a) Long-term debt
____ (b) Inventories
____ (c) Accounts payable
____ (d) Prepaid expenses
____ (e) Equipment
____ (f) Accrued liabilities
____ (g) Accounts receivable
____ (h) Cash
____ (i) Bonds payable
____ (j) Patents

24. Dot's Delicious Donuts has the following accounts on its balance sheet:
     (1) Current assets
     (2) Property, plant, and equipment
     (3) Intangible assets
     (4) Other assets
     (5) Current liabilities
     (6) Deferred Federal income taxes
     (7) Long-term debt
     (8) Stockholders' equity
How would each of the following items be classified?
____ (a) Land held for speculation
____ (b) Current maturities on mortgage
____ (c) Common stock
____ (d) Mortgage payable
____ (e) Balances outstanding on credit sales to customers
____ (f) Accumulated depreciation
____ (g) Buildings used in business
____ (h) Accrued payroll
____ (i) Preferred stock
____ (j) Debt outstanding from credit extended by suppliers
____ (k) Patents
____ (l) Land on which warehouse is located
____ (m) Allowance for doubtful accounts
____ (n) Liability due to difference in taxes paid and taxes reported
____ (o) Additional paid-in capital

25. Match the following terms to the correct definitions.

_____ (a) Consolidated financial statements

_____ (b) Current assets

_____ (c) Depreciation

_____ (d) Deferred taxes

_____ (e) Allowance for doubtful accounts

_____ (f) Prepaid expenses

_____ (g) Current maturities

_____ (h) Accrued expense

_____ (i) Par value of stock

_____ (j) Market value of stock

(1) Used up within one year or operating cycle, whichever is longer.

(2) Expenses incurred prior to cash outflow.

(3) Value unrelated to selling price of stock.

(4) Estimation of uncollectible accounts receivable.

(5) Cost allocation of fixed assets other than land.

(6) Expenses paid in advance.

(7) Combined statements of parent company and controlled subsidiary companies.

(8) Price at which stock trades.

(9) Difference in taxes reported and taxes paid.

(10) Portion of debt to be repaid during the upcoming year.

STUDY QUESTIONS AND PROBLEMS

2.1 How can the allowance for doubtful accounts be used to assess earnings quality?

2.2 Why is the valuation of inventories important in financial reporting?

2.3 Why would a company switch to the LIFO method of inventory valuation in an inflationary period?

2.4 Discuss the difference between the straight-line method of depreciation and the accelerated methods. Why do companies use different depreciation methods for tax reporting and financial reporting?

2.5 How is it possible for a company with positive retained earnings to be unable to pay a cash dividend?

2.6 The following data are available for three companies, A, B, and C:

	A	B	C
Inventories	$ 280,000	$ 280,000	$ 280,000
Net fixed assets	400,000	65,000	70,000
Total assets	1,000,000	430,000	650,000

Which company is most likely a retailer? A wholesaler? A manufacturer?

2.7 The F.L.A.C. Corporation sells a single product. The following is information on inventory, purchase, and sales for the first quarter:

		Number of units	Unit cost	Sale price
January 1	Inventory	10,000	$3.00	
January 10	Purchase	4,000	3.50	
January 1–31	Sales	8,000		$5.00
February 6	Purchase	5,000	4.00	
February 25	Purchase	5,000	4.00	
February 1–28	Sales	11,000		5.50
March 10	Purchase	6,000	4.50	

| March 15 | Purchase | 8,000 | 5.00 | |
| March 1–31 | Sales | 12,000 | | 6.50 |

(a) Compute the inventory balance on March 31 and the cost of goods sold expense reported in the quarterly income statement using the following methods: FIFO, LIFO, and average cost.

(b) Discuss the effect of each method on the balance sheet and income statement during periods of inflation.

2.8 The IOU Corporation has a $150,000 note outstanding with 14% annual interest due in semiannual installments on January 31 and July 31. What amount will be shown as accrued interest on a December 31 balance sheet?

2.9 The King Corporation has total annual revenue of $800,000; expenses other than depreciation of $350,000; depreciation expense of $200,000 for tax purposes; and depreciation expense of $130,000 for reporting purposes. The tax rate is 34%. Calculate net income for reporting purposes and for tax purposes. What is the deferred tax liability?

2.10 Explain how treasury stock affects the stockholders' equity section of the balance sheet and the calculation of earnings per share.

2.11 Energaire Inc. reported the following in its consolidated balance sheets at December 31, 2003:

	2003	2002
Accounts receivable, net of allowance accounts (2003, $28,704; 2002, $18,466)	$289,363	$276,204

Analyze Energaire's allowance for doubtful accounts for 2003 and 2002.

2.12 From the following accounts, prepare a balance sheet for Chester Co. for the current calendar year.

Accrued interest payable	$1,400
Property, plant, and equipment	34,000
Inventory	12,400
Additional paid-in capital	7,000
Deferred taxes payable (noncurrent)	1,600
Cash	1,500
Accumulated depreciation	10,500
Bonds payable	14,500
Accounts payable	4,300
Common stock	2,500
Prepaid expenses	700
Land held for sale	9,200
Retained earnings	?
Current portion of long-term debt	1,700
Accounts receivable	6,200
Notes payable	8,700

2.13 Writing Skills Problem

You have read chapter 2 of the text and have noticed that there are no drawings, such as the simulated ski slope and the cans of soup in chapter 1. The nontext material in chapter 2 consists only of tables, which you find a bit dry. Visual modes of expression are an integral part of business writing and often convey ideas better than prose. Visuals are used both to supplement written communication and in some cases to carry the message entirely. Some of the more commonly used forms of visual in technical communication are *drawings, diagrams, bar charts, pie charts, flow charts, line graphs, tables,* and *photographs.* Technical communication can be greatly enhanced by visual forms of expression.

Required: Select some aspect of chapter 2 and design a visual (other than a table) to accompany, supplement, or replace a section of the text.

2.14 Internet Problem

Choose a publicly held corporation (unless your teacher assigns a particular corporation for this assignment) and find the balance sheet and notes to the financial statements in the most recent Form 10-K. The Form 10-K can be located by going to the homepage of the Securities and Exchange Commission and locating the SEC EDGAR Database. The address for the homepage is http://www.sec.gov/.

Using the information you find answer the following questions:

(a) What current assets are included on the balance sheet?

(b) If the company lists accounts receivable and an allowance account, analyze these accounts.

(c) What method does the company use to value inventory?

(d) What depreciation method does the company use?

(e) What assets other than current assets and property, plant, and equipment are included on the balance sheet?

(f) What current liabilities are included on the balance sheet?

(g) How many deferred tax accounts are included on the balance sheet? Under which classification(s) are deferred taxes found? What temporary differences caused the creation of the deferred tax account(s)?

(h) Does the company have long-term debt? How much?

(i) Does the company have commitments and contingencies? If so, what commitments does the company have and for what amount is the company committed? Explain any contingencies.

(j) What stockholders' equity accounts are included on the balance sheet?

2.15 Annual Report Problem

The 1998 PETsMART Annual Report can be found at the following Web site: www.prenhall.com/fraser

Using the annual report, answer the following questions:

(a) Describe the types of assets PETsMART owns. Which assets are the most significant to the company? Using the notes to the financial statements, discuss the accounting methods used to value assets. What other information can be learned about the asset accounts from the notes?

(b) Describe the types of liabilities PETsMART has incurred. Which liabilities are the most significant to the company?

(c) Describe the commitments and contingencies of PETsMART.

(d) Under which classification(s) are deferred taxes listed? What item is the most significant component of deferred taxes?

(e) What equity accounts are included on the balance sheet of PETsMART? What is the Retained Earnings account called? Why?

Intel Corporation Mini-Case

Using the consolidated balance sheets for Intel Corporation for December 30, 1995 and December 31, 1994, and the excerpts from the notes to the financial statements, explain the meaning of each account listed and its importance to users of Intel financial statements.

NOTES TO CONSOLIDATED FINANCIAL STATEMENTS

Investments   Highly liquid investments with insignificant interest rate risk and with original maturities of three months or less are classified as cash and cash equivalents. Investments with maturities greater than three months and less than one year are classified as short-term investments. Investments with maturities greater than one year are classified as long-term investments.

The Company accounts for investments in accordance with SFAS No. 115, "Accounting for Certain Investments in Debt and Equity Securities," effective as of the beginning of fiscal 1994. The Company's policy is to protect the value of its investment portfolio and to minimize principal risk by earning returns based on current interest rates. All of the Company's marketable investments are classified as available-for-sale as of the balance sheet date and are reported at fair value, with unrealized gains and losses, net of tax, recorded in stockholders' equity. The cost of securities sold is based on the specific identification method. Realized gains or losses and declines in value, if any, judged to be other than temporary on available-for-sale securities are reported in other income or expense. Investments in nonmarketable instruments are recorded at the lower of cost or market and included in other assets.

Inventories   Inventories are stated at the lower of cost or market. Cost is computed on a currently adjusted standard basis (which approximates actual cost on a current average or first-in, first-out basis). Inventories at fiscal year-ends were as follows:

(In millions)	1995	1994
Materials and purchased parts	$ 674	$ 345
Work-in-process	707	528
Finished goods	$ 623	$ 296
Total	$2,004	$1,169

CONSOLIDATED BALANCE SHEETS
DECEMBER 30, 1995 AND DECEMBER 31, 1994
(IN MILLIONS EXCEPT PER SHARE AMOUNTS)

	1994	1995
Assets		
Current assets		
Cash and cash equivalents	$ 1,463	$ 1,180
Short-term investments	995	1,230
Accounts receivable, net of allowance for doubtful accounts of $57 ($32 in 1994)	3,116	1,978
Inventories	2,004	1,169
Deferred tax assets	408	552
Other current assets	111	58
Total current assets	8,097	6,167
Property, plant, and equipment:		
Land and buildings	3,145	2,292
Machinery and equipment	7,099	5,374
Construction in progress	1,548	850
	11,792	8,516
Less accumulated depreciation	4,321	3,149
Property, plant, and equipment, net	7,471	5,367
Long-term investments	1,653	2,127
Other assets	283	155
Total assets	$17,504	$13,816
Liabilities and stockholders' equity		
Current liabilities:		
Short-term debt	$ 346	$ 517
Accounts payable	864	575
Deferred income on shipments to distributors	304	269
Accrued compensation and benefits	758	588
Accrued advertising	218	108
Other accrued liabilities	328	538
Income taxes payable	801	429
Total current liabilities	3,619	3,024
Long-term debt	400	392
Deferred tax liabilities	620	389
Put warrants	725	744
Commitments and contingencies		
Stockholders' equity		
Preferred Stock $.001 par value, 50 shares authorized; none issued	—	—
Common Stock, $.001 par value, 1,400 shares authorized; 821 issued and outstanding in 1995 (827 in 1994) and capital in excess of par value	2,583	2,306
Retained earnings	9,557	6,961
Total stockholders' equity	12,140	9,267
Total liabilities and stockholders' equity	$17,504	$13,816

See accompanying notes.

Property, plant, and equipment   Property, plant, and equipment are stated at cost. Depreciation is computed for financial reporting purposes principally by use of the straight-line method over the following estimated useful lives: machinery and equipment, 2–4 years; land and buildings, 4–45 years.

The Company adopted SFAS No. 121, "Accounting for the Impairment of Long-Lived Assets and for Long-Lived Assets to Be Disposed Of," effective as of the beginning of fiscal 1995. This adoption had no material effect on the Company's financial statements.

Deferred income on shipments to distributors   Certain of the Company's sales are made to distributors under agreements allowing price protection and/or right of return on merchandise unsold by the distributors. Because of frequent sales price reductions and rapid technological obsolescence in the industry, Intel defers recognition of such sales until the merchandise is sold by the distributors.

Put Warrants

In a series of private placements from 1991 through 1995, the Company sold put warrants that entitle the holder of each warrant to sell one share of Common Stock to the Company at a specified price. Activity during the past three years is summarized as follows:

		Put warrants outstanding	
(In millions)	*Cumulative premium received*	*Number of warrants*	*Potential obligation*
December 26, 1992	$56	28.0	$373
Sales	62	21.6	561
Expirations	—	(20.0)	(246)
December 25, 1993	118	29.6	688
Sales	76	25.0	744
Exercises	—	(2.0)	(65)
Expirations	—	(27.6)	(623)
December 31, 1994	194	25.0	744
Sales	85	17.5	925
Repurchases	—	(5.5)	(201)
Expirations	—	(25.0)	(743)
December 30, 1995	$279	12.0	$725

The amount related to Intel's potential repurchase obligation has been reclassified from stockholders' equity to put warrants. The 12 million put warrants outstanding at December 30, 1995 expire on various dates between February 1996 and November 1996 and have exercise prices ranging from $38 to $68 per share, with an average exercise price of $60 per share. There is no significant dilutive effect on earnings per share for the periods presented.

Borrowings

Short term debt   Short-term debt and weighted average interest rates at fiscal year-ends were as follows:

(In millions)	1994 Balance	1994 Weighted average interest rate	1995 Balance	1995 Weighted average interest rate
Borrowed under lines of credit	$57	3.2%	$68	3.2%
Reverse purchase agreements payable in non-U.S. currencies	124	9.2%	99	8.0%
Notes payable	2	4.7%	5	4.7%
Short-term portion of long-term debt	—	—	179	11.8%
Drafts payable	163	N/A	166	N/A
Total	$346		$517	

Long-term debt   Long-term debt at fiscal year-ends was as follows:

(In millions)	1995	1994
Payable in U.S. dollars:		
AFICA Bonds due 2013 at 4%	$110	$110
Zero Coupon Notes due 1995 at 11.8%, net of unamortized discount of $8 in 1994	—	179
Other U.S. dollar debt	4	4
Payable in other currencies:		
Irish punt due 2008–2024 at 6%–12%	240	228
Greek drachma due 2001	46	46
Other foreign currency debt	—	4
(Less short-term portion)	—	(179)
Total	$400	$392

Provision for taxes

Significant components of the Company's deferred tax assets and liabilities at fiscal year-ends were as follows:

(In millions)	1995	1994
Deferred tax assets		
Accrued compensation and benefits	$61	$49
Deferred income	127	127
Inventory valuation and related reserves	104	255
Interest and taxes	61	54
Other, net	55	67
	408	552
Deferred tax liabilities		
Depreciation	(475)	(338)
Unremitted earnings of certain subsidiaries	(116)	(51)

Other, net	(29)	—
	(620)	(389)
Net deferred tax (liability) asset	$(212)	$163

Commitments

The Company leases a portion of its capital equipment and certain of its facilities under operating leases that expire at various dates through 2011. Rental expense was $38 million in 1995, $38 million in 1994 and $35 million in 1993. Minimum rental commitments under all noncancelable leases with an initial term in excess of one year are payable as follows: 1996—$25 million; 1997—$20 million; 1998—$15 million; 1999—$12 million; 2000—$10 million; 2001 and beyond—$23 million.

Contingencies

On March 29, 1995, Thorn EMI North America Inc. brought suit in federal court in Delaware against Intel and Advanced Micro Devices, Inc. (AMD) alleging infringement of a U.S. patent relating to processes for manufacturing semiconductors, certain of which processes are utilized in the manufacture of the Company's Pentium and Pentium Pro microprocessors. The plaintiff is seeking injunctive relief and unspecified damages. On September 8, 1995, Intel was granted a motion to sever its case from the AMD case. Trial of the plaintiff's claims against Intel is presently set for June 1996. The Company believes this lawsuit to be without merit and intends to defend the lawsuit vigorously. Although the ultimate outcome of this lawsuit cannot be determined at this time, management, including internal counsel, does not believe that the outcome of this litigation will have a material adverse effect on the Company's financial position or overall trends in results of operations.

The Rival Company Mini-Case

The Rival Company is a leading designer, manufacturer, and marketer of small household appliances, personal care products, fans, space heaters and sump, well, and utility pumps. The company's product lines are sold in a variety of distribution channels in the United States and Canada, including such mass merchants as Kmart, Target, and Wal-Mart, hardware/home centers, department stores, catalog showrooms, drug stores, warehouse clubs, and industrial supply dealers. The company manufactures a substantial majority of the products that are sold under its Rival, Simer, Patton, and White Mountain brand names. Domestic manufacturing provides a competitive advantage relative to rapid delivery, new-product introductions, and quality control. Selected information from Rival Company's 1995 annual report is given on pages 85–89.

REQUIRED:

1. Which two current assets are the most significant? What percentage is each relative to total assets and to net sales? Calculate the percentages for 1995 and 1994. Analyze the percentage trend of these two current assets.

2. Analyze the allowance for doubtful accounts relative to accounts receivable and net sales.

3. What types of inventories does Rival carry? Why? What inventory method does Rival use? Estimate the current cost of inventory for June 30, 1995 and 1994.

4. Based on the inventory valuation method Rival uses, would you expect Rival to have tax savings or pay more in taxes because of its choice of inventory method? Explain your answer. (You do not need to do any calculations.)

5. Which two assets other than current assets are significant to the Rival Company? What percentage is each relative to total assets? Are the relative proportions of these assets what you would expect for an appliance manufacturer? Explain.

6. What caused the increase in the goodwill account for Rival from 1994 to 1995? What other accounts were impacted on the balance sheet of Rival related to the increase in goodwill?

7. Discuss the types of liabilities Rival Company holds and note any significant changes in the liability structure.

8. Under which classifications do deferred income taxes appear in 1995? Explain why deferred income taxes appear in more than one classification. What are the three principal sources of timing differences for Rival? Explain why these timing differences appear as an asset or a liability. Reconcile the numbers appearing on the balance sheet for deferred income taxes to the numbers appearing in Note 6 for 1995.

9. What is the average price paid for one share of Rival Company's common stock? What is the market value of one share of Rival common stock today? (Rival trades on the NASDAQ under the symbol RIVL.)

10. Has Rival experienced gains or losses due to foreign currency translation of its financial statements?

11. Using the balance sheet and income statement information for Rival, calculate the amount of dividends most likely paid to stockholders for the fiscal year ending June 30, 1995.

THE RIVAL COMPANY AND SUBSIDIARIES
CONSOLIDATED BALANCE SHEETS
IN THOUSANDS

June 30,	1995	1994
Assets		
Current assets:		
Cash	$ 193	$ 119
Accounts receivable	43,492	34,757
Inventories	81,104	50,276
Deferred income tax charges	860	985
Prepaid expenses	835	1,052
Total current assets	126,484	87,189
Property, plant, and equipment, net	27,072	21,980
Goodwill	48,186	38,799
Other assets	2,626	3,499
	$204,368	$151,467
Liabilities and Stockholders' Equity		
Current liabilities:		
Notes payable to bank	$ 37,627	$ 4,600
Current portion of long-term debt	4,000	4,000
Trade accounts payable	14,972	11,010
Accrued interest	1,488	1,462
Income taxes payable	577	106
Other payables and accrued expenses	7,527	5,648
Total current liabilities	66,191	27,126
Long-term debt, less current portion	42,000	46,000
Deferred income taxes	2,372	2,237
Stockholders' equity:		
Common stock, $0.01 par value.		
Authorized 15,000,000 shares; issued, 9,740,330 in 1995 and 9,308,060 in 1994; outstanding, 9,714,933 in 1995 and 9,282,663 in 1994	97	93
Paid-in capital	45,366	40,176
Foreign currency translation	(395)	(409)
Treasury stock, at cost	(310)	(310)
Retained earnings	49,047	36,554
Total stockholders' equity	93,805	76,104
Commitments and contingencies	$204,368	$151,467

FINANCIAL HIGHLIGHTS IN THOUSANDS

For the Fiscal Year Ended June 30	1995	1994
Summary of Operations		
Net sales	$231,711	$229,233
Net earnings	13,985	14,317

THE RIVAL COMPANY AND SUBSIDIARIES
NOTES TO CONSOLIDATED FINANCIAL STATEMENTS

1. Summary of Significant Accounting Policies

Principles of Consolidation   The Consolidated Financial Statements include the accounts of The Rival Company and its wholly-owned subsidiaries: Pollenex Corporation ("Pollenex"), Patton Electric Company, Inc. ("Patton"), Patton Electric (Hong Kong) Limited ("PEHK"), Rival Manufacturing Company of Canada, Ltd. ("Rival-Canada") and Waverly Products Company Ltd. All significant intercompany account balances and transactions have been eliminated in consolidation.

Inventories   Approximately 55% of the Company's inventories are stated at the lower of LIFO (last-in, first-out method) cost or market. The balance of the inventories are stated at the lower of FIFO (first-in, first-out) cost or market.

Depreciation   Depreciation on property, plant and equipment is computed on a straight-line basis over the estimated useful lives of the assets which range from 3 to 10 years on machinery and equipment and 10 to 40 years on buildings and improvements.

Goodwill   The excess of the purchase price paid in the 1986 acquisition of the Company over the estimated fair value of the net assets acquired (goodwill) is being amortized on a straight-line basis over a period of forty years. The goodwill resulting from subsequent acquisitions is being amortized on a straight-line basis over periods ranging from 15 to 30 years. The Company assesses the recoverability of goodwill by determining whether the amortization of the goodwill balance over its remaining life can be recovered through undiscounted future operating cash flows. Goodwill is reflected in the accompanying Consolidated Balance Sheets net of accumulated amortization of $10,485,000 and $9,158,000 at June 30, 1995 and 1994, respectively.

Deferred Debt Expense   Deferred debt expense is amortized over the terms of the related debt using the interest method.

Income Taxes   The Company and its domestic subsidiaries file a consolidated federal income tax return.

   The Company accounts for income taxes under Statement of Financial Accounting Standards No. 109, "Accounting for Income Taxes." Statement No. 109 requires an asset and liability method of accounting for income taxes. Under the asset and liability method, deferred tax assets and liabilities are recognized for the future tax consequences attributable to differences between the financial statement carrying amounts of existing assets and liabilities and their respective tax bases. Deferred tax assets and liabilities are measured using enacted tax rates expected to be recovered or settled. Under Statement No. 109, the effect on deferred tax assets and liabilities of a change in tax rates is recognized in earnings in the period that includes the enactment date.

2. Acquisitions

On April 21, 1995, the Company acquired substantially all of the assets of Patton Electric Company, Inc. ("Patton"), a manufacturer of fans and space heaters for consumer and industrial use with annual sales of approximately $40 million. As part of the transaction, the Company also acquired certain assets of an affiliated corporation, Giant Lion Trading, Ltd., ("GLT"), and acquired all of the outstanding stock of a second affiliated corporation, Patton Electric (Hong Kong) Limited.

At closing, as consideration for the acquisition, the Company issued 850,000 shares of its common stock which were valued at $11.9 million, paid cash of $25.3 million and assumed certain other liabilities including trade accounts payable of Patton. The acquisition was accounted for as a purchase and, accordingly, the purchase price was allocated to the assets acquired and the liabilities assumed based upon their respective fair values. The purchase price and the allocation of such amount to assets acquired and liabilities assumed is summarized as follows:

	(in thousands)
Common stock issued	$11,900
Cash paid at closing	25,269
	$37,169
Inventory	25,393
Accounts receivable	6,481
Property, plant and equipment	4,943
Other assets	41
Goodwill	10,714
Liabilities assumed	(10,403)
	$37,169

3. Accounts Receivable

Accounts receivable consist of:

at June 30,	1995	1994
	(in thousands)	
Trade	$45,154	$36,415
Other	247	35
	45,401	36,450
Less allowance for collection losses and discounts	(1,909)	(1,693)
	$43,492	$34,757

4. Inventories

Inventories consist of:

at June 30,	1995	1994
	(in thousands)	
Raw materials	$33,221	$18,188
Work in process	1,741	1,356
Finished goods	49,924	33,970
	84,886	53,514
Valuation to LIFO	(3,782)	(3,238)
	$81,104	$50,276

If LIFO inventories had been stated at the lower of FIFO cost or market, earnings before income taxes would have been $544,000, $223,000 and $34,000 higher for the years ended June 30, 1995, 1994 and 1993, respectively.

5. Property, Plant and Equipment

Property, plant and equipment is summarized as follows:

at June 30,	1995	1994
	(in thousands)	
Land	$633	$545
Buildings and improvements	14,432	10,932
Machinery and equipment	30,184	27,914
Furniture and fixtures	3,411	2,845
	48,660	42,236
Less accumulated depreciation	(21,588)	(20,256)
	$27,072	$21,980

6. Income Taxes

The tax effects of temporary differences that result in deferred assets and (liabilities) are presented below. There were no valuation allowances provided for deferred tax assets.

at June 30,	1995	1994
	(in thousands)	
Depreciation	$(1,904)	$(1,731)
Inventory	(1,550)	(1,291)
Pension plan costs	(626)	(613)
Total deferred tax liabilities	(4,080)	(3,635)
Bad debts	406	450
Reserves not currently deductible	1,804	1,639
Other	358	294
Total deferred tax assets	2,568	2,383
Net deferred tax liabilities	$(1,512)	$(1,252)

MANAGEMENT DISCUSSION AND ANALYSIS
OF FINANCIAL CONDITION AND RESULTS OF OPERATIONS

The Company's operations require significant amounts of working capital, particularly during the fall of each year. Sales are on terms which generally range from 30 days to 75 days, resulting in substantial accounts receivable balances. Due to the seasonal nature of the business, the Company builds inventory levels during the spring and summer in anticipation of a heavy August through November selling season for Rival and Pollenex products. Historically, inventory levels peak in late July or early August.

Inventories of Patton were $23.8 million as of June 30, 1995. Such inventories were much higher than historical levels at the date of the acquisition. Management believes that Patton inventories will be reduced substantially over the next twelve months. The Company relies on revolving credit loans to finance these working capital requirements. Because of the acquisitions of the Simer Pump business with its peak sales in the spring and Patton with its fans selling primarily in the late spring and summer, the Company's borrowings will likely be less seasonal in the future.

CHAPTER

3

Income Statement and Statement of Stockholders' Equity

Learning about earnings, the bottom line,
Is very important most of the time.
A phony number
Just may encumber
Those folks trying to make more than a dime.

—A. ORMISTON[1]

The operating performance of a business firm has traditionally been measured by its success in generating earnings—the "bottom line." Investors, creditors, and analysts eagerly await companies' earnings reports. One objective of this book is to broaden the reader's perspective of operating success to consider such yardsticks as "cash flow from operations" as well as net income. In this chapter, however, the focus will be on the income statement and how a company arrives at its "bottom line."

The *income statement,* also called the *statement of earnings,* presents revenues, expenses, net income, and earnings per share for an accounting period, generally a

---

[1] According to the *New Book of Knowledge* (1985) by Grolier Incorporated, limericks are difficult to write. Limericks, a form of nonsense-verse, consist of five lines, of which lines one, two, and five rhyme and have from eight to eleven syllables each; lines three and four rhyme with five to seven syllables each. Although thousands exist in literature, it is estimated that only 200 are probably genuine, flawless examples. Readers may submit limericks for possible inclusion in future editions!

year or a quarter. (The terms *income* and *earnings* are used interchangeably throughout the book.) The *statement of stockholders' equity* is an important link between the balance sheet and the income statement. This statement documents the changes in the balance sheet equity accounts from one accounting period to the next. Companies may choose to report the information on the statement of stockholders' equity in a supplementary schedule or in a note to the financial statements rather than preparing a formal financial statement. Annual reports include three years of income statements and stockholder's' equity information.

R.E.C. Inc. prepares a formal statement of stockholders' equity. Both the income statement and statement of stockholders' equity will be discussed in this chapter using the R.E.C. Inc. statements as the basis for a description of each statement and the accounts that typically appear in the statements.

The Income Statement

Regardless of the perspective of the financial statement user—investor, creditor, employee, competitor, supplier, regulator—it is essential to understand and analyze the earnings statement. But it is also important that the analyst realize that a company's

---

EXHIBIT 3.1

R.E.C., INC.
CONSOLIDATED STATEMENTS OF EARNINGS AND RETAINED EARNINGS
FOR THE YEARS ENDED DECEMBER 31, 2002, 2001, AND 2000
(IN THOUSANDS EXCEPT PER SHARE AMOUNTS)

	2002	2001	2000
Net Sales	$215,600	$153,000	$140,700
Cost of goods sold (Note A)	129,364	91,879	81,606
Gross profit	86,236	61,121	59,094
Selling and administrative expenses (Notes A and E)	45,722	33,493	32,765
Advertising	14,258	10,792	9,541
Depreciation and amortization (Note A)	3,998	2,984	2,501
Repairs and maintenance	3,015	2,046	3,031
Operating profit	19,243	11,806	11,256
Other income (expense)			
Interest income	422	838	738
Interest expense	(2,585)	(2,277)	(1,274)
Earnings before income taxes	17,080	10,367	10,720
Income taxes (Notes A and D)	7,686	4,457	4,824
Net Earnings	$ 9,394	$ 5,910	$ 5,896
Basic earnings per common share (Note G)	$ 1.96	$ 1.29	$ 1.33
Diluted earnings per common share (Note G)	$ 1.93	$ 1.26	$ 1.31

The accompanying notes are an integral part of these statements.

report of earnings and other information presented on the income statement are not complete and sufficient barometers of financial performance. The income statement is one of many pieces of a financial statement package, and like the other pieces, the income statement is partially the product of a wide range of accounting choices, estimates, and judgments that affect reported results, just as business policies, economic conditions, and many other variables affect results. How these issues, introduced in chapter 1, affect reported results will continue to be considered throughout this chapter.

It has previously been explained that earnings are measured on an accrual rather than a cash basis, which means that income reported on the income statement is not the same as cash generated during the accounting period. Cash flow from operations and its importance to analysis are covered in chapter 4. The purpose of this chapter is not to minimize the importance of the income statement, however, but to provide a clear context for its interpretation.

The income statement comes in two basic formats and with considerable variation in the degree of detail presented. The earnings statement for R.E.C. Inc. is presented in a *multiple-step* format, which provides several intermediate profit measures—gross profit, operating profit, and earnings before income tax—prior to the amount of net earnings for the period. The *single-step* version of the income statement groups all items of revenue together, then deducts all categories of expense to arrive at a figure for net income. Exhibit 3.2 illustrates the single-step approach if R.E.C. Inc. used that method to report earnings.

Certain special items, if they occur during an accounting period, must be disclosed separately on an income statement, regardless of format. These include discontinued

---

EXHIBIT 3.2

R.E.C., INC.
CONSOLIDATED STATEMENTS OF EARNINGS FOR YEARS ENDED
DECEMBER 31, 2002, 2001, 2000 (IN THOUSANDS EXCEPT PER SHARE AMOUNTS)

	2002	*2001*	*2000*
Income			
Net sales	$215,600	$153,000	$140,700
Interest income	422	838	738
	216,022	153,838	141,438
Costs and Expenses			
Cost of goods sold	129,364	91,879	81,606
Marketing, administrative, and other expenses	66,993	49,315	47,838
Interest expense	2,585	2,277	1,274
Income taxes	7,686	4,457	4,824
Net Earnings	$ 9,394	5,910	5,896
Basic earnings per Common Share	$ 1.96	$ 1.29	$ 1.33
Diluted earnings per Common Share	$ 1.93	$ 1.26	$ 1.31

operations, extraordinary transactions, and the cumulative effect of changes in accounting principles. *Discontinued operations* occur when a firm sells a major portion of its business. The results of continuing operations are shown separately from the operating results of the discontinued portion of the business. Any gain or loss on the disposal is also disclosed separately. *Extraordinary gains and losses* are items that meet two criteria: unusual in nature *and* not expected to recur in the foreseeable future, considering the firm's operating environment. The *cumulative effect of a change in accounting principle* is disclosed when a firm changes an accounting policy, for example, from an accelerated method of depreciation to the straight-line method.

As noted in chapter 2, the FASB passed a new rule, effective in 1998, requiring companies to report *comprehensive income.* According to FASB Statement of Financial Accounting Concepts No. 6, "Elements of Financial Statements," comprehensive income is the change in equity of a company during a period from transactions, other events, and circumstances relating to nonowner sources. It includes all changes in equity during a period except those resulting from investments by owners and distributions to owners. Companies are required to report total comprehensive income in one of three ways:

on the face of its income statement,
in a separate statement of comprehensive income, or
in its statement of stockholders' equity.

Data are presented in corporate income statements for three years to facilitate comparison and to provide evidence regarding trends of revenues, expenses, and net earnings. Because R.E.C. Inc. has only net earnings and no other comprehensive income, the company does not have a statement of comprehensive income. The statements for R.E.C. Inc. are consolidated, which means that the information presented is a combination of the results for R.E.C. Inc. and its wholly owned subsidiaries. The disclosure of comprehensive income and the accounting methods used for subsidiary investments will be discussed later in the chapter under the headings "Comprehensive Income" and "Other Issues—Cost vs. Equity."

NET SALES

Total sales revenue for each year of the three-year period is shown net of returns and allowances. A *sales return* is a cancellation of a sale, and a *sales allowance* is a deduction from the original sales invoice price. Since sales are the major revenue source for most companies, the trend of this figure is a key element in performance measurement. Although most of the analysis of R.E.C. Inc.'s financial statements will be conducted in chapter 5, the reader can look for clues on the income statement.

It would appear, for instance, that R.E.C. Inc. had a much better sales year in 2002 than 2001: sales increased 40.9% ($62.6 million) between 2001 and 2002, compared with an 8.7% ($12.3 million) growth between 2000 and 2001. If a company's sales are increasing (or decreasing), it is important to determine whether the change is a result of price, volume, or a combination of both. Are sales growing because the firm is increasing prices or because more units are being sold, or both? It would seem that, in general, higher quality earnings would be the product of both volume and price increases (during inflation). The firm would want to sell more units and keep prices increasing at least in line with the rate of inflation. The reasons for sales growth (or decline) are covered in a firm's Management Discussion and Analysis section of the annual or 10-K report (see chapter 1).

A related issue is whether sales are growing in "real" (inflation-adjusted) as well as "nominal" (as reported) terms. Disclosures regarding inflation accounting are no longer required, as discussed in chapter 1. The change in sales in nominal terms can be readily calculated from the figures reported on the income statement. An adjustment of the reported sales figure with the Consumer Price Index (CPI) (or some other measure of general inflation) will enable the analyst to make a comparison of the changes in real and nominal terms. To make the calculation to compare real with nominal sales, begin with the sales figures reported in the income statement, and adjust years prior to the current year with the CPI or some other price index. For R.E.C. Inc., the nominal growth rate was already calculated to be 40.9%. Assuming the CPIs for 2002 and 2001 are 322.2 and 311.1, respectively, the adjusted or real sales figure for 2001 is $158,459, (322.2/311.1) × $153,000. Sales when adjusted for inflation still increased 36.1% from 2001 to 2002, but at a smaller rate. Note A (see Exhibit 1.2) to the R.E.C. Inc. financial statements indicates that new store openings have occurred that could explain the large sales growth in the past year.

The remainder of the income statement reveals management's ability to translate sales dollars into profits.

COST OF GOODS SOLD

The first expense deduction from sales is the cost to the seller of products sold to customers. This expense is called cost of goods sold or cost of sales. The amount of cost of goods sold for any accounting period, as explained in chapter 2, will be affected by the cost flow assumption used to value inventory. R.E.C. Inc. uses the LIFO method, which means that the last purchases made during the year have been charged to expense. The LIFO method generally results in the matching of current costs with current revenues and therefore produces higher quality earnings than either FIFO or average cost.

If a company using the LIFO method reduces inventory during the accounting period and liquidates the base LIFO layer, as discussed in chapter 2, there will be an increase in earnings as a result. When LIFO liquidations occur, earnings are enhanced. A base LIFO layer reduction reduces the quality of earnings in the sense that there is an improvement in operating profit from what would generally be considered a negative occurrence: inventory reductions. Base LIFO layer reductions and their effects on earnings are quantified in the notes to the financial statements. In considering the future, ongoing potential of the company, it would be appropriate to exclude from earnings the effect of LIFO liquidations because a firm would not want to continue benefiting from inventory shrinkages.

The relationship between cost of goods sold and net sales—called the cost of *goods sold percentage*—is an important one for profit determination because cost of goods sold is the largest expense item for many firms.

	2002		2001		2000	
Cost of goods sold	$\dfrac{129,364}{215,600}$	= 60.0%	$\dfrac{91,879}{153,000}$	= 60.1%	$\dfrac{81,606}{140,700}$	= 58.0%
Net sales						

The cost of goods sold percentage for R.E.C. Inc. increased between 2000 and 2001. Since then, the firm either has controlled costs more effectively and/or has been able to pass along price increases to customers. The cost of goods sold percentage will vary significantly by industry, according to markup policies and other factors. For example, the cost of goods sold percentage for jewelry retailers averages 49.5%, compared with 77.8% for retailers of groceries and meats.[2]

GROSS PROFIT

The difference between net sales and cost of goods sold is called gross profit or gross margin. Gross profit is the first step of profit measurement on the multiple-step income statement and is a key analytical tool in assessing a firm's operating performance. The gross profit figure indicates how much profit the firm is generating after deducting the cost of products sold. Gross profit, expressed as a percentage of net sales, is the gross profit margin.

	2002	2001	2000
$\dfrac{\text{Gross profit}}{\text{Net sales}}$	$\dfrac{86,236}{215,600} = 40.0\%$	$\dfrac{61,121}{153,000} = 39.9\%$	$\dfrac{59,094}{140,700} = 42.0\%$

OPERATING EXPENSE

R.E.C. Inc. discloses five categories of operating expense: selling and administrative, advertising, lease payments (disclosed in Note E), depreciation and amortization, and repairs and maintenance. These are all areas over which management exercises discretion and that have considerable impact on the firm's current and future profitability. Thus, it is important to track these accounts carefully in terms of trends, absolute amounts, relationship to sales, and relationship to industry competitors.

Selling and administrative expenses are expenses relating to the sale of products or services and to the management of the business. They include salaries, rent, insurance, utilities, supplies, and sometimes depreciation and advertising expense. R.E.C. Inc. provides separate disclosures for advertising and for depreciation and amortization. Note A to the R.E.C. Inc. financial statements indicates that the firm includes the expenses related to the opening of new stores in selling and administrative expense.

Advertising costs are or should be a major expense in the budgets of companies for which marketing is an important element of success. This topic was discussed in chapter 1. As a retail firm operating in a competitive industry, recreational products, R.E.C. Inc. spends 6 to 7 cents of every sales dollar for advertising, as indicated by the ratio of advertising to net sales:

	2002	2001	2000
$\dfrac{\text{Advertising}}{\text{Net sales}}$	$\dfrac{14,258}{215,600} = 6.6\%$	$\dfrac{10,792}{153,000} = 7.1\%$	$\dfrac{9,541}{140,700} = 6.8\%$

Lease payments include the costs associated with operating rentals of leased facilities for retail outlets. Note E to the financial statements explains the agreements that

---

[2] Robert Morris Associates, *Annual Statement Studies,* Philadelphia, PA, 1998.

apply to the rental arrangements and presents a schedule of minimum annual rental commitments. Observation of the sharp rise in lease payments for R.E.C. Inc. between 2001 and 2002, from $7.1 million to $13.1 million—an increase of 84%—would indicate an expansion of the firm's use of leased space.

The property leasing arrangement used by R.E.C. Inc. is called an *operating lease,* which is a conventional rental agreement with no ownership rights transferring to the lessee at the termination of the rental contract. Another commonly used type of leasing arrangement is a *capital lease.* Capital leases are, in substance, a "purchase" rather than a "lease." If a lease contract meets any one of four criteria—transfers ownership to the lessee, contains a bargain purchase option, has a lease term of 75% or more of the leased property's economic life, or has minimum lease payments with a present value of 90% or more of the property's fair value—the lease must be capitalized by the lessee according to the requirements of FASB Statement No. 13, "Accounting for Leases."

Both the balance sheet and the income statement are affected by a capital lease. An asset and a liability are recorded on the lessee's balance sheet equal to the present value of the lease payments to be made under the contract. The asset account reflects what is, in essence, the purchase of an asset; and the liability is the obligation incurred in financing the purchase. Each lease payment is apportioned partly to reduce the outstanding liability and partly to interest expense. The asset account is amortized with amortization expense recognized on the income statement, just as a purchased asset would be depreciated.

DEPRECIATION AND AMORTIZATION

The cost of assets other than land that will benefit a business enterprise for more than a year is allocated over the asset's service life rather than expensed in the year of purchase. Land is an exception to the rule because land is considered to have an unlimited useful life. The cost allocation procedure is determined by the nature of the long-lived asset. *Depreciation* is used to allocate the cost of tangible fixed assets such as buildings, machinery, equipment, furniture and fixtures, and motor vehicles. *Amortization* is the process applied to the cost expiration of intangible assets such as patents, copyrights, trademarks, licenses, franchises, and goodwill. The cost of acquiring and developing natural resources—oil and gas, other minerals, and standing timber—is allocated through *depletion.* The amount of expense recognized in any accounting period will depend on the level of investment in the relevant asset; estimates with regard to the asset's service life and residual value; and for depreciation, the method used.

R.E.C. Inc. recognizes annual depreciation expense for the firm's buildings and equipment and amortization expense for the leasehold improvements on rental property. Note A to the R.E.C. Inc. financial statements explains the company's procedures relating to depreciation and amortization: "Depreciation and Amortization: Property, plant, and equipment is stated at cost. Depreciation expense is calculated principally by the straight-line method based upon estimated useful lives for buildings. Estimated useful lives of leasehold improvements represent the remaining term of the lease in effect at the time the improvements are made." Remember that for tax purposes, most firms use the Modified Accelerated Cost Recovery System for depreciation.

With any expense on the income statement, the analyst should evaluate the amount and trend of the expenditure as well as its relationship to the volume of firm activity that is relevant to the expense. For a firm like R.E.C. Inc., one would expect a fairly constant relationship between the investment in buildings, leasehold improvements, and equipment on the balance sheet and the annual expense recorded for depreciation and amortization on the income statement.

	2002	2001
$\dfrac{\text{Depreciation and amortization}}{\text{Buildings, leasehold improvements, equipment}}$	$\dfrac{3,998}{39,796} = 10.0\%$	$\dfrac{2,984}{25,696} = 11.6\%$

The percentage of depreciation and amortization expense has decreased somewhat, possibly due to the fact that new assets were placed in service during 2002 for only a part of the year, rendering less than a full year's depreciation and amortization. To help put these accounts in a broader context, chapter 5 will include an analysis of long-run trends by using data from earlier years as well as the current year's financial statements.

Repairs and maintenance are the annual costs of repairing and maintaining the firm's property, plant, and equipment. Expenditures in this area should correspond to the level of investment in capital equipment and to the age and condition of the company's fixed assets. Similar to research and development and advertising and marketing expenses, inadequate allowance for repair and maintenance can impair the ongoing success of an organization. This category, like depreciation, should be evaluated in relation to the firm's investments in fixed assets.

	2002	2001
$\dfrac{\text{Repairs and maintenance}}{\text{Buildings, leasehold improvements, equipment}}$	$\dfrac{3,015}{39,796} = 7.6\%$	$\dfrac{2,046}{25,696} = 8.0\%$

Firms in industries other than retail will have different expenses that should also be evaluated. For example, the trend of research and development expenses relative to net sales is an important measurement to evaluate for high technology and pharmaceutical companies.

OPERATING PROFIT

Operating profit (also called EBIT or earnings before interest and taxes) is the second step of profit determination on the R.E.C. Inc. earnings statement and measures the overall performance of the company's operations: sales revenue less the expenses associated with generating sales. The figure for operating profit provides a basis for assessing the success of a company apart from its financing and investing activities and separate from tax considerations. The *operating profit margin* is calculated as the relationship between operating profit and net sales:

	2002	2001	2000
$\dfrac{\text{Operating profit}}{\text{Net sales}}$	$\dfrac{19,243}{215,600} = 8.9\%$	$\dfrac{11,806}{153,000} = 7.7\%$	$\dfrac{11,256}{140,700} = 8.0\%$

The ratio indicates that R.E.C. Inc. strengthened its return on operations in 2002 after a dip in 2001.

OTHER INCOME (EXPENSE)

This category includes revenues and costs other than from operations, such as dividend and interest income, interest expense, gains (losses) from investments, and gains (losses) from the sale of fixed assets. R.E.C. Inc. recognizes as other income the interest earned on its investments in marketable securities and as other expense the interest paid on its debt. The relative amounts will be dependent upon the level of investments and the amount of debt outstanding, as well as the prevailing level of interest rates.

Under the requirements of FASB Statement No. 115, discussed in chapter 2, firms (primarily financial institutions and insurance companies) that carry debt and equity securities classified as "trading securities" report these investments on the balance sheet at market value with any unrealized gains and losses included in earnings. Since 1996, FASB Statement No. 123, "Accounting for Stock-Based Compensation," has required companies to disclose the impact of employee stock option costs on net earnings in notes to the financial statements. The board is encouraging companies to deduct the cost of options from earnings, but few companies are expected to do so.

In the assessment of earnings quality (discussed in chapter 1 and appendix A), it is important that the analyst consider the materiality and the variability of the nonoperating items of income—for example, gains and losses on the sale of major capital assets, accounting changes, extraordinary items, investment income from temporary investments in cash equivalents, and investment income recognized under the equity method (covered later in this chapter).

EARNINGS BEFORE INCOME TAXES

Earnings before income taxes is the profit recognized before the deduction of income tax expense. Income taxes are discussed in notes to the financial statements describing the difference between the reported figure for income taxes and the actual amount of income taxes paid (see the discussion of deferred income taxes in chapter 2). For R.E.C. Inc., refer to Note A, which explains why the differences occur, and Note D, which quantifies the reconciliation between taxes paid and tax expense reported on the income statement. R.E.C. Inc.'s average reported tax rate would be calculated by dividing income taxes on the income statement by earnings before taxes.

	2002	2001	2000
$\dfrac{\text{Income taxes}}{\text{Earnings before income taxes}}$	$\dfrac{7,686}{17,080} = 45.0\%$	$\dfrac{4,457}{10,367} = 43.0\%$	$\dfrac{4,824}{10,720} = 45.0\%$

NET EARNINGS

Net earnings, or "the bottom line," represents the firm's profit after consideration of all revenue and expense reported during the accounting period. The *net profit margin* shows the percentage of profit earned on every sales dollar.

	2002	2001	2000
$\dfrac{\text{Net earnings}}{\text{Net sales}}$	$\dfrac{9,394}{215,600} = 4.4\%$	$\dfrac{5,910}{153,000} = 3.9\%$	$\dfrac{5,896}{140,700} = 4.2\%$

EARNINGS PER COMMON SHARE

Earnings per common share is the net earnings available to common stockholders for the period divided by the average number of common stock shares outstanding. This figure shows the return to the common stock shareholder for every share owned. R.E.C. Inc. earned $1.96 per share in 2002, compared with $1.29 per share in 2001 and $1.33 per share in 2000.

Companies with complex capital structures—which means existence of convertible securities (such as bonds convertible into common stock), stock options, and warrants—must calculate two amounts for earnings per share: *basic* and *diluted.* If convertible securities were converted into common stock and/or the options and warrants were exercised, there would be more shares outstanding for every dollar earned, and the potential for dilution is accounted for by the dual presentation. R.E.C. Inc. has a complex capital structure and therefore presents both basic and diluted earnings per share. In Note G to the financial statements, R.E.C. Inc. discloses the reconciliation of the basic and diluted earnings per share computations for the three-year period ended December 31, 2002. The diluted earnings per share number is slightly lower each year compared to the basic earnings per share due to the dilutive effect of stock options that employees could exercise in the future.

Another issue that an analyst should consider in assessing earnings quality is any material changes in the number of common stock shares outstanding that will cause a change in the computation of earnings per share. Changes in the number of shares outstanding result from such transactions as treasury stock purchases and the purchase and retirement of a firm's own common stock.

COMPREHENSIVE INCOME

As discussed in chapter 2 and earlier in this chapter, companies must now report total comprehensive income either on the face of the income statement, in the statement of stockholders' equity, or in a separate financial statement. Although Pfizer Inc. chooses to report total comprehensive income in the statement of shareholders' equity, if a separate statement had been used, it would appear as illustrated in Exhibit 3.3.

Currently, there are four items that may comprise a company's other comprehensive income: *foreign currency translation effects, unrealized gains and losses, additional pension liabilities,* and *cash flow hedges.* These items are outlined below; however, a detailed

EXHIBIT 3.3

PFIZER INC. STATEMENTS OF COMPREHENSIVE INCOME FOR THE YEARS ENDED
DECEMBER 31, 1998, 1997, 1996 (IN MILLIONS)

	1998	*1997*	*1996*
Net income	$3,351	$2,213	$1,929
Other comprehensive income/(expense), net of tax			
Currency translation adjustment	(74)	(253)	(32)
Net unrealized gain (loss) on available-for-sale securities	(2)	20	15
Minimum pension liability	(73)	3	(1)
Total comprehensive income	$3,202	$1,983	$1,911

discussion of these topics is beyond the scope of this text. A more complete discussion of these four areas can be found in most intermediate or advanced accounting textbooks.

Foreign currency translation effects are the result of disclosures specified in FASB Statement No. 52, "Foreign Currency Translation." When U.S. firms operate abroad, the foreign financial statements must be translated into U.S. dollars at the end of the accounting period. Because the value of the dollar changes in relation to foreign currencies, there are gains and losses that can result from the translation process. These exchange gains and losses, which fluctuate from period to period, are "accumulated" in the stockholders' equity section in most cases.[3]

According to the provisions of FASB Statement No. 115, discussed in chapter 2, *unrealized gains and losses* on investments in debt and equity securities classified as available-for-sale are reported in comprehensive income. Cumulative net unrealized gains and losses are reported in the accumulated other comprehensive income section of stockholders' equity on the balance sheet.

Additional pension liabilities are reported as other comprehensive income when the accumulated benefit obligation is greater than the fair market value of plan assets less the balance in the accrued pension liability account or plus the balance in the deferred pension asset account. Pension accounting is discussed in appendix A.

Companies using *cash flow hedges* (derivatives designated as hedging the exposure to variable cash flows of a forecasted transaction) are required to initially report any gain or loss from a change in the fair market value of the cash flow hedge in other comprehensive income and subsequently reclassify the amount into earnings when the forecasted transaction affects earnings.[4]

The Statement of Stockholders' Equity

The statement of stockholders' equity details the transactions that affect the balance sheet equity accounts during an accounting period. Exhibit 3.4 shows the changes that have occurred in the equity accounts of R.E.C. Inc. Changes to the common stock and additional paid-in capital accounts are due to employees exercising their stock options. The retained earnings account has been increased each year by the net earnings and reduced by the cash dividends that R.E.C. Inc. has paid to their common stockholders. (R.E.C. Inc.'s dividend payment policy is discussed in chapter 5.)

In 2002, R.E.C. Inc. paid cash dividends of $.33 per share on average shares outstanding (Note G) of 4,792,857 for a total of $1,581,643. The amount of the dividend payment was reduced from $.41 per share in 2001 and 2000. Although R.E.C. Inc. paid no stock dividends, the financial statement user should be aware of the accounting treatment of these dividends.

Stock dividends are the issuance to existing shareholders of additional shares in proportion to current ownership. When a stock dividend is declared, the retained earnings account is decreased by the market value of the shares issued in the case of a

---

[3] Exceptions are when the U.S. company designates the U.S. dollar as the "functional" currency for the foreign entity—such is the case, for example, when the foreign operations are simply an extension of the parent company's operations. Under this circumstance, the foreign translation gains and losses are included in the calculation of net income on the income statement.

[4] "Accounting for Derivative Instruments and Hedging Activities," *FASB Statement of Financial Accounting Standards No. 133, 1998.*

EXHIBIT 3.4

R.E.C. INC.
CONSOLIDATED STATEMENTS OF STOCKHOLDERS' EQUITY FOR THE YEARS ENDED
DECEMBER 31, 2002, 2001, AND 2000
(IN THOUSANDS)

	Common Stock		Additional	Retained	
	Shares	*Amount*	*Paid-In Capital*	*Earnings*	*Total*
Balance at December 31, 1999	4,340	$4,340	$857	$24,260	$29,457
Net earnings				5,896	5,896
Proceeds from sale of shares from exercise of stock options	103	103	21		124
Cash dividends				(1,841)	(1,841)
Balance at December 31, 2000	4,443	$4,443	$878	$28,315	$33,636
Net earnings				5,910	5,910
Proceeds from sale of shares from exercise of stock options	151	151	32		183
Cash dividends				(1,862)	(1,862)
Balance at December 31, 2001	4,594	$4,594	$910	$32,363	$37,867
Net earnings				9,394	9,394
Proceeds from sale of shares from exercise of stock options	209	209	47		256
Cash dividends				(1,582)	(1,582)
Balance at December 31, 2002	4,803	$4,803	$957	$40,175	$45,935

small stock dividend (less than 20% to 25% of the number of shares outstanding) or by the par value of the stock in the case of a *large stock dividend* (more than 20% to 25% of the number of shares outstanding). For example, if a company with 100,000 ($1 par) common shares outstanding issues a 10% stock dividend at a time when the market value of the stock is $3, the retained earnings account would be reduced by $30,000:

$$(100,000 \times .10) \times \$3 = \$30,000$$

If a 50% stock dividend were paid, the deduction would be $50,000:

$$(100,000 \times .5) \times \$1 = \$50,000$$

From the stockholders' viewpoint, receipt of stock dividends, unlike a cash dividend, represents nothing of tangible value. When a cash dividend is paid the shareholder receives cash, and the company's assets and retained earnings are reduced. Payment of a stock dividend does not affect assets or liabilities but results only in an adjustment within the equity section of the balance sheet: the retained earnings' balance is reduced, and the stock account (or stock and paid-in capital) is increased by the same amount. The shareholder has more shares, but the proportion of ownership in the company is exactly the same; the net asset value (assets minus liabilities) of the company is exactly the same. The market value of the stock should drop in proportion to the additional shares issued.

Stock splits also result in the issuance of additional shares to the shareholder and are generally executed by a company in order to lower the market price of the firm's shares. For example, assume that a company with 2 million outstanding shares of $4 par value stock, selling at $100 per share, declares a 4–1 stock split. A shareholder with 100 shares would end up with 400 shares after the split. There is no accounting entry required for the issuing company, but a memorandum item would note the change in the par value of the stock from $4 to $1, and the change in the total number of shares outstanding from 2 million to 8 million. Theoretically, the price would fall to $25, and the value of shareholders' holdings would remain unchanged. Companies frequently execute stock splits in order to make common shares more "affordable" for the average investor.

Transactions other than the recognition of net profit/loss and the payment of dividends can cause changes in the retained earnings balance. These include prior period adjustments and certain changes in accounting principles. Prior period adjustments result primarily from the correction of errors made in previous accounting periods; the beginning retained earnings balance is adjusted for the year in which the error is discovered. Some changes in accounting principles, such as a change from LIFO to any other inventory method, also cause an adjustment to retained earnings for the cumulative effect of the change. Retained earnings can also be affected by transactions in a firm's own shares.

A more detailed statement of shareholders' equity is illustrated in Exhibit 3.5. Notice that Pfizer Inc. has not only the same accounts (Common Stock, Additional Paid-In Capital, and Retained Earnings) as R.E.C Inc., but also three other equity accounts: Employee Benefit Trusts, Treasury Stock, and Accumulated Other Comprehensive Income/(Expense.) (These accounts were described in chapter 2.)

The stockholders' equity statement enables the analyst to trace any changes in equity accounts. Consider, for example, the accumulated other comprehensive income (expense) account. Pfizer Inc. had a positive $163 million balance in this account at the beginning of 1996, but by the end of 1998 this account was a negative $234 million. Looking at the detail on the statement of shareholders' equity in Exhibit 3.5, one can see that this decrease was largely caused by foreign currency translation losses as well as an increased pension liability. Each equity account can be analyzed in the same way.

OTHER ISSUES—COST VS. EQUITY

An additional issue that users sometimes encounter in attempting to evaluate financial statement data is the method—cost or equity—employed to account for investments in the voting stock of other companies. This method is not an issue for R.E.C. Inc. because the parent owns 100% of the voting stock in its subsidiaries; R.E.C. Inc. and its subsidiaries are, in substance, one consolidated entity. Where one firm owns more than 50% of the voting stock of another company, the parent company can obviously control the business operations, financial policies, and dividend declarations of the subsidiary, and consolidated financial statements are prepared with the disclosures relating to consolidation policies provided in the financial statement notes. The accounting rules underlying the preparation of consolidated financial statements, while similar to the equity method, are extremely complicated and beyond the scope of this book.[5]

---

[5] Accounting for consolidated financial statements is fully discussed and explained in advanced accounting textbooks.

Questions regarding use of cost or equity come into play for stock investments of less than 50%, where consolidated financial statements are not prepared.

Accounting rules permit two different methods to account for stock investments of less than 50%. The *equity method* allows the investor proportionate recognition of the investee's net income, irrespective of the payment or nonpayment of cash dividends; under the *cost method,* the investor recognizes investment income only to the extent of any cash dividends received. At issue in the choice of accounting methods is whether the investor exercises control over the investee.

Accounting Principles Board Opinion No. 18 specifies that the equity method of accounting should be used when the investor can exercise *significant influence* over the investee's operating and financing policies. No problem exists where there is ownership of 50% or more because, clearly, one company can control the other. But at what level below 50% ownership can one firm substantially influence the affairs of another firm? Although there can be exceptions, 20% ownership of voting stock is generally considered to be evidence of substantial influence. There are, however, circumstances in which less than 20% ownership reflects control and cases where more than 20% does not. Such factors as the extent of representation on investee's board of directors, major intercompany transactions, technological dependence, and other relationships would be considered in the determination.

Use of the equity method is justified on a theoretical basis because it fits the requirements of the accrual basis of accounting. The investor's share in investee income is recorded by the investor in the period in which it is earned, rather than as cash is received. Analysts, however, should be aware of whether a company uses the cost or the equity method. What difference does it make whether a company uses the cost or equity method? An illustration should help provide the answer.

Assume that Company A acquires exactly 20% of the voting common stock of Company B for $400,000. Company B reports $100,000 earnings for the year and pays $25,000 in cash dividends. For Company A, the income recognition in the earnings statement and the noncurrent investment account on the balance sheet would be entirely different depending upon the accounting method used for the investment.

	Cost	Equity
Income statement: investment income	$ 5,000	$ 20,000
Balance sheet: investment account	$400,000	$415,000

The cost method allows recognition of investment income only to the extent of any cash dividends actually received ($25,000 × .20), and the investment account is carried at cost.[6] The equity method permits the investor to count as income the percentage interest in investee's earnings.

Company B's earnings	$100,000
Company A's percent ownership	× .20
Company A's investment income	$ 20,000

---

[6] Or market, depending on the provisions of FASB Statement No. 115; this statement does not apply to investments accounted for under the equity method.

EXHIBIT 3.5

PFIZER INC. CONSOLIDATED STATEMENT OF SHAREHOLDERS' EQUITY (IN MILLIONS)

	Common Stock		Additional Paid-In Capital
	Shares	*Par Value*	*Capital*
Balance January 1, 1996	1,371	$69	$1,200
Comprehensive income:			
Net income			
Other comprehensive expense—net of tax:			
Currency translation adjustment			
Net unrealized gain on available-for-sale securities			
Minimum pension liability			
Total other comprehensive expense			
Total comprehensive income			
Cash dividends declared			
Stock option transactions	7	—	124
Purchases of common stock			
Employee benefit trust transactions—net			341
Other			28
Balance December 31, 1996	1,378	69	1,693
Comprehensive income:			
Net income			
Other comprehensive expense—net of tax			
Currency translation adjustment			
Net unrealized gain or available-for-sale securities			
Minimum pension liability			
Total other comprehensive expense			
Total comprehensive income			
Cash dividends declared			
Stock option transaction	9	—	343
Purchases of common stock			
Employee benefit trusts transactions—net			1,177
Other	1	—	26
Balance December 31, 1997	1,388	69	3,239
Comprehensive income:			
Net income			
Other comprehensive expense—net of tax:			
Currency tanslation adustment			
Net unrealized loss an available-for-sale securities			
Minimum pension liability			
Total other comprehensive expense			
Total comprehensive income			
Cash dividends declared			
Stock option transactions	18	1	747
Purchases of common stock			
Employee benefit trusts transactions—net			1,633
Other	1	—	27
Balance December 31, 1998	1,407	$70	$5,646

See Notes to Consolidated Financial Statements, which are an integral part of these statements.

Employee Benefit Trusts		Treasury Stock		Retained Earnings	Accum. Other Comprehensive Inc./(Exp.)	Total
Shares	Cost	Shares	Cost			
(37)	$(1,170)	(96)	$(1,615)	$6,859	$163	$5,506
				1,929		1,929
					(32)	(32)
					15	15
					(1)	(1)
					(18)	(18)
						1,911
				(771)		(771)
		10	156			280
		(1)	(27)			(27)
1	(318)					23
		—	4			32
(36)	(1,488)	(87)	(1,487)	8,017	145	6,954
				2,213		2,213
					(253)	(253)
					20	20
					3	3
					(230)	(230)
						1,983
				(881)		(881)
		4	68			411
		(11)	(586)			(586)
—	(1,158)	—	7			26
						26
(36)	(2,646)	(94)	(1,993)	9,349	(85)	7,933
				3,351		3,351
					(74)	(74)
					(2)	(2)
					(73)	(73)
					(149)	(149)
						3,202
				(1,261)		(1,261)
		—	(18)			730
		(19)	(1,912)			(1,912)
2	(1,554)	—	12			91
						27
(34)	$(4,200)	(113)	$(3,911)	$11,439	$(234)	$8,810

Under the equity method, the investment account is increased by the amount of investment income recognized and is reduced by the amount of cash dividends received.

Investment at cost	$400,000
Investment income	+ 20,000
Cash dividends received	− 5,000
Investment account	$415,000

Use of the equity method somewhat distorts earnings in the sense that income is recognized even though no cash may ever be received. The theoretical justification for the equity method is that it is presumed that the investor (Company A), through its control of voting shares, could cause Company B to pay dividends. In reality, this may not be true, and Company A is permitted to recognize more income than is received in cash.

One of the adjustments to net income (illustrated in chapter 4) to calculate cash flow from operations is to deduct the amount by which income recognized under the equity method of accounting exceeds cash received from dividends. For Company A this amount would be $15,000 (investment income $20,000 less cash dividends $5,000). It is also equal to the increase in the balance sheet investment account (ending balance $415,000 less original cost $400,000). For comparative purposes it would be appropriate to eliminate this noncash portion of earnings.

Earnings Quality, Inflation, Cash Flow, Segmental Accounting

Additional topics that are directly related to the income statement are covered in other sections of the book. The assessment of the quality of reported earnings is an essential element of income statement analysis. The qualitative interpretation of earnings is discussed in chapter 1 and appendix A.

The impact of inflation on reported earnings is covered in chapter 1.

The earnings figure reported on the income statement is rarely the same as the cash generated during an accounting period. Because it is cash that a firm needs to service debt, pay suppliers, invest in new capital assets, and pay cash dividends, cash flow from operations is a key ingredient in analyzing operating performance. The calculation of cash flow from operations, how it differs from reported earnings, and the interpretation of cash flow as a performance measure are discussed in chapter 4.

Appendix B deals with the supplementary information reported by companies that operate in several different business segments. Segmental data include revenue, operating profit or loss, assets, depreciation and amortization, and capital expenditures by industry components. These disclosures facilitate the analysis of operating performance and contribution by each segment of a diversified company.

SELF-TEST

Solutions are provided in appendix D.
_____ 1. What does the income statement measure for a firm?
    (a) The changes in assets and liabilities that occurred during the period.
    (b) The financing and investment activities for a period.
    (c) The results of operations for a period.
    (d) The financial position of a firm for a period.

_____ 2. Which financial statement can be disclosed in a supplementary schedule or in a note to the financial statements?
    (a) The balance sheet.
    (b) The statement of stockholders' equity.
    (c) The statement of cash flows.
    (d) The income statement.

_____ 3. Which of the following items need *not* be disclosed separately in the income statement?
    (a) Salary expense.
    (b) Selling a major business segment.
    (c) Extraordinary transactions.
    (d) Cumulative effect of changes in accounting principles.

_____ 4. Why are data presented in income statements for three years?
    (a) The IRS requires a three-year presentation for tax purposes.
    (b) A three-year presentation discourages manipulation of earnings by management.
    (c) Income statements for three years facilitate comparison and provide evidence regarding trends of revenues, expenses, and net earnings.
    (d) An income statement for only one year would be meaningless.

_____ 5. What is the largest expense item for most firms?
    (a) Gross profit.
    (b) Depreciation.
    (c) Operating expense.
    (d) Cost of goods sold.

_____ 6. What is the basic difference between an operating lease and a capital lease?
    (a) A capital lease is, in substance, a purchase, whereas an operating lease is a rental agreement.
    (b) An operating lease transfers ownership to the lease.
    (c) Capital leases must meet four criteria.
    (d) Capital leases must have a lease term of 90% or more of the leased property's economic life.

_____ 7. Which of the following statements is incorrect with regard to capital leases?
    (a) The balance sheet and the income statement are affected by a capital lease.
    (b) Each lease payment is apportioned partly to interest expense and partly to reduce a liability.
    (c) The liability account is amortized just as a purchased asset would be depreciated.
    (d) An asset and a liability are recorded on the lessee's balance sheet equal to the present value of the lease payments to be made under the contract.

_____ 8. Which of the following assets will not be depreciated over its service life?
    (a) Buildings.
    (b) Furniture.
    (c) Equipment.
    (d) Land.

_____ 9. How are costs of assets that benefit a firm for more than one year allocated?
    (a) Depreciation.
    (b) Depletion and amortization.
    (c) Costs are divided by service lives of assets and allocated to repairs and maintenance

(d) Both (a) and (b).

_____ 10. Why should the expenditures for repairs and maintenance correspond to the level of investment in capital equipment and to the age and condition of that equipment?

(a) Repairs and maintenance expense is calculated in the same manner as depreciation expense.

(b) Inadequate repairs of equipment can impair the operating success of a business enterprise.

(c) It is a generally accepted accounting principle that repairs and maintenance expense is generally between 5% and 10% of fixed assets.

(d) Repairs and maintenance are depreciated over the remaining life of the assets involved.

_____ 11. Why is the figure for operating profit important?

(a) This is the figure used for calculating federal income tax expense.

(b) The figure for operating profit provides a basis for assessing the success of a company apart from its financing and investment activities and separate from its tax status.

(c) The operating profit figure includes all operating revenues and expenses as well as interest and taxes related to operations.

(d) The figure for operating profit provides a basis for assessing the wealth of a firm.

_____ 12. What are three profit measures calculated from the income statement?

(a) Gross profit margin, operating profit margin, net profit margin.

(b) Gross profit margin, cost of goods sold percentage, EBIT.

(c) Operating profit margin, net profit margin, repairs and maintenance to fixed assets.

(d) None of the above.

_____ 13. When is a dual presentation of basic and diluted earnings per share required?

(a) When a company has a complex capital structure.

(b) When convertible securities were in fact converted.

(c) When a company has a simple capital structure.

(d) When a company has pension liabilities.

_____ 14. What is the impact of a stock dividend on the financial statements?

(a) Cash is reduced on the balance sheet, and common stock is increased.

(b) The proportion of ownership in the company will increase.

(c) The retained earnings balance is reduced, and the stock account is increased by the same amount.

(d) The retained earnings account is decreased by the par value of the shares issued in the case of a small stock dividend or by the market value in the case of a large dividend.

_____ 15. Which of the following cause a change in the retained earnings account balance?

(a) Prior period adjustment.

(b) Payment of dividends.

(c) Net profit or loss.

(d) All of the above.

_____ 16. What is a statement of shareholders' equity?

(a) It is the same as a retained earnings statement.

(b) It is a statement that reconciles only the treasury stock account.

(c) It is a statement that summarizes changes in the entire shareholders' equity section of the balance sheet.

(d) It is a statement reconciling the difference between stock issued at par value and stock issued at market value.

_____ 17. What accounts can be found on a statement of stockholders' equity?

(a) Investments in other companies.

(b) Treasury stock, accumulated other comprehensive income and retained earnings.

(c) Market value of treasury stock.

(d) Both (a) and (c).

_____ 18. Why can the equity method of accounting for investments in the voting stock of other companies cause distortions in net earnings?

(a) Income is recognized where no cash may ever be received.

(b) Significant influence may exist even if the ownership of voting stock is less than 20%.

(c) Income should be recognized in accordance with the accrual method of accounting.

(d) Income is recognized only to the extent of cash dividends received.

19. Match the following terms with the correct definitions:

_____ (a) Depreciation	_____ (h) Cost method
_____ (b) Depletion	_____ (i) Single-step format
_____ (c) Amortization	_____ (j) Multiple-step format
_____ (d) Gross profit	_____ (k) Basic earnings per share
_____ (c) Operating profit	_____ (l) Diluted earnings per share
_____ (f) Net profit	_____ (m) Operating lease
_____ (g) Equity method	_____ (n) Capital lease

Definitions:

(1) Proportionate recognition of investee's net income for investments in voting stock of other companies.

(2) Presentation of income statement that provides several intermediate profit measures.

(3) Conventional rental agreement with no ownership rights transferring to the lessee at the termination of the contract.

(4) Allocation of costs of tangible fixed assets.

(5) Difference between sales revenue and expenses associated with generating sales.

(6) Recognition of income from investments in voting stock of other companies to the extent of cash dividend received.

(7) Rental agreement that is, in substance, a purchase.

(8) Difference between net sales and cost of goods sold.

(9) Allocation of costs of acquiring and developing natural resources.

(10) Earnings per share figure calculated by dividing the average number of common stock shares outstanding into the net earnings available to common stockholders.

(11) Presentation of income statement that groups all revenue items, then deducts all expenses, to arrive at net income.

(12) Earnings per share figure based on the assumption that all potentially dilutive securities have been converted to common stock.

(13) Allocation of costs of intangible assets.

(14) Difference between all revenues and expenses.
20. The following categories appear on the income statement of Joshua Jeans Company:
    (a) Net sales
    (b) Cost of sales
    (c) Operating expenses
    (d) Other revenue / expense
    (e) Income tax expense

Classify the following items according to income statement category:
_____ (1) Depreciation expense
_____ (2) Interest revenue
_____ (3) Sales revenue
_____ (4) Advertising expense
_____ (5) Interest expense
_____ (6) Sales returns and allowance
_____ (7) Federal income taxes
_____ (8) Repairs and maintenance
_____ (9) Selling and administrative expenses
_____ (10) Cost of products sold
_____ (11) Dividend income
_____ (12) Lease payments

STUDY QUESTIONS AND PROBLEMS

3.1 What is the difference between a multiple-step and a single-step format of the earnings statement?

3.2 Under what circumstances must a lease be capitalized?

3.3 Discuss the differences between depreciation, amortization, and depletion.

3.4 What is the importance of evaluating the repairs and maintenance expense account on an income statement?

3.5 Explain what can be found on a statement of stockholders' equity.

3.6 Why is the bottom line figure, net income, not necessarily a good indicator of a firm's financial success?

3.7 An excerpt from the Sun Company's annual report is presented below. Calculating any profit measures deemed necessary, discuss the implications of the profitability of the company.

SUN COMPANY INCOME STATEMENTS
FOR THE YEARS ENDED DECEMBER 31, 2003, 2002, AND 2001

	2003	2002	2001
Net sales	$236,000	$195,000	$120,000
Cost of goods sold	186,000	150,000	85,000
Gross profit	$ 50,000	$ 45,000	$ 35,000
Operating expenses	22,000	18,000	11,000
Operating profit	$ 28,000	$ 27,000	$ 24,000
Income taxes	12,000	11,500	10,500
Net income	$ 16,000	$ 15,500	$ 13,500

3.8   Star, Inc. has 400,000 $1 par common shares outstanding currently valued at $20. If the company issues a 15% stock dividend, what will be the effect on the equity section of the balance sheet? What about a 40% stock dividend?

3.9   Big Company purchased 25% of the voting common stock of Little Company on January 1 and paid $500,000 for the investment. Little Company reported $250,000 of earnings for the year and paid $50,000 cash dividends. Calculate investment income and the balance sheet investment account for Big Company under the cost method and under the equity method.

3.10   Prepare a multiple-step income statement for Coyote, Inc. from the following single-step step statement.

Net sales	$1,833,000
Interest income	13,000
	1,846,000
Costs and expenses:	
Cost of good sold	1,072,000
Selling expenses	279,000
General and admin. expenses	175,000
Depreciation	14,000
Interest expense	16,000
Income tax expense	116,000
Net income	$ 174,000

3.11 Writing Skills Problem

Income statements are presented for the Elf Corporation for the years ending December 31, 2001, 2000, and 1999.

ELF CORPORATION
INCOME STATEMENTS FOR THE YEARS ENDING DECEMBER 31,
(MILLIONS OF DOLLARS)

	2001	2000	1999
Sales	700	650	550
Cost of goods sold	350	325	275
Gross profit	350	325	275
Operating expenses:			
Administrative	100	100	100
Advertising and marketing	50	75	75
Operating profit	200	150	100
Interest expense	70	50	30
Earnings before tax	130	100	70
Tax expense (.50)	65	50	35
Net income	65	50	35

Required: Write a one paragraph *analysis* of Elf Corporation's profit performance for the period.

To the Student: The focus of this exercise is on *analyzing* financial data rather than simply *describing* the numbers and trends. Analysis involves breaking the information into parts for study, relating the pieces, making comparisons, drawing conclusions, and evaluating cause and effect.

3.12 Internet Problem

Look up the FASB Home Page on the Internet at the following address: http://www.rutgers.edu/accounting/raw/fasb/. Find the current list of technical projects that are currently on the board's agenda. Choose one of the projects that will impact the income statement. Describe the potential change and how the income statement may be impacted.

3.13 Annual Report Problem

The 1998 PETsMART Annual Report can be found at the following Web site: www.prenhall.com/fraser

(a) Using the Consolidated Statements of Operations, analyze the profitability of PETsMART by calculating and discussing profit measures for the past three years.

(b) Using the Consolidated Statements of Stockholders' Equity for PETsMART answer the following questions:

   (1) Why has the common stock and additional paid in capital accounts increased during the past three years?

   (2) Has the retained earnings account increased or decreased during the past three years? Explain the cause of the changes to this account.

   (3) Explain the meaning of the "Deferred Compensation" account. (Hint: Read Note 10.)

   (4) What item(s) does PETsMART have that affect "Accumulated Other Comprehensive Income (Loss)"? Explain whether these items have increased or decreased equity.

Time Warner Mini-Case

Time Warner Inc. is the world's largest media and entertainment company with interests in four fundamental areas of business: *Cable Networks,* consisting principally of interests in cable television programming; *Publishing,* consisting principally of interests in magazine publishing, book publishing and direct marketing; *Entertainment,* consisting principally of interests in recorded music and music publishing, filmed entertainment, television production and television broadcasting; and *Cable,* consisting principally of interests in cable television systems. A majority of Time Warner's interests in filmed entertainment, television production, television broadcasting, and cable television systems, and a portion of its interests in cable television programming are held through Time Warner Entertainment Company, L. P. ("TWE"). Time Warner does not consolidate TWE for financial reporting purposes. Selected information from Time Warner's 1998 annual report is given on pages 114 to 116.

REQUIRED:

1. Analyze the profitability of Time Warner by calculating and discussing expense and profit measures for all three years, 1998, 1997 and 1996. Your analysis should also include an explanation of the income tax rate and all unusual, extraordinary, and nonrecurring items.
2. Recommend any adjustments to the 1998 net loss you think would be necessary to develop a more relevant earnings figure that would reflect Time Warner's future earnings potential. Explain each recommended adjustment and calculate the adjusted net earnings for future comparative purposes.
3. Using the Statement of Shareholders' Equity, answer the following questions:
   a. What is the Retained Earnings account called on Time Warner's financial statements? Why?
   b. The Retained Earnings account for Time Warner has declined from 1996 to 1998. For the three-year period as a whole, calculate percentages to show which items are primarily responsible for this decline. (Do not do this calculation on a yearly basis.)
   c. How was Time Warner able to pay cash dividends when the company experienced losses (applicable to common shares) for all three years?
   d. What other items of comprehensive income or loss were recorded over the three-year period from 1996 to 1998? Did these items increase or decrease comprehensive income (loss) relative to net income (loss)?

CONSOLIDATED STATEMENT OF OPERATIONS

Years Ended December 31 (millions, except per share amounts)	1998	1997	1996
Revenues[a]	$14,582	$13,294	$10,064
Cost of revenues[a][b]	8,210	7,542	5,922
Selling, general, and administrative[a][b]	4,876	4,481	3,176
Operating expenses	13,086	12,023	9,098
Business segment operating income	1,496	1,271	966
Equity in pretax income of Entertainment Group[a]	356	686	290
Interest and other, net[a]	(1,180)	(1,044)	(1,174)
Corporate expenses[a]	(86)	(81)	(78)
Income before income taxes	586	832	4
Income taxes	(418)	(531)	(160)
Income (loss) before extraordinary item	168	301	(156)
Extraordinary loss on retirement of debt, net of $37 and $22 million income tax benefit in 1997 and 1996, respectively	—	(55)	(35)
Net income (loss)	168	246	(191)
Preferred dividend requirements[c]	(540)	(319)	(257)
Net loss applicable to common shares	$ (372)	$ (73)	$ (448)
Basic and diluted loss per common share:			
Loss before extraordinary item	$ (.31)	$ (.01)	$ (.48)
Net loss	$ (.31)	$ (.06)	$ (.52)
Average common shares	1,194.7	1,135.4	862.4

(a) Includes the following income (expense) resulting from transactions with the Entertainment Group and other related companies for the years ended December 31, 1998, 1997, and 1996, respectively: revenues—$487 million, $384 million, and $224 million: cost of revenues—$(322) million, $(245) million, and $(177) million; selling, general, and administrative—$(40) million, $(53) million, and $34 million; equity in pretax oncome of Entertainment Group—$105 million, $5 million, and $(29) million; interest and other, net—$(9) million. $(36) million, and $(33) million; and corporate expenses—$72 million, $72 million, and $69 million.

(b) Includes depreciation and amortization expense of: $ 1,178 $ 1,294 $ 988

(c) Preferred dividend requirements of 1998 include a one-time effect of $234 million ($.19 loss per common share) relating to the premium paid in connection with the redemption of the Company's 10 1/4% Series M exchangeable preferred stock ("Series M Preferred Stock") at an aggregate cost of approximately $2.1 billion.

CONSOLIDATED STATEMENT OF SHAREHOLDERS' EQUITY

	Preferred Stock	*Common Stock*	*Paid-in Capital*	*Accumulated Deficit*	*Total*
Balance at December 31, 1995	$30	$776	$5,034	$(2,173)	$3,667
Net loss				(191)	(191)
Increase in unrealized gains on securities, net of $11 million tax expense				17	17
Foreign currency translation adjustments				9	9
Comprehensive income (loss)				(165)	(165)
Common stock dividends				(155)	(155)
Preferred stock dividends				(257)	(257)
Issuance of common and preferred stock in the CVI acquistion	6	6	668		680
Reduction in par value of common and preferred stock due to TBS Transaction	(32)	(774)	806		—
Issuance of common stock in the TBS Transaction		3	6,024		6,027
Repurchases of Time Warner common stock			(456)		(456)
Shares issued pursuant to stock option, dividend reinvestment and benefit plans			163	(8)	155
Other			6		6
Balance at December 31, 1996	4	11	12,245	(2,758)	9,502
Net income				246	246
Decrease in unrealized gains on securities, net of $89 million tax benefit[a]				(128)	(128)
Foreign currency translation adjustments				(76)	(76)
Comprehensive income (loss)				42	42
Common stock dividends				(204)	(204)
Preferred stock dividends				(319)	(319)
Issuance of common stock in connection with the TBS Transaction			67		67
Repurchases of Time Warner common stock			(344)		(344)
Shares issued pursuant to stock option, dividend reinvestment and benefit plans			711	(98)	613
Other			(4)	3	(1)
Balance at December 31, 1997	4	11	12,675	(3,334)	9,356
Net income				168	168
Foreign currency translation adjustments				4	4
Increase in realized and unrealized losses on derivative financial instruments, net of $13 million tax benefit				(20)	(20)
Cumulative effect of change in accounting for derivative financial instruments, net of $3 million tax benefit				(18)	(18)
Comprehensive income (loss)				134	134
Common stock dividends				(216)	(216)
Preferred stock dividends				(540)	(540)
Issuance of common stock in connection with the conversion of zero-coupon convertible notes due 2013			1,150		1,150
Issuance of common stock in connection with the conversion of convertible preferred stock	(2)	1	151	(150)	—
Repurchases of Time Warner common stock		(1)	(2,239)		(2,240)
Shares issued pursuant to stock option, dividend reinvestment, and benefit plans		1	1,397	(190)	1,208
Balance at December 31, 1998	$2	$12	$13,134	$(4,296)	$8,852

(a) Includes a $13 million reduction (net of a $9 million tax effect) related to realized gains on the sale of securities in 1997. In prior periods, this amount was included in comprehensive income as a component of Time Warner's unrealized gains on securities.

INCOME TAXES

The differences between income taxes expected at the U.S. federal statutory income tax rate of 35% and income taxes provided are as set forth below. The relationship between income before income taxes and income tax expense is most affected by the amortization of goodwill and certain other financial statement expenses that are not deductible for income tax purposes.

Years Ended December 31, (millions)	1998	1997	1996
Taxes on income at U.S. federal statutory rate	$205	$291	$ 2
State and local taxes, net of federal tax benefits	20	58	26
Nondeductible goodwill amortization	170	170	131
Other nondeductible expenses	13	11	10
Foreign income taxed at different rates, net of U.S. foreign tax credits	—	9	4
Other	10	(8)	(13)
Total	$418	$531	$160

Compaq Computer Corporation Mini-Case

Compaq Computer Corporation is a global information technology company. The Consolidated Statements of Income for Compaq for the years ended December 31, 1998, 1997, and 1996 and selected notes to the financial statements are given on pages 117 to 118. When preparing its income statements, Compaq segregates revenues and cost of goods sold into two industry segments: Products and Services.

REQUIRED:

Analyze the profitability of Compaq by calculating and discussing profit measures for all three years. Your analysis should also include an explanation of the year-to-year changes in gross profit by pinpointing the specific causes of those changes a discussion of amounts spent on research and development and an explantion of the income tax rate.

COMPAQ COMPUTER CORPORATION
CONSOLIDATED STATEMENTS OF INCOME

Year Ended December 31 (in Millions, Except per Share Amounts)	1998	1997	1996
Revenue:			
Products	$ 27,372	$24,122	$19,611
Services	3,797	462	398
Total revenue	31,169	24,584	20,009
Cost of sales:			
Products	21,383	17,500	14,565
Services	2,597	333	290
Total cost of sales	23,980	17,833	14,855
Selling, general and administrative expense	4,978	2,947	2,507
Research and development costs	1,353	817	695
Purchased in-process technology	3,196	208	—
Restructuring and asset impairment charges	393	—	52
Merger-related costs	—	44	—
Other income and expense, net	(69)	(23)	17
	9,851	3,993	3,271
Income (loss) before provision for income taxes	(2,662)	2,758	1,883
Provision for income taxes	81	903	565
Net income (loss)	$(2,743)	$ 1,855	$ 1,318
Earnings (loss) per common share:			
Basic	$ (1.71)	$ 1.23	$ 0.90
Diluted	$ (1.71)	$ 1.19	$ 0.87
Shares used in computing earnings (loss) per common share:			
Basic	1,608	1,505	1,472
Diluted	1,608	1,564	1,516

ACQUISITIONS

On June 11, 1998, Compaq consummated its acquistion of Digital. Digital was an industry leader in implementing and supporting networked business solutions in multi-vendor environments based on high performance platforms and had an established global service and support team.

Approximately $3.2 billion of the purchase price represents purchased in-process technology that had not yet reached technological feasibility and had no alternative future use. Accordingly, this amount was immediately expensed in the Consolidated Statement of Income upon consummation of the acquisition.

RESTRUCTURING AND ASSET IMPAIRMENT CHARGES

In June 1998, Compaq's management approved restructuring plans, which included initiatives to integrate operations of Compaq and Digital, consolidate duplicative facilities, improve service delivery, and reduce overhead. Total restructuring costs of approximately $1.7 billion were recorded in the second quarter related to these initiatives, $1.5 billion of which related to Digital that was recorded as a component of the preliminary purchase price allocation and $286 million of which related to Compaq that was charged to operations.

During 1998, Compaq also recorded a $107 million charge related to asset impairments. The asset impairments resulted from the write down to fair market value, less costs to sell, for assets taken out of service and held for sale or disposal. The majority of this charge related to the impairment of $74 million of intangible assets associated with the acquisition of a company during 1995 that developed, manufactured, and supplied fast ethernet hubs, switches, and related products. In May 1998, management decided to close the manufacturing facility and abandoned the technologies acquired through this acquisition and discontinued all related products.

PROVISION FOR INCOME TAXES

The components of income (loss) before provision for income taxes were as follows:

Year Ended December 31 (in millions)	1998	1997	1996
Domestic	$(4,782)	$1,789	$ 929
Foreign	2,120	969	954
	$(2,662)	$2,758	$1,883

The provision for income taxes charged to operations was as follows:

Year Ended December 31 (in millions)	1998	1997	1996
Current tax expense (benefit)			
U.S. federal	$ (92)	$ 430	$ 672
State and local	(9)	30	34
Foreign	312	241	238
Total current	211	701	944
Deferred tax expense (benefit)			
U.S. federal	(429)	194	(332)
State and local	(11)	2	(19)
Foreign	310	6	(28)
Total deferred	(130)	202	(379)
Total provision	$ 81	$ 903	$ 565

The reasons for the differences between income tax expense and amounts calculated using the U.S. statutory rate of 35% were as follows:

Year Ended December 31 (in millions)	1998	1997	1996
Tax expense (benefit) at U.S. statutory rate	$ (932)	$ 965	$ 659
Foreign tax effect, net	(40)	(88)	(105)
Nondeductible purchased in-process technology	1,119	73	—
Release of valuation allowance	(77)	(30)	(7)
Other, net	11	(17)	18
	$ 81	$ 903	$ 565

4

Statement of Cash Flows

"Joan and Joe: A Tale of Woe"

Joe added up profits and went to see Joan,
Assured of obtaining a much-needed loan.
When Joe arrived, he announced with good cheer:
"My firm has had an outstanding year,
"And now I need a loan from your bank."
Eyeing the statements, Joan's heart sank.
"Your profits are fine," Joan said to Joe.
"But where, oh where, is your company's cash flow?
I'm sorry to say: the answer is 'no'."

—L. FRASER

The statement of cash flows, required by Statement of Financial Accounting Standards No. 95, represents a major step forward in accounting measurement and disclosure because of its relevance to financial statement users. Ample evidence has been provided over the years by firms of every conceivable size, structure, and type of business operation that it is possible for a company to post a healthy net income but still not have the cash needed to pay its employees, suppliers, and bankers. The statement of cash flows, which replaced the statement of changes in financial position in 1988, provides information about cash inflows and outflows during an accounting period. On the statement, cash flows are segregated by *operating activities, investing activities,* and *financing activities.*[1] The mandated focus on cash in this statement results in a more

---

[1] Financing and investing activities not involving cash receipts and payments—such as the exchange of debt for stock or the exchange of property—are reported in a separate schedule on the statement of cash flows.

useful document than its predecessor. A positive net income figure on the income statement is ultimately insignificant unless a company can translate its earnings into cash, and the only source in financial statements for learning about cash generation is the statement of cash flows.

The objectives of this chapter are twofold: (1) to explain how the statement of cash flows is prepared and (2) to interpret the information presented in the statement, including a discussion of the significance of cash flow from operations as an analytical tool in assessing financial performance. Readers may legitimately ask at this point why it is necessary to wade through the preparation of this statement in order to understand and use the information it contains. This chapter provides a far more extensive (some would say tedious) treatment of the preparation of the statement—its underpinnings—than the chapters on the balance sheet, income statement, and statement of stockholders' equity. The reasons for this approach are several, including its relative newness in the required financial statement package, its complexity both to users and preparers, and its extreme importance as an analytical tool. Understanding the statement is greatly enhanced by understanding how it is developed from the balance sheet and income statement; knowing the nuts and bolts helps the analyst utilize its disclosures to maximum effectiveness.

The Consolidated Statements of Cash Flows for R.E.C. Inc., shown in Exhibit 4.1, will serve as the background for an explanation of how the statement is prepared and a discussion of its usefulness for financial analysis.

Preparing a Statement of Cash Flows

Preparing the statement of cash flows begins with a return to the balance sheet, covered in chapter 2. The statement of cash flows requires a reordering of the information presented on a balance sheet. The balance sheet shows account balances at the end of an accounting period, and the statement of cash flows shows changes in those same account balances between accounting periods. The statement is called a statement of *flows* because it shows *changes over time rather than the absolute dollar amount of the accounts at a point in time.* Because a balance sheet balances, the changes in all of the balance sheet accounts balance, and the changes that reflect cash inflows less the changes that result from cash outflows will equal the changes in the cash account.

The statement of cash flows is prepared in exactly that way: by calculating the changes in all of the balance sheet accounts, including *cash;* then listing the changes in all of the accounts except cash as *inflows* or *outflows;* and categorizing the flows by *operating, financing,* or *investing* activities. The *inflows less the outflows balance to and explain the change in cash.*

In order to classify the account changes on the balance sheet, it is first necessary to review the definitions of the four parts of a statement of cash flows:

- cash;
- operating activities;
- investing activities; and
- financing activities.

Cash includes cash and highly liquid short-term marketable securities, also called cash equivalents. Marketable securities are included as cash for R.E.C. Inc., because

EXHIBIT 4.1

R.E.C. INC.
CONSOLIDATED STATEMENTS OF CASH FLOWS
FOR THE YEARS ENDED DECEMBER 31, 2002, 2001, AND 2000
(IN THOUSANDS)

	2002	2001	2000
Cash Flow from Operating Activities—Direct Method			
Cash received from customers	$214,990	$149,661	$140,252
Interest received	422	838	738
Cash paid to suppliers for inventory	(132,933)	(99,936)	(83,035)
Cash paid to employees (S&A expenses)	(32,664)	(26,382)	(25,498)
Cash paid for other operating expenses	(29,728)	(21,350)	(20,848)
Interest paid	(2,585)	(2,277)	(1,274)
Taxes paid	(7,478)	(4,321)	(4,706)
Net cash provided (used) by operating activities	$ 10,024	($3,767)	$ 5,629
Cash Flow from Investing Activities			
Additions to property, plant, and equipment	(14,100)	(4,773)	(3,982)
Other investing activities	295	0	0
Net cash provided (used) by investing activities	($13,805)	($4,773)	($3,982)
Cash Flow from Financing Activities			
Sales of common stock	256	183	124
Increase (decrease) in short-term borrowings (includes current maturities of long-term debt)	(30)	1,854	1,326
Additions to long-term borrowings	5,600	7,882	629
Reductions of long-term borrowings	(1,516)	(1,593)	(127)
Dividends paid	(1,582)	(1,862)	(1,841)
Net cash provided (used) by financing activities	$ 2,728	$ 6,464	$ 111
Increase (decrease) in cash and marketable securities	($1,053)	($2,076)	$ 1,758
Supplementary Schedule			
Cash Flow from Operating Activities—Indirect Method			
Net income	$ 9,394	$ 5,910	$ 5,896
Noncash revenue and expense included in net income:			
Depreciation	3,998	2,984	2,501
Deferred income taxes	208	136	118
Cash provided (used) by current assets and liabilities:			
Accounts receivable	(610)	(3,339)	(448)
Inventories	(10,272)	(7,006)	(2,331)
Prepaid expenses	247	295	(82)
Accounts payable	6,703	(1,051)	902
Accrued liabilities	356	(1,696)	(927)
Net cash provided (used) by operations	$ 10,024	($3,767)	$ 5,629

The accompanying notes are an integral part of these statements.

they represent, as explained in chapter 2, short-term highly liquid investments that can be readily converted into cash. They include U.S. Treasury bills, certificates, notes, and bonds; negotiable certificates of deposit at financial institutions; and commercial paper. Some companies will separate marketable securities into two accounts: (1) cash and cash equivalents and (2) short-term investments. When this occurs, the short-term investments are classified as investing activities.

Operating activities include delivering or producing goods for sale and providing services and the cash effects of transactions and other events that enter into the determination of income.

INFLOWS

> Sales of goods
> Revenue from services
> Returns on interest earning assets (interest)
> Returns on equity securities (dividends)

OUTFLOWS

> Payments for purchases of inventories
> Payments for operating expenses (salaries, rent, insurance, etc.)
> Payments for purchases from suppliers other than inventory
> Payments to lenders (interest)
> Payments for taxes

Investing activities include (1) acquiring and selling or otherwise disposing of (a) securities that are not cash equivalents and (b) productive assets that are expected to benefit the firm for long periods of time and (2) lending money and collecting on loans.

INFLOWS

> Sales of long-lived assets such as property, plant, and equipment
> Sales of debt or equity securities of other entities (except securities treated as cash equivalents)
> Returns from loans (principal) to others

OUTFLOWS

> Acquisitions of long-lived assets
> Purchases of debt or equity securities of other entities (except trading securities)
> Loans (principal) to others

Financing activities include borrowing from creditors and repaying the principal and obtaining resources from owners and providing them with a return on the investment.

INFLOWS

> Proceeds from borrowing
> Proceeds from issuing the firm's own equity securities

OUTFLOWS

Repayment of debt principal

Repurchase of a firm's own shares

Payment of dividends

With these definitions in mind, consider Exhibit 4.2, a worksheet for preparing the statement of cash flows that shows comparative 2002 and 2001 balance sheet accounts for R.E.C. Inc. Included in this exhibit is a column with the account balance changes and the category (or categories) that applies to each account. Explanations of how each account change is used in a statement of cash flow will be provided in subsequent sections of this chapter.

(1)(2) Cash and marketable securities are cash. The changes in these two accounts—a net decrease of $1,053 thousand (decrease in marketable securities of $2,732 thousand less increase in cash of $1,679 thousand)—will be explained by the changes in all of the other accounts. This means that for the year ending 2002, the cash outflows have exceeded the cash inflows by $1,053 thousand.

(3)(4)(5) Accounts receivable, inventories, and prepaid expenses are all operating accounts relating to sales of goods, purchases of inventories, and payments for operating expenses.

(6) The net increase in property, plant, and equipment is an investing activity reflecting purchases of long-lived assets.

(7) The change in accumulated depreciation and amortization is classified as operating because it will be used as an adjustment to operating expenses or net income to determine cash flow from operating activities.

(8) Other assets are holdings of land held for resale, representing an investing activity.

(9) Accounts payable is an operating account because it arises from purchases of inventory.

(10) (11) Notes payable and current maturities of long-term debt result from borrowing (debt principal), a financing activity.

(12) Accrued liabilities are operating because they result from the accrual of operating expenses such as wages, rent, salaries, and insurance.

(13) The change in deferred income taxes is categorized as operating because it is part of the adjustment of tax expense to calculate cash flow from operating activities.

(14) The change in long-term debt, principal on borrowings, is a financing activity.

(15)(16) Common stock and paid-in capital are also financing activities because the changes result from sales of the firm's own equity shares.

(17) The change in retained earnings, as explained in chapter 3, is the product of two activities: (18) net income for the period, which is operating; and (19) the payment of cash dividends, which is a financing activity.

The next step is to transfer the account changes to the appropriate area of a statement of cash flows.[2] In doing so, a determination must also be made of what

---

[2] Several alternative formats can be used for presenting the statement of cash flows, provided that the statement is reconciled to the change in cash and shows cash inflows and outflows from operating, financing, and investing activities.

EXHIBIT 4.2

R.E.C. INC.
WORKSHEET FOR PREPARING STATEMENT OF CASH FLOWS
(IN THOUSANDS)

	2002	2001	Change (2002–2001)	Category
Assets				
(1) Cash	$ 4,061	$ 2,382	$ 1,679	Cash
(2) Marketable securities	5,272	8,004	(2,732)	Cash
(3) Accounts receivable (net)	8,960	8,350	610	Operating
(4) Inventories	47,041	36,769	10,272	Operating
(5) Prepaid expenses	512	759	(247)	Operating
(6) Property, plant, and equipment	40,607	26,507	$14,100	Investing
(7) Accumulated depreciation and amortization	(11,528)	(7,530)	(3,998)	Operating
(8) Other assets	373	668	(295)	Investing
Liabilities and Stockholders' Equity				
Liabilities				
(9) Accounts payable	14,294	7,591	6,703	Operating
(10) Notes payable—banks	5,614	6,012	(398)	Financing
(11) Current maturities of long-term debt	1,884	1,516	368	Financing
(12) Accrued liabilities	5,669	5,313	356	Operating
(13) Deferred income taxes	843	635	208	Operating
(14) Long-term borrowings*	21,059	16,975	4,084	Financing
Stockholders' Equity				
(15) Common stock	4,803	4,594	209	Financing
(16) Additional paid-in capital	957	910	47	Financing
(17) Retained earnings**	40,175	32,363	7,812	**
*(14) Additions to long-term borrowings			$5,600	Financing
(14) Reductions of long-term borrowings			(1,516)	Financing
(14) Net change in long-term debt			$4,084	
**(18) Net income (operating)			$9,394	Operating
(19) Dividends paid (financing)			(1,582)	Financing
(17) Change in retained earnings			$7,812	

constitutes an inflow and what constitutes an outflow when analyzing the change in an account balance. The following table should help:

Inflow	Outflow
− Asset account	+ Asset account
+ Liability account	− Liability account
+ Equity account	− Equity account

The table indicates that a decrease in an asset balance and an increase in liability and equity accounts are inflows.[3] Examples from Exhibit 4.2 are the decrease in other assets (cash inflow from the sale of property not used in the business), the increase in long-term debt (cash inflow from borrowing), and the increase in common stock and additional paid-in capital (cash inflow from sales of equity securities). Outflows are represented by the increase in inventories (cash outflow to purchase inventory) and the decrease in notes payable (cash outflow to repay borrowings).

Note that accumulated depreciation appears in the asset section but actually is a contra-asset or credit balance account because it reduces the amount of total assets. Accumulated depreciation is shown in parentheses on the balance sheet and has the same effect as a liability account.

Another complication occurs from the impact of *two transactions in one account*. For example, the net increase in retained earnings has resulted from the combination of net income for the period, which increases the account, and the payment of dividends, which reduces the account. Multiple transactions can also affect other accounts, such as property, plant, and equipment if a firm both acquires and sells capital assets during the period, and debt accounts, if the firm both borrows and repays principal.

Calculating Cash Flow from Operating Activities

The R.E.C. Inc. Consolidated Statements of Cash Flows begins with cash flow from operating activities. This represents the cash generated *internally*. In contrast, investing and financing activities provide cash from *external* sources. Two methods are used for calculating and presenting cash flow from operating activities: the direct method and the indirect method.[4] Both methods are illustrated for R.E.C. Inc. and explained in the chapter. The *direct method* shows cash collections from customers, interest and dividends collected, other operating cash receipts, cash paid to suppliers and employees, interest paid, taxes paid, and other operating cash payments. The *indirect method* starts with net income and adjusts for deferrals; accruals; noncash items, such as depreciation and amortization; and nonoperating items, such as gains and losses on asset sales. The direct and indirect methods yield identical figures for net cash flow from operating activities because the underlying accounting concepts are the same.

DIRECT METHOD

Exhibit 4.3 illustrates the calculation of net cash flow from operating activities by the direct method. This method translates each item on the accrual-based income statement to a cash revenue or expense item. The calculation of cash flow from operating activities in Exhibit 4.3 represents an approximation of the *actual* receipts and payments of cash required by the direct method.

---

[3] In accounting terminology, an inflow results from the decrease in a debit balance account or an increase in a credit balance account; an outflow results from the increase in a debit balance account or the decrease in a credit balance account.

[4] FASB Statement No. 95 recommends presentation of the direct method in the primary statement with the indirect method provided as supplementary information; firms are permitted to use either method.

EXHIBIT 4.3

R.E.C. INC.
NET CASH FLOW FROM OPERATING ACTIVITIES
DIRECT METHOD

Sales	− Increase in accounts receivable + Decrease in accounts receivable + Increase in deferred revenue − Decrease in deferred revenue	= Cash collections from customers
Cost of Goods Sold	+ Increase in inventory − Decrease in inventory − Increase in accounts payable + Decrease in accounts payable	= Cash paid to suppliers
Salary Expense	−Increase in accrued salaries payable + Decrease in accrued salaries payable	= Cash paid to employees
Other Operating Expenses	−Depreciation, amortization, depletion expense for period + Increase in prepaid expenses − Decrease in prepaid expenses − Increase in accrued operating expenses + Decrease in accrued operating expenses	= Cash paid for other operating expenses
Interest Revenue	− Increase in interest receivable + Decrease in interest receivable	= Cash revenue from interest
Interest Expense	− Increase in accrued interest payable + Decrease in accrued interest payable	= Cash paid for interest
Investment Income	− Increase in investment account from equity income* + Decrease in investment account from equity income**	= Cash revenue from dividends
Tax Expense	− Increase in deferred tax liability + Decrease in deferred tax liability − Decrease in deferred tax asset + Increase in deferred tax asset − Increase in accrued taxes payable + Decrease in accrued taxes payable − Decrease in prepaid tax + Increase in prepaid tax	= Cash paid for taxes

Net cash flow from operating activities

---

*Amount by which equity income recognized exceeds cash dividends received.

**Amount by which cash dividends received exceed equity income recognized.

The steps shown in Exhibit 4.3 will be used to explain the calculation of net cash flow from operating activities on the R.E.C. Inc. Statement of Cash Flows for 2002.

R.E.C. Inc. Direct Method

Sales	$215,600	
Increase in accounts receivable	(610)	
Cash collections on sales		214,990
Cost of goods sold	129,364	
Increase in inventory	10,272	
Increase in accounts payable	(6,703)	
Cash payments for supplies		132,933
Selling and administrative expenses		32,664
Other operating expenses	34,329	
Depreciation and amortization	(3,998)	
Decrease in prepaid expense	(247)	
Increase in accrued liabilities	(356)	
Cash paid for other operating expense		29,728
Interest revenue		422
Interest expense		2,585
Tax expense	7,686	
Increase in deferred tax liability	(208)	
Cash paid for taxes		7,478
Net cash flow from operating activities		$ 10,024

The increase in *accounts receivable* is subtracted from sales revenue because more sales revenue was recognized in the income statement than was received in cash.

The increase in *inventories* is added to cost of goods sold because more cash was paid to purchase inventories than was included in cost of goods sold expense; that is, cash was used to purchase inventory that has not yet been sold.

The increase in *accounts payable* is subtracted from cost of goods sold because R.E.C. Inc. was able to defer some payments to suppliers for purchases of inventory; more cost of goods sold expense was recognized than was actually paid in cash.

Depreciation and amortization expense is subtracted from other operating expenses. Remember that depreciation represents a cost allocation, not an outflow of cash. The acquisition of the capital asset was recognized as an investing cash outflow (unless it was exchanged for debt or stock) in the statement of cash flows for the period in which the asset was acquired. So depreciation itself does not require any outflow of cash in the year it is recognized. Deducting depreciation expense in the current year's statement of cash flows would be double counting. Amortization is similar to depreciation—an expense that enters into the determination of net income but that does not require an outflow of cash. Depletion would be handled in the same manner as depreciation and amortization. The depreciation and amortization expense for R.E.C. Inc. in 2002 is equal to the change in the balance sheet accumulated depreciation and amortization account. If the firm had dispositions of capital assets during the accounting period, however, the balance sheet change would not equal the expense recognition for the period because some of the account change would have resulted from the elimination of accumulated depreciation for the asset that was removed. The appropriate figure to subtract would be depreciation and amortization expense from the earnings statement.

The decrease in *prepaid expense* is subtracted from other operating expenses because the firm is recognizing as expense in 2002 items for which cash was paid in the previous year; that is, the firm is utilizing on a net basis some of the prior years' pre-payments.

The increase in *accrued liabilities* is subtracted from other operating expenses because R.E.C. Inc. has recognized more in expense on the income statement than has been paid in cash.

Finally, the increase in the *deferred tax liability* account is subtracted from tax expense to obtain cash payments for taxes. The deferred tax liability, explained in chapter 2, was created as a reconciliation between the amount of tax expense reported on the income statement and the cash actually paid or payable to the IRS. If a deferred tax liability increases from one year to the next, tax expense deducted on the earnings statement to arrive at net income has exceeded cash actually paid for taxes. Thus, an increase in the deferred tax liability account is subtracted from tax expense to arrive at cash from operations. A decrease in deferred tax liabilities would be added. A change in deferred tax assets would be handled in the opposite way from the deferred tax liability.

Exhibit 4.3 includes other possible adjustments, not present for R.E.C. Inc., that would be made to calculate net cash flow from operating activities by the direct method.

INDIRECT METHOD

Exhibit 4.4 illustrates the steps necessary to convert net income to cash flow from operating activities. The steps shown in Exhibit 4.4 will be used to explain the calculation of cash flow from operating activities for R.E.C. Inc. using the indirect method. Exhibit 4.4 includes some adjustments not present for R.E.C. Inc.

R.E.C., Inc. Indirect Method	
Net income	$ 9,394
Noncash nonoperating items	
+ Depreciation and amortization expense	3,998
+ Increase in deferred tax liability	208
Cash provided (used) by current assets, liabilities	
− Increase in accounts receivables	(610)
− Increase in inventory	(10,272)
+ Decrease in prepaid expenses	247
+ Increase in accounts payable	6,703
+ Increase in accrued liabilities	356
Net cash flow from operating activities	$10,024

Depreciation and amortization are added back to net income because they reflect the recognition of a noncash expense (see preceding discussion).

EXHIBIT 4.4

R.E.C. INC.
NET CASH FLOW FROM OPERATING ACTIVITIES
INDIRECT METHOD

Net income*

Noncash/Nonoperating revenue and expense included in income:

+ Depreciation, amortization, depletion expense for period

+ Increase in deferred tax liability
− Decrease in deferred tax liability
+ Decrease in deferred tax asset
− Increase in deferred tax asset

− Increase in investment account from equity income**
+ Decrease in investment account from equity income***

+ Increase in deferred revenue
  Decrease in deferred revenue

− Gain on sale of assets
+ Loss on sale of assets

Cash provided (used) by current assets and liabilities

+ Decrease in accounts receivable
− Increase in accounts receivable

+ Decrease in inventory
− Increase in inventory

+ Decrease in prepaid expenses
− Increase in prepaid expenses

+ Decrease in interest receivable
− Increase in interest receivable

+ Increase in accounts payable
− Decrease in accounts payable

+ Increase in accrued liabilities
− Decrease in accrued liabilities

Net cash flow from operating activities

*Before extraordinary items, accounting changes, discontinued operations.

**Amount by which equity income exceeds cash dividends received.

***Amount by which cash dividends received exceed equity income recognized.

The *deferred tax liability* account, as discussed in chapter 2 and the preceding section, reconciles the difference between tax expense recognized in the calculation of net income and the tax expense actually paid. The increase in the liability account for R.E.C. Inc. is added back to net income because more tax expense was recognized in the calculation of net income than was actually paid for taxes.

The increase in *accounts receivable* is deducted because more sales revenue has been included in net income than has been collected in cash from customers.

The increase in *inventory* is subtracted because R.E.C. Inc. has purchased more inventory than has been included in cost of goods sold. Cost of goods sold used in calculating net income includes only the inventory actually sold.

The decrease in *prepaid expenses* is added back because the firm has recognized an expense in the current period for which cash was paid in an earlier period, on a net basis.

The increase in *accounts payable* is added because less has been paid to suppliers for purchases of inventory than was included in cost of goods sold.

The increase in *accrued liabilities* is an addition to net income because it reflects the recognition of expense, on a net basis, prior to the payment of cash.

There are other potential adjustments, not required for R.E.C. Inc., that enter into the net income adjustment for noncash expense and revenues. One such item is the recognition of investment income from unconsolidated subsidiaries by the equity method of accounting, discussed in chapter 3. When a company uses the equity method, earnings can be recognized in the income statement in excess of cash actually received from dividends, or the reverse can occur, for example, in the case of a loss recorded by an investee. For a firm using the equity method, there would be a deduction from net income for the amount by which investment income recognized exceeded cash received. Other potential adjustment items include changes relating to deferred income, deferred expense, the amortization of bond discounts and premiums, extraordinary items, and gains or losses on sales of long-lived assets.

Although *gains and losses from asset sales* are included in the calculation of net income, they are not considered an operating activity. A gain should be deducted from net income, and a loss should be added to net income to determine cash flow from operating activities. The entire proceeds from sales of long-lived assets are included as investing inflows.

Cash Flow from Investing Activities

Additions to *property, plant, and equipment* represent a net addition to R.E.C. Inc.'s buildings, leasehold improvements, and equipment, a cash outflow of $14.1 million. Other investing activities for R.E.C. Inc. result from a decrease in the *other assets* account on the balance sheet, which represent holdings of investment properties. The sale of these assets has provided a cash inflow of $295 thousand.

Cash Flow from Financing Activities

As a result of the exercise of stock options, R.E.C. Inc. issued new shares of stock during 2002. The total cash generated from stock sales amounted to $256 thousand. Note that two accounts on the balance sheet—*common stock* and *additional paid-in capital*—combine to explain this change:

Common stock	$209	Inflow
Additional paid-in capital	47	Inflow
	256	Total inflow

The two accounts *notes payable to banks* and *current maturities of long-term debt* (carried as a current liability since the principal is payable within a year) jointly explain R.E.C. Inc.'s net reduction in short-term borrowings in 2002 of $30 thousand:

Notes payable—banks	($398)	Outflow
Current maturities of long-term debt	368	Inflow
	($ 30)	Net outflow

In preparing the statement of cash flows, long-term borrowings should be segregated into two components: additions to long-term borrowings and reductions of long-term borrowings. This information is provided in Note C, Long-Term Debt, to the R.E.C. Inc. financial statements where detail on the various long-term notes is provided. The two figures—additions to long-term debt and reductions of long-term debt—on the R.E.C. Inc. statement of cash flows reconcile the change in the *long-term debt* account on the R.E.C. Inc. balance sheet:

Additions to long-term borrowings	$5,600	Inflow
Reductions of long-term borrowings	(1,516)	Outflow
Increase in long term debt	$4,084	

The payment of cash dividends by R.E.C. Inc. in 2002 of $1.582 million is the final item in the financing activities section. The change in *retained earnings* results from the combination of net income recognition and the payment of cash dividends; this information is provided in the R.E.C. Inc. Statement of Retained Earnings:

Net income	$9,394	Inflow
Dividends paid	(1,582)	Outflow
Change in retained earnings	$7,812	

It should be noted that the *payment* of cash dividends is the financing outflow; the *declaration* of a cash dividend would not affect cash.

Change in Cash

To summarize the cash inflows and outflows for 2002 for R.E.C. Inc., the net cash provided by operating activities, plus the net cash provided by financing activities, less the net cash used by investing activities produced a net decrease in *cash* and *marketable securities* for the period:

Net cash provided by operating activities	$10,024
Net cash provided by financing activities	2,728
Net cash used by investing activities	(13,805)
Decrease in cash and marketable securities	(1,053)

The three-year statements of cash flows for R.E.C. Inc. are provided in Exhibit 4.5. The statement for 2001 and 2000 would be prepared using the same process that was illustrated for 2002.

EXHIBIT 4.5

R.E.C. INC.
CONSOLIDATED STATEMENTS OF CASH FLOWS
FOR THE YEARS ENDED DECEMBER 31, 2002, 2001, AND 2000
(IN THOUSANDS)

	2002	2001	2000
Cash Flow from Operating Activities—Direct Method			
Cash received from customers	$214,990	$149,661	$140,252
Interest received	422	838	738
Cash paid to suppliers for inventory	(132,933)	(99,936)	(83,035)
Cash paid to employees (S&A Expenses)	(32,664)	(26,382)	(25,498)
Cash paid for other operating expenses	(29,728)	(21,350)	(20,848)
Interest paid	(2,585)	(2,277)	(1,274)
Taxes paid	(7,478)	(4,321)	(4,706)
Net cash provided (used) by operating activities	$ 10,024	($ 3,767)	$ 5,629
Cash Flows from Investing Activities			
Additions to property, plant, and equipment	(14,100)	(4,773)	(3,982)
Other investing activities	295	0	0
Net cash provided (used) by investing activities	($ 13,805)	($ 4,773)	($ 3,982)
Cash Flow from Financing Activities			
Sales of common stock	256	183	124
Increase (decrease) in short-term borrowings (includes current maturities of long-term debt)	(30)	1,854	1,326
Additions to long-term borrowings	5,600	7,882	629
Reductions of long-term borrowings	(1,516)	(1,593)	(127)
Dividends paid	(1,582)	(1,862)	(1,841)
Net cash provided (used) by financing activities	$ 2,728	$ 6,464	$ 111
Increase (decrease) in cash and marketable securities	($ 1,053)	($ 2,076)	$ 1,758
Supplementary Schedule			
Cash Flow from Operating Activities—Indirect Method			
Net income	$ 9,394	$ 5,910	$ 5,896
Noncash revenue and expense included in net income			
Depreciation and amortization	3,998	2,984	2,501
Deferred income taxes	208	136	118
Cash provided (used) by current assets and liabilities			
Accounts receivable	(610)	(3,339)	(448)
Inventories	(10,272)	(7,006)	(2,331)
Prepaid expenses	247	295	(82)
Accounts payable	6,703	(1,051)	902
Accrued liabilities	356	(1,696)	(927)
Net cash provided (used) by operations	$ 10,024	($ 3,767)	$ 5,629

Analyzing the Statement of Cash Flows

The statement of cash flows is an important analytical tool for creditors, investors, and other users of financial statement data in order to help determine the following about a business firm:

- its ability to generate cash flows in the future;
- its capacity to meet obligations for cash;
- its future external financing needs;
- its success in productively managing investing activities; and
- its effectiveness in implementing financing and investing strategies.

To begin the analysis of a statement of cash flows, it is essential to understand the importance of cash flow from operations, the first category on the statement.

CASH FLOW FROM OPERATIONS

It is possible for a firm to be highly profitable and not be able to pay dividends or invest in new equipment. It is possible for a firm to be highly profitable and not be able to service debt. It is also possible for a firm to be highly profitable and go bankrupt. W. T. Grant is one of the classic examples.[5] How? The problem is cash. Consider the following questions:

1. You are a banker evaluating a loan request from a prospective customer. What is your primary concern when making a decision regarding approval or denial of the loan request?
2. You are a wholesaler of goods and have been asked to sell your products on credit to a potential buyer. What is the major determining factor regarding approval or denial of the credit sale?
3. You are an investor in a firm and rely on the receipt of regular cash dividends as part of your return on investment. What must the firm generate in order to pay dividends?

In each case, the answer is *cash*. The banker must decide whether or not the prospective borrower will have the cash to meet interest and principal payments on the debt. The wholesaler will sell goods on credit only to those customers who can satisfy their accounts. A company can pay cash dividends only by producing cash.

The ongoing operation of any business depends upon its success in generating cash from operations. It is cash that a firm needs to satisfy creditors and investors. Temporary shortfalls of cash can be satisfied by borrowing or other means, such as selling long-lived assets, but ultimately a company must generate cash.

Cash flow from operations has become increasingly important as an analytical tool to determine the financial health of a business enterprise. Periods of high interest rates and inflation contributed to the enhanced attention paid to cash flow by investors and creditors. When interest rates are high, the cost of borrowing to cover short-term cash can be out of reach for many firms seeking to cover temporary cash shortages. Periods of inflation distort the meaningfulness of net income, through the understatement of depreciation and cost of goods sold expenses, making other measures of oper-

---

[5]   J. A. Largay and C. P. Stickney, "Cash Flows, Ratio Analysis, and the W. T. Grant Bankruptcy," *Financial Analysts Journal,* July-August 1980.

ating performance and financial success important. Even when interest rates and inflation are low, there are other factors that limit the usefulness of net income as a barometer of financial health. Consider the case of Nocash Corporation.

NOCASH CORPORATION

The Nocash Corporation had sales of $100,000 in its second year of operations, up from $50,000 in the first year. Expenses, including taxes, amounted to $70,000 in year 2, compared with $40,000 in year 1. The comparative income statements for the two years indicate substantial growth, with year 2 earnings greatly improved over those reported in year 1.

NOCASH CORPORATION
INCOME STATEMENT FOR YEAR 1 AND YEAR 2

	Year 1	Year 2
Sales	$50,000	$100,000
Expenses	40,000	70,000
Net income	$10,000	$ 30,000

So far, so good—a tripling of profit for Nocash. There are some additional facts, however, that are relevant to Nocash's operations but that do not appear on the firm's income statement:

1. In order to improve sales in year 2, Nocash eased its credit policies and attracted customers of a substantially lower quality than in year 1.
2. Nocash purchased a new line of inventory near the end of year 1, and it became apparent during year 2 that the inventory could not be sold, except at substantial reductions below cost.
3. Rumors regarding Nocash's problems with regard to accounts receivable and inventory management prompted some suppliers to refuse the sale of goods on credit to Nocash.

The effect of these additional factors can be found on Nocash's balance sheet.

NOCASH CORPORATION
BALANCE SHEET AT DECEMBER 31

	Year 1	Year 2	$Change
Cash	$2,000	$2,000	0
Accounts Receivable	10,000	30,000	+20,000 [1]
Inventories	10,000	25,000	+15,000 [2]
Total assets	$22,000	$57,000	+35,000
Accounts payable	7,000	2,000	−5,000 [3]
Notes payable—to banks	0	10,000	+10,000
Equity	15,000	45,000	+30,000
Total liabilities & equity	$22,000	$57,000	+35,000

[1] Accounts receivable increased at a faster pace than sales as a result of deterioration in customer quality.

[2] Ending inventory increased and included items that would ultimately be sold at a loss.

[3] Nocash's inability to purchase goods on credit caused a reduction in accounts payable.

If Nocash's net income is recalculated on a cash basis, the following adjustments would be made, using the account balance changes between year 1 and year 2:

Net income	$30,000
(1) Accounts receivable	(20,000)
(2) Inventories	(15,000)
(3) Accounts payable	(5,000)
Cash income	($10,000)

(1) The increase in accounts receivable is subtracted because more sales revenue was recognized in computing net income than was collected in cash.

Sales recognized in net income		$100,000
Sales collected		
Beginning accounts receivable	$10,000	
Plus: sales, year 2	100,000	
Less: ending accounts receivable	(30,000)	80,000
Difference between net income and cash flow		$ 20,000

(2) The increase in inventory is deducted, reflecting the cash outflow for inventory purchases in excess of the expense recognized through cost of goods sold.

Purchases for inventory*	$75,000
Less: cost of goods sold	(60,000)
Difference between net income & cash flow	$15,000

(3) The decrease in accounts payable is deducted because the cash payments to suppliers in year 2 were greater than the amount of expense recorded. (In essence, cash was paid for some year 1 accounts as well as year 2 accounts.)

Payments to suppliers**	$80,000
Less: purchases for inventory*	75,000
Difference between net income and cash flow	$ 5,000
*Ending inventory	$25,000
Plus: Cost of goods sold	60,000
Less: Beginning inventory	(10,000)
*Purchases	$75,000
**Beginning accounts payable	$ 7,000
Plus: Purchases	75,000
Less: Ending accounts payable	(2,000)
**Payments	$80,000

How did Nocash cover its $10,000 cash shortfall? Note the appearance of a $10,000 note payable to banks on the year 2 balance sheet. The borrowing has enabled Nocash to continue to operate, but unless the company can begin to generate cash from operations, its problems will compound. Bankers sometimes refer to this problem as a company's "selling itself out of business." The higher the cost of borrowing, the more costly and difficult it will be for Nocash to continue to operate.

HELP FROM A STATEMENT OF CASH FLOWS

The statement of cash flows provides the figure "net cash flow from operating activities." A condensed Statement of Cash Flows for R.E.C. Inc. (using the indirect method because it provides detail on changes in relevant balance sheet accounts) is shown in Exhibit 4.6. The analyst should be concerned with the following in reviewing this information:

- The success or failure of the firm in generating cash from operations.
- The underlying causes of the positive or negative operating cash flow.
- The magnitude of positive or negative operating cash flow.
- Fluctuations in cash flow from operations over time.

For R.E.C. Inc. the first point of significance is the negative cash flow from operations in 2001 ($3,767 million). It should be noted that the *negative cash flow* occurred for a year in which the company reported *positive net income* of $5,910 million. The cash flow crunch was apparently caused primarily by a substantial growth in accounts receivable and inventories. Those increases were partly the result of the firm's expansion policies, and it would also be important to evaluate the quality of receivables and inventory—that is, are they collectable and salable? R.E.C. Inc. was able to recover in 2002, returning to strongly positive cash generation of $10.024 million, in spite of the continuation of inventory growth to support the expansion. The company obtained good supplier credit in 2002 and controlled the growth in

---

EXHIBIT 4.6

R.E.C. INC.
CONDENSED CONSOLIDATED STATEMENTS OF CASH FLOWS FOR THE YEARS
ENDED DECEMBER 31, 2002, 2001, AND 2000 (IN THOUSANDS)

	2002	*2001*	*2000*
Cash Flow from Operating Activities			
Net income	$9,394	$5,910	$5,896
Noncash expenses and revenues included in income			
Depreciation and amortization	3,998	2,984	2,501
Deferred income taxes	208	136	118
Cash Provided by (used for) Current Assets and Liabilities			
Accounts receivable	(610)	(3,339)	(448)
Inventories	(10,272)	(7,006)	(2,331)
Prepaid expenses	247	295	(82)
Accounts payable	6,703	(1,051)	902
Accrued liabilities	356	(1,696)	(927)
Net cash provided (used) by operating activities	$10,024	($3,767)	$5,629

accounts receivable. It will be necessary to monitor R.E.C. Inc.'s cash flow from operations closely and, in particular, the management of inventories. Inventory growth is desirable when supporting an expansion of sales but undesirable when like Nocash Corporation, the inventory is not selling or is selling only at discounted prices.

The calculation of cash flow from operations illustrated for R.E.C. Inc. can be made for any company from its balance sheet and income statement, using the procedures outlined in the examples. Cash flow from operations is especially important for those firms that are heavily invested in inventories and that use trade accounts receivables and payables as a major part of ordinary business operations. Such problems as sales growth that is too rapid, slow-moving or obsolete inventory, price discounting within the industry, a rise in accounts receivable of inferior quality, and the tightening of credit by suppliers can all impair the firm's ability to generate cash from operations and lead to serious financial problems, including bankruptcy.

SUMMARY ANALYSIS OF THE STATEMENT OF CASH FLOWS

Exhibit 4.7 presents a summary table to facilitate the analysis of a statement of cash flows, including cash flow from operating activities. The top part of the exhibit shows the inflows and outflows over the three-year period from 2000 to 2002 for R.E.C. Inc. in dollar amounts. The lower portion of Exhibit 4.7 shows the cash inflows as a percentage of total inflows and the outflows as a percentage of total outflows.

First consider the dollar amounts. It is apparent that the magnitude of R.E.C. Inc.'s activity has increased sharply over the three-year period, with total cash inflows increasing from $7.7 million to $16.2 million and cash outflows from $6.0 million to $17.2 million. The major increase in cash outflows is capital asset expansion, and the increases in inflows have been the result of operations and long-term borrowings. The firm also has used liquid cash assets to support growth: note that cash and marketable securities decreased in 2001 and 2002.

In percentage terms, it is noteworthy that operations supplied 62% of needed cash in 2002 and 73% in 2000. As a result of negative cash from operations in 2001, the firm had to borrow heavily, with debt (short-term and long-term) accounting for 98% of 2001 inflows. The stronger operating cash production in 2002 supported the substantial capital expansion (82% of cash outflow for investments in property, plant, and equipment) with only 35% external debt financing. Also interesting is the trend of R.E.C. Inc.'s reducing dividend payments—in dollar amounts in 2002, and in percentage terms in both 2001 and 2002.

The purpose of the summary table is to provide an approach to analyzing a statement of cash flows. This type of analysis can be used for any firm that provides comparative cash flow data. The information in the summary table underlines the importance of internal cash generation—from operations—and the implications for investing and financing activities when this does and does not occur.

The next step is to integrate the analysis of cash flows into an overall analysis of R.E.C. Inc.'s financial condition and performance in chapter 5.

EXHIBIT 4.7

R.E.C. INC.
SUMMARY ANALYSIS STATEMENT OF CASH FLOWS

	2002	2001	2000
Inflows (thousands)			
Operations	$10,024	$0	$5,629
Sales of other assets	295	0	0
Sales of common stock	256	183	124
Additions to short-term debt	0	1,854	1,326
Additions to long-term debt	5,600	7,882	629
Total	$16,175	$9,919	$7,708
Outflows (thousands)			
Operations	$0	$3,767	$0
Purchase of property, plant, and equipment	14,100	4,773	3,982
Reductions of short-term debt	30	0	0
Reductions of long-term debt	1,516	1,593	127
Dividends paid	1,582	1,862	1,841
Total	$17,228	$11,995	$5,950
Change in cash and marketable securities	($1,053)	(2,076)	$1,758
Inflows (percent of total)			
Operations	62.0%	0.0%	73.0%
Sales and other assets	1.8	0.0	0.0
Sales of common stock	1.6	1.8	1.6
Additions to short-term debt	0.0	18.7	17.2
Additions to long-term debt	34.6	79.5	8.2
Total	100.0%	100.0%	100.0%
Ouflows (percent of total)			
Operations	0.0%	31.4%	0.0%
Purchase of property, plant, and equipment	81.8	40.0	66.9
Reductions in short-term debt	0.2	0.0	0.0
Reductions in long-term debt	8.8	13.2	2.1
Dividends paid	9.2	15.4	31.0
Total	100.0%	100.0%	100.0%

SELF-TEST

Solutions are provided in appendix D.

_____ 1. The statement of cash flows segregates cash inflows and outflows by:
   (a) Operating and financing activities.
   (b) Financing and investing activities.
   (c) Operating and investing activities.
   (d) Operating, financing, and investing activities.

2. How would short-term investments in marketable securities be classified?
   (a) If the marketable securities are essentially equivalent to cash, then they could be classified with cash.
   (b) Investing activities.
   (c) Financing activities.
   (d) Both (a) and (b).

3. How would revenue from sales of goods and services be classified?
   (a) Operating outflow.
   (b) Operating inflow.
   (c) Investing inflow.
   (d) Financing inflow.

4. How would payments for taxes be classified?
   (a) Operating outflow.
   (b) Operating inflow.
   (c) Investing outflow.
   (d) Financing outflow.

5. How would the sale of a building be classified?
   (a) Operating outflow.
   (b) Operating inflow.
   (c) Investing inflow.
   (d) Financing inflow.

6. How would the repayment of debt principal be classified?
   (a) Operating outflow.
   (b) Operating inflow.
   (c) Investing outflow.
   (d) Financing outflow.

7. What type of accounts are accounts receivable and inventory?
   (a) Cash accounts.
   (b) Operating accounts.
   (c) Financing accounts.
   (d) Investing accounts.

8. What type of accounts are notes payable and current maturities of long-term debt?
   (a) Cash accounts.
   (b) Operating accounts.
   (c) Financing accounts.
   (d) Investing accounts.

9. The change in retained earnings is affected by which of the following?
   (a) Net income and common stock.
   (b) Net income and paid-in capital.
   (c) Net income and payment of dividends.
   (d) Payment of dividends and common stock.

10. Which method of calculating cash flow from operations requires the adjustment of net income for deferrals, accruals, noncash, and nonoperating expenses?
   (a) The direct method.
   (b) The indirect method.
   (c) The inflow method.

(d) The outflow method.

_____ 11. An inflow of cash would result from which of the following?
  (a) The increase in an asset account other than cash.
  (b) The decrease in an asset account other than cash.
  (c) The decrease in an equity account.
  (d) The decrease in a liability account.

_____ 12. An outflow of cash would result from which of the following?
  (a) The decrease in an asset account other than cash.
  (b) The increase in a liability account.
  (c) The decrease in a liability account.
  (d) The increase in an equity account.

_____ 13. What are internal sources of cash?
  (a) Cash inflows from operating activities.
  (b) Cash inflows from investing activities.
  (c) Cash inflows from financing activities.
  (d) All of the above.

_____ 14. What are external sources of cash?
  (a) Cash inflows from operating activities.
  (b) Cash inflows from investing activities.
  (c) Cash inflows from financing activities.
  (d) Both (b) and (c).

_____ 15. Which of the following items is included in the adjustment of net income to obtain cash flow from operating activities?
  (a) Depreciation expense for the period.
  (b) The change in deferred taxes.
  (c) The amount by which equity income recognized exceeds cash received.
  (d) All of the above.

_____ 16. Which statement is true for gains and losses from capital asset sales?
  (a) They do not affect cash and are excluded from the statement of cash flows.
  (b) They are included in cash flows from operating activities.
  (c) They are included in cash flows from investing activities.
  (d) They are included in cash flows from financing activities.

_____ 17. Which of the following current assets is included in the adjustment of net income to obtain cash flow from operating activities?
  (a) Accounts receivable.
  (b) Inventory.
  (c) Prepaid expenses.
  (d) All of the above.

_____ 18. Which of the following current liability accounts is included in the adjustment of expenses to obtain cash flow from operating activities?
  (a) Accounts payable.
  (b) Notes payable and current maturities of long-term debt.
  (c) Accrued liabilities.
  (d) Both (a) and (c).

_____ 19. How is it possible for a firm to be profitable and still go bankrupt?
  (a) Earnings have increased more rapidly than sales.
  (b) The firm has positive net income but has failed to generate cash from operations.

    (c) Net income has been adjusted for inflation.

    (d) Sales have not improved even though credit policies have been eased.

____ 20. Why has cash flow from operations become increasingly important as an analytical tool?

    (a) Inflation has distorted the meaningfulness of net income.

    (b) High interest rates can put the cost of borrowing to cover short-term cash needs out of reach for many firms.

    (c) Firms may have uncollected accounts receivable and unsalable inventory on the books.

    (d) All of the above.

____ 21. Which of the following statements is false?

    (a) A negative cash flow can occur in a year in which net income is positive.

    (b) An increase in accounts receivable represents accounts not yet collected in cash.

    (c) An increase in accounts payable represents accounts not yet collected in cash.

    (d) To obtain cash flow from operations, the reported net income must be adjusted.

____ 22. Which of the following could lead to cash flow problems?

    (a) Obsolete inventory, accounts receivable of inferior quality, easing of credit by suppliers.

    (b) Slow-moving inventory, accounts receivable of inferior quality, tightening of credit by suppliers.

    (c) Obsolete inventory, increasing notes payable, easing of credit by suppliers.

    (d) Obsolete inventory, improved quality of accounts receivable, easing of credit by suppliers.

Questions 23–30 are based on the *direct method* of presenting cash flow from operating activities. Indicate whether the following items will be added (A) or subtracted (S) to/from the relevant revenue or expense item in the calculation of cash flow from operating activities.

____ 23. Decrease in accounts receivable to calculate cash collections from sales.

____ 24. Decrease in inventories to calculate cash paid to suppliers.

____ 25. Increase in accounts payable to calculate cash paid to suppliers.

____ 26. Decrease in accrued salaries payable to calculate cash paid to employees.

____ 27. Depreciation expense for the period to calculate cash paid for operating expenses.

____ 28. Increase in prepaid expenses to calculate cash paid for operating expense.

____ 29. Decrease in accrued interest payable to calculate cash paid for interest expense.

____ 30. Increase in deferred tax liability to calculate cash paid for tax expense.

The following information is available for Jacqui's Jewelry and Gift Store:

Net income	$ 5,000
Depreciation expense	2,500
Increase in deferred tax liabilities	500
Decrease in accounts receivable	2,000
Increase in inventories	9,000
Decrease in accounts payable	5,000
Increase in accrued liabilities	1,000

Increase in property and equipment	14,000
Increase in short-term notes payable	19,000
Decrease in long-term bonds payable	4,000

Use the *indirect method* to answer questions 31–34.

____ 31. What is net cash flow from operating activities?
    (a) ($3,000)
    (b) ($1,000)
    (c) $5,000
    (d) $13,000

____ 32. What is net cash flow from investing activities?
    (a) $14,000
    (b) ($14,000)
    (c) $21,000
    (d) ($16,000)

____ 33. What is net cash flow from financing activities?
    (a) $15,000
    (b) ($15,000)
    (c) $17,000
    (d) ($14,000)

____ 34. What is the change in cash?
    (a) ($3,000)
    (b) $3,000
    (c) $2,000
    (d) ($2,000)

STUDY QUESTIONS AND PROBLEMS

4.1 Identify the following as financing activities (F) or investing activities (I):
    (a) Purchase of equipment
    (b) Purchase of treasury stock
    (c) Reduction of long-term debt
    (d) Sale of building
    (e) Resale of treasury stock
    (f) Increase in short-term debt
    (g) Issuance of common stock
    (h) Purchase of land
    (i) Purchase of common stock of another firm
    (j) Payment of cash dividends
    (k) Gain on sale of land
    (l) Repayment of debt principal

4.2 Indicate which of the following current assets and current liabilities are operating accounts (O) and thus included in the adjustment of net income to cash flow from operating activities and which are cash (C), investing (I), or financing (F) accounts.
    (a) Accounts payable
    (b) Accounts receivable

(c) Notes payable (to bank)
(d) Marketable securities
(e) Accrued expenses
(f) Inventory
(g) Notes receivable—officers
(h) Current portion of long-term debt
(i) Dividends payable
(j) Income taxes payable
(k) Interest payable
(l) Certificates of deposit

4.3 Condensed financial statements for Luna Enterprises are provided below.

LUNA ENTERPRISES
COMPARATIVE BALANCE SHEETS
DECEMBER 31, 20X9 AND 20X8

	20X9	20X8
Cash	$ 1,200	$ 950
Accounts receivable	1,750	1,200
Inventory	1,150	1,450
Plant and equipment	4,500	3,900
Accumulated depreciation	(1,200)	(1,100)
Long-term investments	900	1,150
Total Assets	8,300	7,550
Accounts payable	1,100	800
Accrued wages payable	250	350
Bonds payable	1,100	1,400
Capital stock	1,000	1,000
Paid-in Capital	400	400
Retained earnings	4,450	3,600
Total Liabilities and Equity	$ 8,300	$ 7,550

INCOME STATEMENT
FOR YEAR ENDED DECEMBER 31, 20X9

Sales	$ 9,500
Cost of Goods Sold	6,650
Gross Profit	2,850
Other Expenses	
Selling	1,200
Depreciation	100
Interest	150
Income tax	350
Net income	$ 1,050
Cash Dividends	200

(a) Prepare a statement of cash flows using the indirect method.

(b) Compute cash flow from operating activities by the direct method.

4.4   The following income statement and balance sheet information are available for two firms: Firm A operates in a retail trade industry and Firm B in a service oriented industry. Firm A paid $5,000 in dividends; Firm B paid $35,000 in dividends during 20X9.

(a) Prepare a statement of cash flows for each firm.

(b) Analyze the difference in the two firms.

INCOME STATEMENT
FOR YEAR ENDED DECEMBER 31, 20X9

	Firm A	Firm B
Sales	$1,000,000	$1,000,000
Cost of Goods Sold	700,000	700,000
Gross Profit	300,000	300,000
Other Expenses		
Selling and administrative	120,000	115,000
Depreciation	10,000	30,000
Interest Expense	20,000	5,000
Earnings before taxes	150,000	150,000
Income Tax Expense	75,000	75,000
Net Income	$ 75,000	$ 75,000

CHANGES IN BALANCE SHEET ACCOUNTS
DECEMBER 31, 20X8, TO DECEMBER 31, 20X9

	Firm A	Firm B
Cash	$+ 5,000	$+ 5,000
Cash equivalents	− 5,000	+ 5,000
Accounts Receivable	+40,000	+ 5,000
Inventory	+40,000	−10,000
Property, plant, and equipment	+20,000	+70,000
Less accumulated depreciation	(+10,000)	(+30,000)
Total Assets	$+90,000	$+45,000
Accounts payable	$−20,000	$− 5,000
Notes payable (current)	+17,000	+ 2,000
Long-term debt	+20,000	−10,000
Deferred taxes (nonconcurrent)	+ 3,000	+18,000
Stockholders' equity	+70,000	+40,000
Total liability and equity	$+90,000	$+45,000

4.5   The following comparative balance sheets, income statement, and additional information are available for Little Bit Inc.

Required: Prepare a statement of cash flows for 20X9 and analyze the statement.

	December 31, 20X9 and 20X8	
	20X9	*20X8*
Cash	$ 12,000	$ 7,000
Accounts receivable (net)	190,000	125,000
Inventory	280,000	210,000
Prepaid rent	25,000	18,000
Total current assets	$ 507,000	$360,000
Plant and equipment	$ 500,000	$450,000
Less accumulated depreciation	(105,000)	(95,000)
Plant and equipment (net)	$ 395,000	$355,000
Land held for investment	165,000	150,000
Total assets	$1,067,000	$865,000
Accounts payable	$ 175,000	$150,000
Notes payable—banks	179,000	61,000
Accrued salaries payable	43,000	52,000
Total current liabilities	$ 397,000	$263,000
Long-term debt	210,000	190,000
Deferred taxes	105,000	95,000
Total liabilities	712,000	548,000
Common stock ($1 par)	110,000	100,000
Additional paid-in capital	70,000	60,000
Retained earnings	175,000	157,000
Total liabilities and equity	$1,067,000	$865,000

Income Statement for 20X9		
Sales		$950,000
Cost of goods sold		650,000
Gross profit		$300,000
Selling and administrative	$ 100,000	
Depreciation	60,000	
Other operating	45,000	205,000
Operating Profit		$ 95,000
Other Income		
Gain on sale of building		5,000
Other expense		
Interest		40,000
Earnings before tax		$ 60,000
Tax expense		20,000
Net Income		40,000

Additional Information

1. A building with original cost of $100,000 and accumulated depreciation of $50,000 was sold for $55,000.
2. Land for investment was purchased at a cost of $15,000.
3. Long-term debt of $20,000 was repaid.
4. 10,000 shares of common stock were sold for $2 per share.

4.6 The following cash flows were reported by Techno Inc. in 20X8 and 20X7.

(In thousands)	20X8	20X7
Net income	$316,354	$242,329
Noncash charges (credits) to income		
Depreciation and amortization	68,156	62,591
Deferred taxes	15,394	22,814
	399,904	327,734
Cash Provided (Used) by Operating Assets and Liabilities:		
Receivables	(288,174)	(49,704)
Inventories	(159,419)	(145,554)
Other current assets	(1,470)	3,832
Accounts payable, accrued liabilities	73,684	41,079
Total Cash Provided by Operations	24,525	177,387
Investment Activities		
Additions to plant and equipment	(94,176)	(93,136)
Other investment activities	14,408	(34,771)
Net Investment Activities	(79,768)	(127,907)
Financing Activities		
Purchases of treasury stock	(45,854)	(39,267)
Dividends paid	(40,290)	(22,523)
Net changes in short-term borrowings	125,248	45,067
Additions to long-term borrowings	135,249	4,610
Repayments of long-term borrowings		(250,564)
Net Financing Activities	165,353	(262,677)
Increase (Decrease) in Cash	110,110	(213,197)
Beginning Cash Balance	78,114	291,311
Ending Cash Balance	188,224	78,114

(a) What method does Techno use to calculate cash flows from operating activities?

(b) Explain the difference between net income and cash flow from operating activities for Techno in 20X8.

(c) Analyze Techno Inc.'s cash flows for 20X8 and 20X7.

4.7 Analyze the 20X9 Consolidated Statement of Cash flows for BeeBop International Ltd.

BEEBOP INTERNATIONAL LTD.
CONSOLIDATED STATEMENTS OF CASH FLOWS
(IN THOUSANDS)

	Year Ended December 31		
	20X9	*20X8*	*20X7*
Cash flows from operating activities			
Net income	$175,000	$137,000	$165,200
Adjustment to reconcile net income to net cash provided by operating activities:			
Depreciation and amortization	28,500	18,190	7,525
Gain on sale of business segment	(10,960)	—	—
Changes in operating assets and liabilities			
Decrease (increase) in assets:			
Accounts receivable	(6,475)	(66,700)	(43,100)
Inventory	35,600	(53,960)	(81,400)
Prepaid expenses	(5,025)	(5,110)	(11,940)
Increase (decrease) in liabilities			
Accounts payable and accrued expenses	33,465	1,335	20,380
Income taxes payable	14,815	(1,490)	4,460
Total adjustments	89,920	(107,735)	(104,075)
Net cash provided by operating activities	264,920	29,265	61,125
Cash flows from investing activities:			
Payment to acquire property and equipment	(18,400)	(31,950)	(28,630)
Payments for business acquisitions, net of cash acquired	(32,850)	(14,770)	(198,900)
Cash received from sale of business segment	1,110		
Net cash used by investing activities	(50,140)	(46,720)	(227,530)
Cash flows from financing activities:			
Net borrowings (repayments) short-term debt	(105,560)	(14,755)	45,040
Proceeds from issuance of common stock	—	—	125,625
Proceeds from issuance of common stock to employees	8,400	2,880	1,805
Dividends paid	(33,965)	(25,455)	(22,275)
Repayments of long-term debt	(11,760)	(120)	(250)
Proceeds from long-term debt	—	96,465	7,765
Net cash (used) provided by financing activities	(142,885)	59,015	157,710
Net increase (decrease) in cash	71,895	41,560	(8,695)
Cash at beginning of year	99,500	60,100	66,000
Cash at end of year	$171,395	$101,660	$ 57,305

4.8 Writing Skills Problem

Write a short article (250 words) for a local business publication in which you explain why cash flow from operations is important information for small business owners.

4.9 Internet Problem

Locate the most recent statement of cash flows for Amazon.com on the Securities & Exchange Commission's EDGAR Database at http://www.sec.gov/.

(a) For the three years of cash flow information reported for the company, is cash flow from operations higher or lower than the net income (loss) reported?

(b) For each year, explain what has caused the cash flow from operations to be different from the reported net income (loss).

4.10 Annual Report Problem

The 1998 PETsMART Annual Report can be found at the following Web site: www.prenhall.com/fraser

Analyze the Consolidated Statements of Cash Flows for PETsMART for the past three years.

PETsMART Mini-Case

Your friend, Tom, is interested in investing in PETsMART, a company he just heard about. He is concerned, however, due to the recurring net losses the company has incurred. Despite these losses, the company's stock price has continued to increase. Tom knows you have been taking business classes while at college and asks if you would look at PETsMART's statement of cash flows. He has heard this statement is critical to assessing a company, but he is unfamiliar with its content. Tom gives you a copy of the statement of cash flows as well as some other information he has gathered from the company's annual report.

REQUIRED:

1. Analyze the statement of cash flows for PETsMART for the past three years ended in January, 1996, 1995, 1994.
2. Using the information from the letter to the stockholders and your cash flow analysis, evaluate the investment potential of PETsMART.
3. What information other than the financial statements would be helpful in making this investment decision?

CONSOLIDATED STATEMENTS OF CASH FLOWS

Fiscal Year Ended (In Thousands)	January 28, 1996	January 29, 1995	January 30, 1994
Cash Flows From (Used in) Operating Activities:			
Net loss	$ (2,803)	$ (9,830)	$ (9,135)
Adjustments to reconcile net loss to net cash from (used in) operating activities:			
Depreciation and amortization	21,819	18,571	10,369
Loss on disposal of property and equipment	11,082	3,134	224
Changes in assets and liabilities:			
Receivables	(10,105)	(9,207)	(5,633)
Merchandise inventories	(35,512)	(56,520)	(45,008)
Prepaid expenses and other current assets	(497)	(4,194)	(2,008)
Other assets	(18,947)	(4,901)	(5,090)
Accounts payable	46,426	6,496	30,896
Accrued payroll and employee benefits	3,576	3,893	3,614
Accrued occupancy expense	2,128	2,835	1,068
Other accrued expenses	2,599	7,648	3,950
Deferred rents	1,453	3,372	3,170
Other liabilities	(915)	203	204
Net cash (used in) operating activities	20,304	(38,500)	(13,379)
Cash Flows From (Used in) Investing Activities:			
Purchases of leaseholds, fixtures, and equipment	(35,256)	(45,041)	(33,423)
Purchases of property held for sale and leaseback	(16,285)	(16,300)	(18,800)
Purchases of investments	—	(6,782)	(2,954)
Proceeds from sales of investments	3,999	5,030	707
Proceeds from sale of property held for sale and leaseback	9,561	24,985	10,213
Net cash (used in) investing activities	(37,981)	(38,108)	(44,257)
Cash Flows From (Used in) Financing Activities:			
Net proceeds from issuance of stock—			
Preferred stock	—	7,934	22,131
Common stock	9,067	1,736	165,876
Borrowings from bank credit facility	54,100	21,852	13,488
Repayment of bank credit facility	(46,067)	(20,310)	(8,170)
Payment on capital lease obligations	(11,885)	(6,146)	(4,515)
Distributions to Sporting Dog shareholders	—	(423)	(464)
Tax benefit resulting from exercise of stock options	2,219	451	449
Net cash from financing activities	7,434	5,094	188,795
Foreign Currency Translation Gains (Losses)	(46)	4	—
Increase (Decrease) in Cash And Cash Equivalents	(10,289)	(71,510)	131,159
Cash and Cash Equivalents at Beginning of Year	84,518	156,028	24,869
Cash and Cash Equivalents at End of Year	$ 74,229	$ 84,518	$ 156,028

CORPORATE PROFILE

Founded in 1987 in Phoenix, Arizona, PETsMART is the nation's leading operator of superstores specializing in pet food, pet supplies and pet services. As of March 29, 1996, the Company operated 283 superstores in 33 states and anticipates operating approximately 312 superstores in 35 states by the end of fiscal 1996. The average PETsMART superstore is 25,000 square feet. The superstores stock more than 12,000 items and offer the most complete assortment of products and services available for household pets. PETsMART, which employs approximately 11,000 associates, guarantees its customers the lowest price on all of the products it sells.

Through its catalog subsidiaries, the Company is the leading direct marketer of pet-related and equine products. Sporting Dog Specialties and its affiliates sell pet supplies and products for small and large animals to individuals and small businesses through five catalogs, while the Company's most recent acquisition, State Line Tack, is a worldwide catalog retailer specializing in discount brand name tack, riding apparel and equine supplies.

PETsMART has been a publicly held company since July 1993, and its stock is traded over the counter on The Nasdaq Stock Market under the symbol "PETM."

TO OUR STOCKHOLDERS

1995 was a great year for your Company. In financial terms, sales exceeded $1 billion, while net income, excluding merger and nonrecurring charges, rose sixfold from $3.3 million in 1994 to $23.1 million in 1995. Earnings per share, excluding merger and non-recurring charges and any related tax benefits, increased from $0.07 in 1994 to $0.44 per share in 1995.

Outstanding Sales and Earnings Growth

Net sales for the year were $1.03 billion, an increase of 26% over the $818 million reported on a restated basis last year. Comparable store sales increased 12.5%, excluding the Petstuff and Pet Food Giant stores, primarily reflecting the maturing of our store base during the year.

During 1995, the Company achieved record profitability. Operating income for 1995, excluding merger and nonrecurring charges, amounted to $41.1 million, a 407% increase over the $8.1 million reported for 1994 on a comparable basis. Net loss for 1995 declined to $2.8 million from a net loss of $9.8 million for 1994. However, net loss in both years included merger and nonrecurring charges and recognition of tax benefits from net operating loss carryforwards arising from acquisitions. Excluding the above items, net income increased, on a comparable basis, from $3.3 million (or $0.07 per share) for fiscal 1994, to $23.1 million (or $0.44 per share) in fiscal 1995, an increase of 600%.

Financial Strength

Our balance sheet remains strong. Stockholders' equity rose 9.1% to end the year at $266.9 million. Our fiscal year concluded with $74.2 million in cash and a $65 million revolving credit facility. In total, the available capacity of our credit facility and cash represented nearly $125 million of liquidity at year end. This liquidity provides your

Company with significant flexibility to fund its anticipated growth. We expect to become an overall cash generator in 1996.

Royal Appliance Mfg. Co. and Subsidiaries Mini-Case

As the vice president of lending for Gilbert National Bank, you are in charge of giving final approval on all loan applications. Gilbert National Bank is currently trying to acquire new corporate clients and Royal Appliance Mfg. Co. and Subsidiaries has approached the bank to request a substantial line of credit. Kathy Kuebbing, one of your loan officers, has been working with the company and has recommended approval. She submitted the following summary of her analysis:

Royal Appliance Manufacturing Company

(Submitted by Kathy Kuebbing)

Royal Appliance owns numerous trademarks in the vacuum cleaner industry, including the famous product line introduced in 1984, the Dirt Devil Hand Vac. Since 1984, the Company has made significant progress in gaining market share. At the end of 1992 Royal had a 20% market share in the upright vacuum cleaner market, just 8% behind the industry leader. The tremendous gain in market share should continue since Royal has doubled advertising and promotion expenditures in each of the three past years. The company has also increased spending in engineering and product development. Net sales have increased 229% from 1990 to 1992. Despite the large increase in advertising and engineering expenditures, Royal has still managed to increase net earnings 72% from 1990 to 1992. The company also has a strong working capital position. Current assets, comprised mainly of accounts receivable and inventories, are 2.5 times greater than current liabilities. Other noncurrent debt includes a revolving credit agreement and capital lease obligations. This company, which just began selling stock to the public in 1991, is a high growth company that I highly recommend for funding.

You note that Kathy's analysis did not consider the statement of cash flows, which you decide to review before making a final decision.

ROYAL APPLIANCE MFG. CO. AND SUBSIDIARIES
CONDENSED CONSOLIDATED STATEMENTS OF CASH FLOWS
FOR THE YEARS ENDED DECEMBER 31
(DOLLARS IN THOUSANDS)

	1990	1991	1992
Cash flows from operating activities:			
Net income	$11,714	$ 32,800	$ 20,151
Adjustments to reconcile net income to net cash provided by (used in) operating activities			
Depreciation and amortization	1,404	2,868	6,246
Compensatory effect of stock options			
(Increase) decrease in assets:	—	—	39
Trade accounts receivable, net	(17,933)	(7,213)	(2,557)
Inventories	(9,847)	(30,317)	(35,281)
Refundable and deferred income taxes	—	(2,935)	(1,154)
Prepaid expenses and other	(313)	(80)	(1,891)
Other	515	(780)	(767)
Increase (decrease) in liabilities:			
Trade accounts payable	4,524	14,306	(8,166)
Accrued advertising and promotion	3,972	2,149	2,908
Accrued salaries, benefits, and payroll taxes	181	1,986	(725)
Accrued warranty and customer returns	—	2,041	5,011
Accrued income taxes	—	—	5,894
Accrued interest and other	390	591	236
Other	—	—	(183)
Total adjustments	(17,107)	(17,384)	(30,390)
Net cash (used in) provided by operations	(5,393)	15,416	(10,239)
Cash flows from investing activities:			
Purchases of tooling, property, plant, and equipment net	(4,663)	(9,512)	(31,876)
Increase in tooling deposits	—	(4,622)	(618)
Net cash (used in) investing activities	(4,663)	(14,134)	(32,494)
Cash flows from financing activities:			
Proceeds from bank debt	31,992	108,010	210,928
Payments on bank debt	(17,500)	(122,273)	(154,564)
Purchase of treasury shares	—	—	(12,973)
Payments on capital lease obligations	(46)	(61)	(206)
S corporation dividends	(4,975)	(28,429)	—
Proceeds of share offering	—	42,237	—
Proceeds from (payment on) note payable	2,000	(2,000)	—
Other	24	(150)	—
Net cash provided by (used in) financing activities	11,495	(2,666)	43,185
Effect of exchange rate changes on cash	(137)	62	(452)
Net increase (decrease) in cash	1,302	(1,322)	—
Cash at beginning of year	20	1,322	—
Cash at the end of year	$ 1,322	$ —	$ —
Supplemental disclosure of cash flow information:			
Cash payments for:			
Interest, net of capitalized interest	$ 2,629	$ 2,846	$ 3,057
Income taxes	$ —	$ 15,686	$ 8,136
Supplemental schedule of noncash investing and financing activities:			
Capital assets acquired under capital leases	$ —	$ 7,270	$ —
Reinstatement of deferred tax benefit	$ —	$ 923	$ —

REQUIRED:

1. Analyze the statement of cash flows for Royal Appliance Mfg. Company for the past three years, 1990 through 1992.
2. Using the statement submitted by Kathy and your cash flow analysis, evaluate the credit worthiness of Royal Appliance Mfg. Co. and Subsidiaries.
3. Explain what information you gain from the statement of cash flows that cannot be found directly from the balance sheet or income statement.
4. What information, other than the financial statements, would be helpful in making this credit decision?

CHAPTER

5

The Analysis of Financial Statements

Ratios are tools, and their value is limited when used alone. The more tools used, the better the analysis. For example, you can't use the same golf club for every shot and expect to be a good golfer. The more you practice with each club, however, the better able you will be to gauge which club to use on one shot. So too, we need to be skilled with the financial tools we use.

—DIANNE MORRISON,
Chief Executive Officer, R.E.C. Inc.

The preceding chapters have covered in detail the form and content of the four basic financial statements found in the annual reports of U.S. firms: the balance sheet, the income statement, the statement of retained earnings or statement of stockholders' equity, and the statement of cash flows. This chapter will develop tools and techniques for the interpretation of financial statement information.

Objectives of Analysis

Before beginning the analysis of any firm's financial statements, it is necessary to specify the objectives of the analysis. The objectives will vary depending upon the perspective of the financial statement user and the specific questions that are addressed by the analysis of the financial statement data.

A *creditor* is ultimately concerned with the ability of an existing or prospective borrower to make interest and principal payments on borrowed funds. The questions raised in a credit analysis should include:

- What is the *borrowing cause*? What do the financial statements reveal about the reason a firm has requested a loan or the purchase of goods on credit?
- What is the firm's *capital structure*? How much debt is currently outstanding? How well has debt been serviced in the past?
- What will be the *source of debt repayment*? How well does the company manage working capital? Is the firm generating cash from operations?

The credit analyst will use the historical record of the company, as presented in the financial statements, to answer such questions and to predict the potential of the firm to satisfy future demands for cash, including debt service.

The *investor* attempts to arrive at an estimation of a company's future earnings stream in order to attach a value to the securities being considered for purchase or liquidation. The investment analyst poses such questions as:

- What is the company *performance record,* and what are the *future expectations*? What is its record with regard to growth and stability of earnings? Of cash flow from operations?
- How much *risk* is inherent in the firm's existing capital structure? What are the *expected returns,* given the firm's current condition and future outlook?
- How successfully does the firm compete in its industry, and how well positioned is the company to hold or improve its *competitive position?*

The investment analyst also uses historical financial statement data to forecast the future. In the case of the investor, the ultimate objective is to determine whether the investment is sound.

Financial statement analysis from the standpoint of *management* relates to all of the questions raised by creditors and investors because these user groups must be satisfied in order for the firm to obtain capital as needed. Management must also consider its employees, the general public, regulators, and the financial press. Management looks to financial statement data to determine:

- How *well* has the firm performed and *why*? What *operating areas* have contributed to success and which have not?
- What are the *strengths and weaknesses* of the company's financial position?
- What *changes* should be implemented in order to improve future performance?

Financial statements provide insight into the company's current status and lead to the development of policies and strategies for the future. It should be pointed out, however, that management also has responsibility for preparing the financial statements. The analyst should be alert to the potential for management to influence the outcome of financial statement reporting in order to appeal to creditors, investors, and other users. It is important that any analysis of financial statements include a careful reading of the notes to the financial statements, and it may be helpful to supplement the analysis with other material in the annual report and with other sources of information apart from the annual report.

Sources of Information

The financial statement user has access to a wide range of data sources in the analysis of financial statements. The objective of the analysis will dictate to a considerable degree not only the approach taken in the analysis but also the particular resources that should be consulted in a given circumstance. The beginning point, however, should always be the financial statements themselves and the notes to the financial statements. In addition, the analyst will want to consider the following resources.

AUDITOR'S REPORT

The report of the independent auditor contains the expression of opinion as to the fairness of the financial statement presentation. Most auditor's reports are *unqualified,* which means that in the opinion of the auditor the financial statements present fairly the financial position, the results of operations, and the cash flows for the periods covered by the financial statements. A *qualified* report, an adverse opinion, or a disclaimer of opinion, is rare and therefore suggests that a careful evaluation of the firm be made. An unqualified opinion with explanatory language should be reviewed carefully by the analyst.

MANAGEMENT DISCUSSION AND ANALYSIS

The Management Discussion and Analysis of the Financial Condition and Results of Operations, discussed in chapter 1, is a section of the annual report that is required and monitored by the SEC. In this section, management presents a detailed coverage of the firm's liquidity, capital resources, and operations. The material can be especially helpful to the financial analyst because it includes facts and estimates not found elsewhere in the annual report. For example, this report is expected to cover forward-looking information such as projections of capital expenditures and how such investments will be financed. There is detail about the mix of price relative to volume increases for products sold. Management must disclose any favorable or unfavorable trends and any significant events or uncertainties that relate to the firm's historical or prospective financial condition and operations.

SUPPLEMENTARY SCHEDULES

Certain supplementary schedules are required for inclusion in an annual report and are frequently helpful to the analysis. For example, companies that operate in several unrelated lines of business provide a breakdown of key financial figures by operating segment. (The analysis of segmental data is covered in appendix B.)

FORM 10-K AND FORM 10-Q

Form 10-K is an annual document filed with the SEC by companies that sell securities to the public and contains much of the same information as the annual report issued to shareholders. It also shows additional detail that may be of interest to the financial analyst, such as schedules listing information about management, a description of material litigation and governmental actions, and elaborations of some financial statement disclosures. Form 10-Q, a less-extensive document, provides quarterly financial information. Both reports are available to the general public on request from the SEC.

OTHER SOURCES

There is a considerable body of material outside of the corporate annual report that can contribute to an analysis of financial statements. Most academic libraries and many public libraries have available computerized search systems and computerized databases that can greatly facilitate financial analysis.[1] Although not a replacement for the techniques that are discussed in this chapter, these research materials supplement and enhance the analytical process as well as provide time-saving features. Computerized financial statement analysis packages are also available that perform some of the ratio calculations and other analytical tools described in this chapter.

Other general resources useful as aids in the analysis of financial statements can be found in the general reference section of public and university libraries. The following sources provide comparative statistical ratios to help determine a company's relative position within its industry:

1. Dun & Bradstreet Information Services, *Industry Norms and Key Business Ratios*. Murray Hill, NJ.
2. Robert Morris Associates, *Annual Statement Studies*. Philadelphia, PA.
3. Standard & Poor's Corporation, *Ratings Handbook* and *Industry Surveys*. New York, NY.
4. Gale Research Inc., *Manufacturing U.S.A. Industry Analyses*. Detroit, MI.

Also helpful to the analyst are the following references, which contain useful investment and financial information about particular companies, industries, and mutual funds:

1. Moody's Investor Service, *Moody's Manuals* and *Moody's Handbook*. New York, NY.
2. Standard & Poor's Corporation, *Corporation Records, The Outlook, Stock Reports,* and *Stock Guide*. New York, NY.
3. Value Line Inc., *The Value Line Investment Survey*. New York, NY.
4. Zack's Investment Research Inc., *Earnings Forecaster*. Chicago, IL.
5. Gale Research Inc., *Market Share Reporter*. Detroit, MI.
6. Dow Jones-Irwin, *The Financial Analyst's Handbook*. Homewood, IL.
7. For mutual funds: Morningstar, *Morningstar Mutual Funds*. Chicago, IL.

The following Web sites contain useful investment and financial information, including company profile and stock prices:

1. SEC EDGAR Database, http://www.sec.gov/edgarhp.htm
2. Hoover's Corporate Directory, http://www.hoovers.com/
3. Stockmaster, http://www.stockmaster.com
4. Dun & Bradstreet, http://www.dnb.com/
5. Standard & Poor's Ratings Services, http://www.ratings.standardpoor.com/ratings.htm
6. CNN Financial Network, http://www.cnnfn.com/

---

[1] One resource that is commonly available in both public and academic libraries is the Infotrak—General Business Index. This CD-ROM database provides indexing to approximately 800 business, trade, and management journals; it has company profiles, investment analyst reports, and a wide range of business news. To learn about the availability and use of this system or other search systems and databases, consult the library's reference librarian or the business reference librarian.

Articles from current periodicals such as *Business Week, Forbes, Fortune,* and *The Wall Street Journal* can add insight into the management and operations of individual firms as well as provide perspective on general economic and industry trends.

Tools and Techniques

Various tools and techniques are used by the financial statement analyst in order to convert financial statement data into formats that facilitate the evaluation of a firm's financial condition and performance, both over time and in comparison with industry competitors. These include common size financial statements, which express each account on the balance sheet as a percentage of total assets and each account on the income statement as a percentage of net sales; financial ratios, which standardize financial data in terms of mathematical relationships expressed in the form of percentages or times; trend analysis, which requires the evaluation of financial data over several accounting periods; structural analysis, which looks at the internal structure of a business enterprise; industry comparisons, which relate one firm with averages compiled for the industry in which it operates; and most important of all, common sense and judgment. These tools and techniques will be illustrated by walking through a financial statement analysis of R.E.C. Inc. This first part will cover number crunching—the preparation of common size financial statements, and the calculation of key financial ratios. The second part will provide the integration of these numbers with other information—such as the statement of cash flows from chapter 4 and background on the economy and the environment in which the firm operates—in order to perform an analysis of R.E.C. Inc. over a five-year period and to assess the firm's strengths, weaknesses, and future prospects.

COMMON SIZE FINANCIAL STATEMENTS

Common size financial statements are a form of ratio analysis that allows the comparison of firms with different levels of sales or total assets by introducing a common denominator. A *common size balance sheet* expresses each item on the balance sheet as a percentage of total assets, and a *common size income statement* expresses each income statement category as a percentage of net sales. Common size statements facilitate the internal or structural analysis of a firm. The common size balance sheet reveals the composition of assets within major categories, for example, cash and cash equivalents relative to other current assets, the distribution of assets in which funds are invested (current, long-lived, intangible), the capital structure of the firm (debt relative to equity), and the debt structure (long-term relative to short-term). The common size income statement shows the relative magnitude of various expenses relative to sales, the profit percentages (gross profit, operating profit, and net profit margins), and the relative importance of "other" revenues and expenses. Common size statements are also useful to evaluate trends and to make industry comparisons. The common size balance sheets and income statements for R.E.C. Inc. are presented in Exhibits 5.1 and 5.2.

Referring first to the common size balance sheet in Exhibit 5.1, it can be seen that inventories have become more dominant over the five-year period in the firm's total asset structure and in 2002 comprised almost half (49.4%) of total assets. Holdings of cash and marketable securities have decreased from a 20% combined level in 1998

EXHIBIT 5.1

R.E.C. INC.
COMMON SIZE BALANCE SHEETS
(PERCENT)

	2002	2001	2000	1999	1998
Assets					
Current Assets					
Cash	4.3	3.1	3.9	5.1	4.9
Marketable securities	5.5	10.6	14.9	15.3	15.1
Accounts receivable, less allowance for doubtful accounts	9.4	11.0	7.6	6.6	6.8
Inventories	49.4	48.4	45.0	40.1	39.7
Prepaid expenses	.5	1.0	1.6	2.4	2.6
Total current assets	69.1	74.1	73.0	69.5	69.1
Property, Plant, and Equipment					
Land	.8	1.1	1.2	1.4	1.4
Buildings and leasehold improvements	19.2	15.7	14.4	14.1	14.5
Equipment	22.6	18.1	17.3	15.9	16.5
Less accumulated depreciation and amortization	(12.1)	(9.9)	(6.9)	(3.1)	(3.0)
Net property, plant, and equipment	30.5	25.0	26.0	28.3	29.4
Other Assets	.4	.9	1.0	2.2	1.5
Total Assets	100.0	100.0	100.0	100.0	100.0
Liabilities and Stockholders' Equity					
Current Liabilities					
Accounts payable	15.0	10.0	13.1	11.4	11.8
Notes payable—banks	5.9	7.9	6.2	4.4	4.3
Current maturities of long-term debt	2.0	2.0	2.4	2.4	2.6
Accrued liabilities	5.9	7.0	10.6	7.7	5.7
Total current liabilities	28.8	26.9	32.3	25.9	24.4
Deferred Federal Income Taxes	.9	.8	.7	.5	.4
Long-Term Debt	22.1	22.4	16.2	14.4	14.9
Total liabilities	51.8	50.1	49.2	40.8	39.7
Stockholders' Equity					
Common stock	5.0	6.1	6.7	7.3	7.5
Additional paid-in capital	1.0	1.2	1.3	1.6	1.8
Retained earnings	42.2	42.6	42.8	50.3	51.0
Total stockholders' equity	48.2	49.9	50.8	59.2	60.3
Total Liabilities and Stockholders' Equity	100.0	100.0	100.0	100.0	100.0

EXHIBIT 5.2

R.E.C. INC.
COMMON SIZE INCOME STATEMENTS
(PERCENT)

	2002	2001	2000	1999	1998
Net Sales	100.0	100.0	100.0	100.0	100.0
Cost of Goods Sold	60.0	60.1	58.0	58.2	58.2
Gross Profit	40.0	39.9	42.0	41.8	41.8
Operating Expenses					
Selling and administrative expenses	21.2	21.8	23.2	20.3	20.0
Advertising	6.6	7.1	6.8	6.4	6.3
Depreciation and amortization	1.9	2.0	1.8	1.4	1.2
Repairs and maintenance	1.4	1.3	2.2	2.7	2.7
Operating Profit	8.9	7.7	8.0	11.0	11.6
Other Income (Expense)					
Interest income	.2	.5	.5	.3	.3
Interest expense	(1.2)	(1.5)	(.9)	(.9)	(1.0)
Earnings before income taxes	7.9	6.7	7.6	10.4	10.9
Income Taxes	3.6	2.9	3.4	5.4	5.7
Net Earnings	4.3	3.8	4.2	5.0	5.2

and 1999 to about 10% in 2002. The company has elected to make this shift in order to accommodate the inventory requirements of new store openings. The firm has opened 43 new stores in the past two years, and the effect of this market strategy is also reflected in the overall asset structure. Buildings, leasehold improvements, equipment, and accumulated depreciation and amortization have increased as a percentage of total assets. On the liability side, the proportion of debt required to finance investments in assets has risen, primarily from long-term borrowing.

The common size income statement shown in Exhibit 5.2 reveals the trends of expenses and profit margins. Cost of goods sold has increased slightly in percentage terms, resulting in a small decline in the gross profit percentage. To improve this margin, the firm will either have to raise its own retail prices, change the product mix, or figure ways to reduce costs on goods purchased for resale. In the area of operating expenses, depreciation and amortization have increased relative to sales, again reflecting costs associated with new store openings. Selling and administrative expenses also rose in 2000 and 2001, but the company controlled these costs more effectively in 2002 relative to overall sales. Operating and net profit percentages will be discussed more extensively in connection with the five-year trends of financial ratios later in the chapter. It can be seen from the common size income statements that both profit percentages deteriorated through 2001 and rebounded in the most recent year as R.E.C. Inc. enjoyed the benefits of an economic recovery and profits from expansion.

KEY FINANCIAL RATIOS

The R.E.C. Inc. financial statements will be used to compute a set of key financial ratios for the years 2002 and 2001. Later in the chapter, these ratios will be evaluated in the context of R.E.C. Inc.'s five-year historical record and in comparison with industry competitors. The four categories of ratios to be covered are (1) liquidity ratios, which measure a firm's ability to meet cash needs as they arise; (2) activity ratios, which measure the liquidity of specific assets and the efficiency of managing assets; (3) leverage ratios, which measure the extent of a firm's financing with debt relative to equity and its ability to cover interest and other fixed charges; and (4) profitability ratios, which measure the overall performance of a firm and its efficiency in managing assets, liabilities, and equity.

Before delving into the R.E.C. Inc. financial ratios, it is important to introduce a word of caution in the use of financial ratios generally. Although extremely valuable as analytical tools, financial ratios also have limitations. They can serve as screening devices, indicate areas of potential strength or weakness, and reveal matters that need further investigation. But financial ratios do not provide answers in and of themselves, and they are not predictive. Financial ratios should be used with caution and common sense, and they should be used in combination with other elements of financial analysis. It should also be noted that there is no one definitive set of key financial ratios, there is no uniform definition for all ratios, and there is no standard that should be met for each ratio. Finally, there are no "rules of thumb" that apply to the interpretation of financial ratios. Each situation should be evaluated within the context of the particular firm, industry, and economic environment.

Figures from the R.E.C. Inc. Consolidated Balance Sheets and Statements of Earnings, Exhibit 5.3, are used to illustrate the calculation of financial ratios for 2002 and 2001, and these financial ratios will subsequently be incorporated into a five-year analysis of the firm.

LIQUIDITY RATIOS: SHORT-TERM SOLVENCY

Current ratio

	2002	2001
$\dfrac{\text{Current assets}}{\text{Current liabilities}}$	$\dfrac{65,846}{27,461} = 2.40 \text{ times}$	$\dfrac{56,264}{20,432} = 2.75 \text{ times}$

The current ratio is a commonly used measure of short-run solvency, the ability of a firm to meet its debt requirements as they come due. Current liabilities are used as the denominator of the ratio because they are considered to represent the most urgent debts, requiring retirement within one year or one operating cycle. The available cash resources to satisfy these obligations must come primarily from cash or the conversion to cash of other current assets. Some analysts eliminate prepaid expenses from the numerator because they are not a potential source of cash but, rather, represent future obligations that have already been satisfied. The current ratio for R.E.C. Inc. indicates that at year-end 2002 current assets covered current liabilities 2.4 times, down from 2001. In order to interpret the significance of this ratio it will be necessary to evaluate the trend of liquidity over a longer period and to compare R.E.C. Inc.'s coverage with

EXHIBIT 5.3

R.E.C. INC.
CONSOLIDATED BALANCE SHEETS AT DECEMBER 31, 2002 AND 2001
(IN THOUSANDS)

	2002	2001
Assets		
Current Assets		
Cash	$ 4,061	$ 2,382
Marketable securities (Note A)	5,272	8,004
Accounts receivable, less allowance for doubtful accounts of $448 in 2002 and $417 in 2001	8,960	8,350
Inventories (Note A)	47,041	36,769
Prepaid expenses	512	759
Total current assets	65,846	56,264
Property, Plant, and Equipment (Notes A, C, and E)		
Land	811	811
Buildings and leasehold improvements	18,273	11,928
Equipment	21,523	13,768
	40,607	26,507
Less accumulated depreciation and amortization	11,528	7,530
Net property, plant, and equipment	29,079	18,977
Other Assets (Note A)	373	668
Total Assets	$95,298	$75,909
Liabilities and Stockholders' Equity		
Current Liabilities		
Accounts Payable	$14,294	$ 7,591
Notes payable—banks (Note B)	5,614	6,012
Current maturities of long-term debt (Note C)	1,884	1,516
Accrued liabilities	5,669	5,313
Total current liabilities	27,461	20,432
Deferred Federal Income Taxes (Notes A and D)	843	635
Long-Term Debt (Note C)	21,059	16,975
Commitments (Note E)		
Total liabilities	49,363	38,042
Stockholders' Equity		
Common stock, par value $1, authorized, 10,000,000 shares; issued, 4,803,000 shares in 2002 and 4,594,000 shares in 2001 (Note F)	4,803	4,594
Additional paid-in capital	957	910
Retained Earnings	40,175	32,363
Total stockholders' equity	45,935	37,867
Total Liabilities and Stockholders' Equity	$95,298	$75,909

The accompanying notes are an integral part of these statements.

EXHIBIT 5.3 (Continued)

R.E.C. INC.
CONSOLIDATED STATEMENTS OF EARNINGS
FOR THE YEARS ENDED DECEMBER 31, 2002, 2001, AND 2000
(IN THOUSANDS EXCEPT PER SHARE AMOUNTS)

	2002	2001	2000
Net sales	$215,600	$153,000	$140,700
Cost of goods sold (Note A)	129,364	91,879	81,606
Gross profit	86,236	61,121	59,094
Selling and administrative expenses (Notes A and E)	45,722	33,493	32,765
Advertising	14,258	10,792	9,541
Depreciation and amortization (Note A)	3,998	2,984	2,501
Repairs and maintenance	3,015	2,046	3,031
Operating profit	19,243	11,806	11,256
Other income (expense)			
Interest income	422	838	738
Interest expense	(2,585)	(2,277)	(1,274)
Earnings before income taxes	17,080	10,367	10,720
Income taxes (Notes A and D)	7,686	4,457	4,824
Net earnings	$ 9,394	$ 5,910	$ 5,896
Basic earnings per common share (Note G)	$1.96	$1.29	$1.33
Diluted earnings per common share (Note G)	$1.92	$1.26	$1.31

The accompanying notes are an integral part of these statements.

industry competitors. It is also essential to assess the composition of the components that comprise the ratio.

As a barometer of short-term liquidity, the current ratio is limited by the nature of its components. Remember that the balance sheet is prepared as of a particular date, and the actual amount of liquid assets may vary considerably from the date on which the balance sheet is prepared. Further, accounts receivable and inventory may not be truly liquid. A firm could have a relatively high current ratio but not be able to meet demands for cash because the accounts receivable are of inferior quality or the inventory is salable only at discounted prices. It is necessary to use other measures of liquidity, including cash flow from operations and other financial ratios that rate the liquidity of specific assets, to supplement the current ratio.

Quick or acid-test ratio

	2002	2001
$\dfrac{\text{Current assets} - \text{Inventory}}{\text{Current liabilities}}$	$\dfrac{65,846 - 47,041}{27,461} = .68$ times	$\dfrac{56,264 - 36,769}{20,432} = .95$ times

The quick or acid-test ratio is a more rigorous test of short-run solvency than the current ratio because the numerator eliminates inventory, considered the least liquid current asset and the most likely source of losses. Like the current ratio and other ratios, there are alternative ways to calculate the quick ratio. Some analysts eliminate prepaid expenses and supplies (if carried as a separate item) from the numerator. The quick ratio for R.E.C. Inc. indicates some deterioration between 2001 and 2002; this ratio must also be examined in relation to the firm's own trends and to other firms operating in the same industry.

Cash flow liquidity ratio

	2002	2001
$\dfrac{\text{Cash + Market securities + CFO*}}{\text{Current liabilities}}$	$\dfrac{4{,}061 + 5{,}272 + 10{,}024}{27{,}461} = .70$ times	$\dfrac{2{,}382 + 8{,}004 + (3{,}767)}{20{,}432} = .32$ times

Another approach to measuring short-term solvency is the cash flow liquidity ratio,[2] which considers cash flow from operating activities (from the statement of cash flows). The cash flow liquidity ratio uses in the numerator, as an approximation of cash resources, cash and marketable securities, which are truly liquid current assets, and cash flow from operating activities, which represents the amount of cash generated from the firm's operations, such as the ability to sell inventory and collect the cash.

Note that both the current ratio and the quick ratio decreased between 2001 and 2002, which could be interpreted as a deterioration of liquidity. But the cash flow ratio increased, indicating an improvement in short-run solvency. Which is the correct assessment? With any ratio, the analyst must explore the underlying components. One major reason for the decreases in the current and quick ratios was the 88% growth in accounts payable in 2002, which could actually be a plus if it means that R.E.C. Inc. strengthened its ability to obtain supplier credit. Also, the firm turned around from negative to positive its generation of cash from operations in 2002, explaining the improvement in the cash flow liquidity ratio and indicating stronger short-term solvency.

ACTIVITY RATIOS: ASSET LIQUIDITY, ASSET MANAGEMENT EFFICIENCY

Average collection period

	2002	2001
$\dfrac{\text{Accounts receivable}}{\text{Average daily sales}}$	$\dfrac{8{,}960}{215{,}600/365} = 15$ days	$\dfrac{8{,}350}{153{,}000/365} = 20$ days

---

* Cash flow from operating activities

[2] For additional reading about this ratio and its applications, see L. Fraser, "Cash Flow from Operations and Liquidity Analysis, A New Financial Ratio for Commercial Lending Decisions," *Cash Flow,* Robert Morris Associates, Philadelphia, PA. For other cash flow ratios, see C. Carslaw, and J. Mills, "Developing Ratios for Effective Cash Flow Statement Analysis," *Journal of Accountancy,* November 1991; D. E. Giacomino and D. E. Mielke, "Cash Flows: Another Approach to Ratio Analysis," *Journal of Accountancy,* March 1993; and John R. Mills and Jeanne H. Yamamura, "The Power of Cash Flow Ratios," *Journal of Accountancy,* October 1998.

The average collection period of accounts receivable is the average number of days required to convert receivables into cash. The ratio is calculated as the relationship between net accounts receivable (net of the allowance for doubtful accounts) and average daily sales (sales/365 days). Where available, the figure for credit sales can be substituted for net sales because credit sales produce the receivables. The ratio for R.E.C. Inc. indicates that during 2002 the firm collected its accounts in 15 days on average, which is an improvement over the 20-day collection period in 2001.

The average collection period helps gauge the liquidity of accounts receivable, the ability of the firm to collect from customers. It may also provide information about a company's credit policies. For example, if the average collection period is increasing over time or is higher than the industry average, the firm's credit policies could be too lenient and accounts receivables not sufficiently liquid. The loosening of credit could be necessary at times to boost sales, but at an increasing cost to the firm. On the other hand, if credit policies are too restrictive, as reflected in an average collection period that is shortening and less than industry competitors, the firm may be losing qualified customers.

The average collection period should be compared with the firm's stated credit policies. If the policy calls for collection within 30 days and the average collection period is 60 days, the implication is that the company is not stringent in collection efforts. There could be other explanations, however, such as temporary problems due to a depressed economy. The analyst should attempt to determine the cause of a ratio that is too long or too short.

Another factor for consideration is the strength of the firm within its industry. There are circumstances that would enable a company in a relatively strong financial position within its industry to extend credit for longer periods than weaker competitors.

Accounts receivable turnover

	2002	2001
$\dfrac{\text{Net sales}}{\text{Accounts receivable}}$	$\dfrac{215,600}{8,960} = 24.06$ times	$\dfrac{153,000}{8,350} = 18.32$ times

The accounts receivable turnover indicates how many times, on average, accounts receivable are collected during the year. R.E.C. Inc. converted accounts receivable into cash 24 times in 2002, up from 18 in 2001. The turnover of receivables, like the average collection period, has improved; the two ratios are measuring the same thing—the quality of receivables and the efficiency of the firm's collection and credit policies. The turnover expresses this information in number of times, and the average collection period measures the process in days. Generally, a high turnover is good because it is evidence of efficiency in converting receivables into cash, but a turnover that is too high may be indicative of credit and collection policies that are overly restrictive.

Inventory turnover

	2002	2001
$\dfrac{\text{Cost of goods sold}}{\text{Inventory}}$	$\dfrac{129,364}{47,041} = 2.75$ times	$\dfrac{91,879}{36,769} = 2.50$ times

Inventory turnover measures the efficiency of the firm in managing and selling inventory. It is a gauge of the liquidity of a firm's inventory. The ratio is sometimes calculated with net sales in the numerator and/or with average inventory as the denominator. The inventory turnover for R.E.C. Inc. was 2.75 times in 2002, an improvement over 2001.

Generally, a high turnover is a sign of efficient inventory management and profit for the firm; the faster inventory sells, the fewer funds are tied up in inventory. But a high turnover can also mean understocking and lost orders, a decrease in prices, a shortage of materials, or more sales than planned. A relatively low turnover could be the result of a company's carrying too much inventory or stocking inventory that is obsolete, slow-moving, or inferior. On the other hand, low turnover could stem from a stockpiling for legitimate reasons, such as increased demand or an expected strike. The analyst should explore the underlying causes of a turnover figure that is out of line one way or the other.

The type of industry is important in assessing inventory turnover. We would expect florists and produce retailers to have a relatively high inventory turnover because they deal in perishable products, whereas retailers of jewelry or farm equipment would have lower turnover but higher profit margins. When making comparisons among firms, it is essential to check the cost flow assumption, discussed in chapter 2, used to value inventory and cost of goods sold.

Fixed asset turnover

	2002	2001
$\dfrac{\text{Net sales}}{\text{Net property, plant, equipment}}$	$\dfrac{215,600}{29,079} = 7.41$ times	$\dfrac{153,000}{18,977} = 8.06$ times

Total asset turnover

	2002	2001
$\dfrac{\text{Net sales}}{\text{Total assets}}$	$\dfrac{215,600}{95,298} = 2.26$ times	$\dfrac{153,000}{75,909} = 2.02$ times

The fixed asset turnover and total asset turnover ratios are two approaches to assessing management's effectiveness in generating sales from investments in assets. The fixed asset turnover considers only the firm's investment in property, plant, and equipment and is extremely important for a capital-intensive firm, such as a manufacturer with heavy investments in long-lived assets. The total asset turnover measures the efficiency of managing all of a firm's assets. Generally, the higher these ratios, the smaller is the investment required to generate sales and thus the more profitable is the firm. When the asset turnover ratios are low relative to the industry or the firm's historical record, either the investment in assets is too heavy and/or sales are sluggish. There may, however, be plausible explanations; for example, the firm may have undertaken an extensive plant modernization or placed assets in service at year-end, which will generate positive results in the long-term.

For R.E.C. Inc., the fixed asset turnover has slipped slightly, but the total asset turnover has improved. The firm's investment in fixed assets has grown at a faster rate

(53%) than sales (41%), and this occurrence should be examined within the frame-work of the overall analysis of R.E.C. Inc. The increase in total asset turnover is the result of improvements in inventory and accounts receivable turnover.

LEVERAGE RATIOS: DEBT FINANCING AND COVERAGE

Debt ratio

	2002	2001
$\dfrac{\text{Total liabilities}}{\text{Total assets}}$	$\dfrac{49{,}363}{95{,}298} = 51.8\%$	$\dfrac{38{,}042}{75{,}909} = 50.1\%$

Long-term debt to total capitalization

	2002	2001
$\dfrac{\text{Long-term debt}}{\text{Long-term debt + Stockholders' equity}}$	$\dfrac{21{,}059}{21{,}059 + 45{,}935} = 31.4\%$	$\dfrac{16{,}975}{16{,}975 + 37{,}867} = 31.0\%$

Debt to equity

	2002	2001
$\dfrac{\text{Total liabilities}}{\text{Stockholders' equity}}$	$\dfrac{49{,}363}{45{,}935} = 1.07 \text{ times}$	$\dfrac{38{,}042}{37{,}867} = 1.00 \text{ times}$

Each of the three debt ratios measures the extent of the firm's financing with debt. The amount and proportion of debt in a company's capital structure is extremely important to the financial analyst because of the tradeoff between risk and return. Use of debt involves risk because debt carries a fixed commitment in the form of interest charges and principal repayment. Failure to satisfy the fixed charges associated with debt will ultimately result in bankruptcy. A lesser risk is that a firm with too much debt has difficulty obtaining additional debt financing when needed or finds that credit is available only at extremely high rates of interest. Although debt implies risk, it also introduces the potential for increased benefits to the firm's owners. When debt is used successfully—if operating earnings are more than sufficient to cover the fixed charges associated with debt—the returns to shareholders are magnified through financial leverage, a concept that is explained and illustrated later in this chapter.

The debt ratio considers the proportion of all assets that are financed with debt. The ratio of long-term debt to total capitalization reveals the extent to which long-term debt is used for the firm's permanent financing (both long-term debt and equity). The debt-to-equity ratio measures the riskiness of the firm's capital structure in terms of the relationship between the funds supplied by creditors (debt) and investors (equity). The higher the proportion of debt, the greater is the degree of risk because creditors must be satisfied before owners in the event of bankruptcy. The equity base provides, in effect, a cushion of protection for the suppliers of debt. Each of the three ratios has increased somewhat for R.E.C. Inc. between 2002 and 2001, implying a slightly riskier capital structure.

The analyst should be aware that the debt ratios do not present the whole picture with regard to risk. There are fixed commitments, such as lease payments, that are similar to debt but are not included in debt. The fixed charge coverage ratio, illustrated later, considers such obligations. Off–balance sheet financing arrangements, discussed in Chapter 1, also have the characteristics of debt and must be disclosed in notes to the financial statements according to the provisions of FASB Statement No. 105. These arrangements should be included in an evaluation of a firm's overall capital structure.

Times interest earned

	2002	2001
$\dfrac{\text{Operating profit}}{\text{Interest expense}}$	$\dfrac{19{,}243}{2{,}585} = 7.4 \text{ times}$	$\dfrac{11{,}806}{2{,}277} = 5.2 \text{ times}$

In order for a firm to benefit from debt financing, the fixed interest payments that accompany debt must be more than satisfied from operating earnings.[3] The more times a company can cover its annual interest expense from operating earnings, the better off will be the firm's investors. Although R.E.C. Inc. increased its use of debt in 2002, the company also improved its ability to cover interest payments from operating profits.

Fixed charge coverage

	2002	2001
$\dfrac{\text{Operating profit} + \text{Lease payments}}{\text{Interest expense} + \text{Lease payments}}$	$\dfrac{19{,}243 + 13{,}058}{2{,}585 + 13{,}058} = 2.1 \text{ times}$	$\dfrac{11{,}806 + 7{,}111}{2{,}277 + 7{,}111} = 2.0 \text{ times}$

The fixed charge coverage ratio is a broader measure of coverage capability than the times interest earned ratio because it includes the fixed payments associated with leasing. Lease payments are added back in the numerator because they were deducted as an operating expense to calculate operating profit. Lease payments are similar in nature to interest expense in that they both represent obligations that must be met on an annual basis. The fixed charge coverage ratio is important for firms that operate extensively with leasing arrangements—either operating leases, used by R.E.C. Inc., or capital leases, a form of property financing described in chapter 3. R.E.C. Inc. experienced a significant increase in the amount of annual lease payments in 2002 but was still able to improve its fixed charge coverage slightly.

Cash flow adequacy

	2002	2001
$\dfrac{\text{Cash flow from operating activities}}{\text{Average annual long-term debt maturities}^4}$	$\dfrac{10{,}024}{2{,}360} = 4.2 \text{ times}$	$\dfrac{(3{,}767)}{2{,}287} = (1.6) \text{ times}$

---

[3] The operating return, operating profit divided by assets, must exceed the cost of debt, interest expense divided by liabilities.

[4] The denominator is calculated by referring to Note C of the financial statements for R.E.C. Inc. The current maturities of the current year are added to the current maturities of the upcoming four years and the total is divided by five.

Credit rating agencies often use cash flow adequacy ratios to evaluate how well a company can cover annual payments of items such as debt, capital expenditures, and dividends from operating cash flow. Cash flow adequacy is generally defined differently by analysts; therefore, it is important to understand what is actually being measured. Cash flow adequacy is being used here to measure a firm's ability to cover long-term debt maturities each year. It is reasonable to expect this ratio to be at least one on average. Companies over the long run should generate enough cash flow from operations to cover investing activities of the firm. If purchases of fixed assets are financed with debt, the company should be capable of covering the principal payments with cash generated by the company. A larger ratio would be expected if the company pays dividends annually because cash used for dividends should be generated internally by the company, rather than by borrowing. As indicated in chapter 4, companies must generate cash to be successful. Borrowing each year to pay dividends and repay debt is a questionable cycle for a company to be in over the long run.

In 2002, R.E.C. Inc. had a cash flow adequacy ratio much greater than one. This represents solid improvement over 2001 when the firm failed to generate cash from operations.

PROFITABILITY RATIOS: OVERALL EFFICIENCY AND PERFORMANCE

Gross profit margin

	2002	2001
$\dfrac{\text{Gross profit}}{\text{Net sales}}$	$\dfrac{86,236}{215,600} = 40.0\%$	$\dfrac{61,121}{153,000} = 39.9\%$

Operating profit margin

	2002	2001
$\dfrac{\text{Operating profit}}{\text{Net sales}}$	$\dfrac{19,243}{215,600} = 8.9\%$	$\dfrac{11,806}{153,000} = 7.7\%$

Net profit margin

	2002	2001
$\dfrac{\text{Net earnings}}{\text{Net sales}}$	$\dfrac{9,394}{215,600} = 4.4\%$	$\dfrac{5,910}{153,000} = 3.9\%$

Gross profit margin, operating profit margin, and net profit margin represent the firm's ability to translate sales dollars into profits at different stages of measurement. The gross profit margin, which shows the relationship between sales and the cost of products sold, measures the ability of a company both to control costs of inventories or manufacturing of products and to pass along price increases through sales to customers. The operating profit margin, a measure of overall operating efficiency, incorporates all of the expenses associated with ordinary business activities. The net profit margin measures profitability after consideration of all revenue and expense, including interest, taxes, and nonoperating items.

There was little change in the R.E.C. Inc. gross profit margin, but the company improved its operating margin. Apparently, the firm was able to control the growth of operating expenses while sharply increasing sales. There was also a slight increase in net profit margin, a flow-through from operating margin, but it will be necessary to look at these ratios over a longer term and in conjunction with other parts of the analysis to explain the changes.

Cash flow margin

	2002	2001
$\dfrac{\text{Cash flow from operating activities}}{\text{Net sales}}$	$\dfrac{10,024}{215,600} = 4.6\%$	$\dfrac{(3,767)}{153,000} = (2.5\%)$

Another important perspective on operating performance is the relationship between cash generated from operations and sales. As pointed out in chapter 4, it is cash, not accrual-measured earnings, that a firm needs to service debt, pay dividends, and invest in new capital assets. The cash flow margin measures the ability of the firm to translate sales into cash.

In 2002, R.E.C. Inc. had a cash flow margin that was greater than its net profit margin, the result of a strongly positive generation of cash. The performance in 2002 represents a solid improvement over 2001 when the firm failed to generate cash from operations and had a negative cash flow margin.

Return on total assets (ROA) or return on investment (ROI)

	2002	2001
$\dfrac{\text{Net earnings}}{\text{Total assets}}$	$\dfrac{9,394}{95,298} = 9.9\%$	$\dfrac{5,910}{75,909} = 7.8\%$

Return on equity (ROE)

	2002	2001
$\dfrac{\text{Net earnings}}{\text{Stockholders' equity}}$	$\dfrac{9,394}{45,935} = 20.5\%$	$\dfrac{5,910}{37,867} = 15.6\%$

Return on investment and return on equity are two ratios that measure the overall efficiency of the firm in managing its total investment in assets and in generating return to shareholders. Return on investment or return on assets indicates the amount of profit earned relative to the level of investment in total assets. Return on equity measures the return to common shareholders; this ratio is also calculated as return on common equity if a firm has preferred stock outstanding. R.E.C. Inc. registered a solid improvement in 2002 of both return ratios.

Cash return on assets

	2002	2001
$\dfrac{\text{Cash flow from operating activities}}{\text{Total assets}}$	$\dfrac{10,024}{95,298} = 10.5\%$	$\dfrac{(3,767)}{75,909} = (5.0\%)$

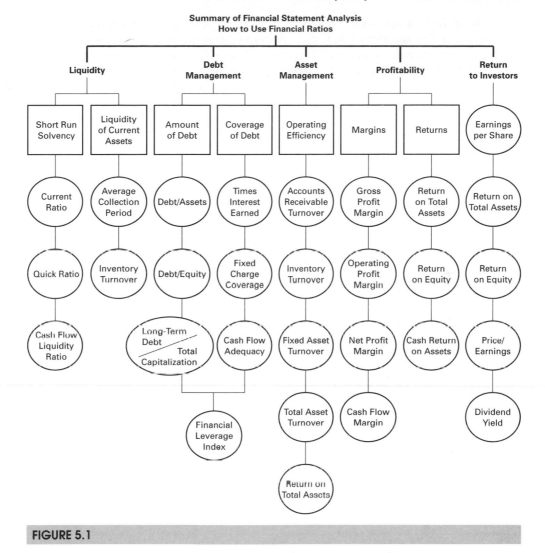

Summary of Financial Statement Analysis
How to Use Financial Ratios

FIGURE 5.1

The cash return on assets offers a useful comparison to return on investment. Again, the relationship between cash generated from operations and an accrual based number allows the analyst to measure the firm's cash generating ability of assets. Cash will be required for future investments.

Figure 5.1 shows in summary form the use of key financial ratios discussed in the chapter.

Analyzing the Data

Would you as a bank loan officer extend $1.5 million in new credit to R.E.C. Inc.? Would you as an investor purchase R.E.C. Inc. common shares at the current market price of $30 per share? Would you as a wholesaler of running shoes sell your products on credit to R.E.C. Inc.? Would you as a recent college graduate accept a position as manager-trainee with R.E.C. Inc.? Would you as the chief financial officer of R.E.C. Inc. authorize the opening of 25 new retail stores during the next two years?

In order to answer such questions, it is necessary to complete the analysis of R.E.C. Inc.'s financial statements, utilizing the common size financial statements and key financial ratios as well as other information presented throughout the book. Ordinarily, the analysis would deal with only one of the above questions, and the perspective of the financial statement user would determine the focus of the analysis. Because the purpose of this chapter is to present a general approach to financial statement analysis, however, the evaluation will cover each of four broad areas that would typically constitute a fundamental analysis of financial statements: (1) background on firm, industry, economy, and outlook; (2) short-term liquidity; (3) capital structure and long-term solvency; and (4) operating efficiency and profitability. From this general approach, each analytical situation can be tailored to meet specific user objectives.

The following table shows the steps of financial statement analysis:

Steps of a Financial Statement Analysis

1. Establish objectives of the analysis.
2. Study the industry in which firm operates and relate industry climate to current and projected economic developments.
3. Develop knowledge of the firm and the quality of management.
4. Evaluate financial statements.
   - Tools: Common size financial statements, key financial ratios, trend analysis, structural analysis, and comparison with industry competitors.
   - Major Areas: Short-term liquidity, capital structure and long-term solvency, operating efficiency and profitability, market ratios, and segmental analysis (when relevant).
5. Summarize findings based on analysis and reach conclusions about firm relevant to the established objectives.

BACKGROUND: ECONOMY, INDUSTRY, AND FIRM

An individual company does not operate in a vacuum. Economic developments and the actions of competitors affect the ability of any business enterprise to perform successfully. It is therefore necessary to preface the analysis of a firm's financial statements with an evaluation of the environment in which the firm conducts business. This process involves blending hard facts with guesses and estimates. Reference to the section entitled "Other Sources" in this chapter may be beneficial for this part of the analysis. A brief section discussing the business climate of R.E.C. Inc. follows.[5]

Recreational Equipment and Clothing Incorporated (R.E.C. Inc.) is the third largest retailer of recreational products in the U.S. The firm offers a broad line of

---

[5] The background section of R.E.C. Inc. is based on an unpublished paper by Kimberly Ann Davis, "A Financial Analysis of Oshman's Sporting Goods, Inc."

sporting goods and equipment and active sports apparel in medium to higher price ranges. R.E.C. Inc. sells equipment used in running, aerobics, walking, basketball, golf, tennis, skiing, football, scuba diving, and other sports; merchandise for camping hiking, fishing, and hunting; men's and women's sporting apparel; gift items; games; and consumer electronic products. The firm also sells sporting goods on a direct basis to institutional customers such as schools and athletic teams.

The general and executive offices of the company are located in Dime Box, Texas, and these facilities were expanded in 2002. Most of the retail stores occupy leased spaces and are located in major regional or suburban shopping districts throughout the southwestern United States. Eighteen new retail outlets were added in late 2001, and 25 new stores were opened in 2002. The firm owns distribution center warehouses located in Arizona, California, Colorado, Utah, and Texas.

The recreational products industry is affected by current trends in consumer preferences, a cyclical sales demand, and weather conditions. The running boom has shifted to walking and aerobics; golf, once on the downswing, is increasing in popularity; by winning the Tour de France, American Lance Armstrong invigorated the cycling industry in the United States. Recreational product retailers also rely heavily on sales of sportswear for their profits, because the markup on sportswear is generally higher than on sports equipment, and these products are also affected by consumer preference shifts. With regard to seasonality, most retail sales occur in November, December, May, and June. Sales to institutions are highest in August and September. Weather conditions also influence sales volume, especially of winter sports equipment—come on, Rocky Mountain snow!

Competition within the recreational products industry is based on price, quality, and variety of goods offered as well as the location of outlets and the quality of services offered. R.E.C. Inc.'s two major competitors are also full-line sporting goods companies. One operates in the northwest and the other primarily in the eastern and southeastern United States, reducing direct competition among the three firms.

The current outlook for the sporting goods industry is promising, following a recessionary year in 2001.[6] Americans have become increasingly aware of the importance of physical fitness and have become more actively involved in recreational activities. The 25-to-44 age group is the most athletically active and is projected to be the largest age group in the United States during the next decade. The southwestern United States is expected to provide a rapidly expanding market because of its population growth and excellent weather conditions for year-round recreational participation.

SHORT-TERM LIQUIDITY

Short-term liquidity analysis is especially important to creditors, suppliers, management, and others who are concerned with the ability of a firm to meet near-term demands for cash. The evaluation of R.E.C. Inc.'s short-term liquidity position began with the preparation and interpretation of the firm's common size balance sheet earlier in the chapter. From that assessment, it was evident that inventories

---

[6] The recession is assumed for purposes of writing this book and does not represent the authors' forecast.

have increased relative to cash and marketable securities in the current asset section, and there has been an increase in the proportion of debt, both short and long-term. These developments were traced primarily to policies and financing needs related to new store openings. Additional evidence useful to short-term liquidity analysis is provided by a five-year trend of selected financial ratios and a comparison with industry averages. Sources of comparative industry ratios include Dun & Bradstreet, *Industry Norms and Key Business Ratios,* New York, NY; Robert Morris Associates, *Annual Statement Studies,* Philadelphia, PA; and Standard & Poor's Corporation, *Industry Surveys,* New York, NY. As a source of industry comparative ratios, the analyst may prefer to develop a set of financial ratios for one or more major competitors.

R.E.C. Inc.	*2002*	*2001*	*2000*	*1999*	*1998*	*Industry Average 2002*
Current ratio	2.40	2.75	2.26	2.18	2.83	2.53
Quick ratio	.68	.95	.87	1.22	1.20	.97
Cash flow liquidity	.70	.32	.85	.78	.68	*
Average collection period	15 days	20 days	13 days	11 days	10 days	17 days
Inventory turnover	2.75	2.50	2.74	2.99	3.20	3.12
Cash flow from operating activities ($ thousands)	10,024	(3,767)	5,629	4,925	3,430	*

*Not available

Liquidity analysis involves something of an impossible task: a prediction of the *future* ability of the firm to meet prospective needs for cash. This prediction is made from the historical record of the firm, and no one financial ratio or set of financial ratios or other financial data can serve as a proxy for future developments. For R.E.C. Inc., the financial ratios are somewhat contradictory.

The current and quick ratios have trended downward over the five-year period, indicating a deterioration of short-term liquidity. On the other hand, the cash flow liquidity ratio improved strongly in 2002 after a year of negative cash generation in 2001. The average collection period for accounts receivable and the inventory turnover ratio—after worsening between 1998 and 2001—also improved in 2002. These ratios measure the quality or liquidity of accounts receivable and inventory. The average collection period increased to a high of 20 days in 2001, which was a recessionary year in the economy, then decreased to a more acceptable 15-day level in 2002.

The common size balance sheet for R.E.C. Inc. revealed that inventories now comprise about half of the firm's total assets. The growth in inventories has been necessary to satisfy the requirements associated with the opening of new retail outlets but has been accomplished by reducing holdings of cash and cash equivalents. This represents a tradeoff of highly liquid assets for potentially less liquid assets. The efficient management of inventories is a critical ingredient for the firm's ongoing liquidity. In 2002, inventory turnover improved in spite of the buildups necessary to stock new stores. Sales demand in 2002 was more than adequate to absorb the 28% increase in inventories recorded for the year.

The major question in the outlook for liquidity is the ability of the firm to produce cash from operations. Problems in 2001 resulted partly from the depressed state of the economy and poor ski conditions, which reduced sales growth. The easing of sales demand hit the company in a year that marked the beginning of a major market expansion. Inventories and receivables increased too fast for the limited sales growth of a recessionary year, and R.E.C. also experienced some reduction of credit availability from suppliers that felt the economic pinch. The consequence was a cash crunch and negative cash flow from operations.

In 2002 R.E.C. Inc. enjoyed considerable improvement, generating more than $10 million in cash from operations and progress in managing inventories and receivables. There appears to be no major problem with the firm's short-term liquidity position at the present time. Another poor year, however, might well cause problems similar to those experienced in 2001. The timing of further expansion of retail outlets will be of critical importance to the ongoing success of the firm.

NET TRADE CYCLE

One additional tool in the assessment of liquidity is the net trade cycle or cash conversion cycle. The normal operating cycle of a firm consists of buying or manufacturing inventory, with some purchases on credit and the creation of accounts payable; selling inventory, with some sales on credit and the creation of accounts receivable; and collecting the cash. The net trade cycle measures this process in number of days and is calculated as follows for R.E.C. Inc.:

	2002	2001
Accounts receivable	15 days	20 days
Average daily sales		
plus		
Inventory	80 days	88 days
Average daily sales*		
minus		
Accounts payable	(24 days)	(18 days)
Average daily sales*		
equals		
Cash conversion cycle	71 days	90 days

*Net sales divided by 365 days

As with other ratios, there are alternative calculations, such as cost of sales, in the denominator of the ratio.

By reducing and thus improving the net trade cycle by 19 days between 2001 and 2002, R.E.C. Inc. has increased cash flow by more than $11 million: 2002 average daily sales of $590,685 × 19 days = $11,223,015. The net trade cycle helps the analyst understand why cash flow generation has improved or deteriorated by analyzing the key balance sheet accounts—accounts receivable, inventory, and accounts payable—that affect cash flow from operating activities.

CAPITAL STRUCTURE AND LONG-TERM SOLVENCY

The analytical process includes an evaluation of the amount and proportion of debt in a firm's capital structure as well as the ability to service debt. Debt implies risk because debt involves the satisfaction of fixed financial obligations. The disadvantage of debt financing is that the fixed commitments must be met in order for the firm to continue operations. The major advantage of debt financing is that, when used successfully, shareholder returns are magnified through financial leverage. The concept of financial leverage can best be illustrated with an example.

EXAMPLE OF FINANCIAL LEVERAGE

Sockee Sock Company has $100,000 in total assets, and the firm's capital structure consists of 50% debt and 50% equity:

Debt	$50,000
Equity	50,000
Total assets	$100,000

$$\text{Cost of debt} = 10\%$$
$$\text{Average tax rate} = 40\%$$

If Sockee has $20,000 in operating earnings, the return to shareholders as measured by the return on equity ratio would be 18%:

Operating earnings	$20,000
Interest expense	5,000
Earnings before tax	15,000
Tax expense	6,000
Net earnings	$ 9,000

Return on equity: 9,000/50,000 = 18%

If Sockee is able to double operating earnings from $20,000 to $40,000, the return on equity will more than double, increasing from 18% to 42%:

Operating earnings	$40,000
Interest expense	5,000
Earnings before tax	35,000
Tax expense	14,000
Net earnings	$21,000

Return on equity: 21,000/50,000 = 42%

The magnified return on equity results from *financial leverage.* Unfortunately, leverage has a double edge. If operating earnings are cut in half from $20,000 to $10,000, the return on equity is more than halved, declining from 18% to 6%:

Operating earnings	$10,000
Interest expense	5,000
Earnings before tax	5,000
Tax expense	2,000
Net earnings	3,000

Return on equity: 3,000/50,000 = 6%

The amount of interest expense is fixed, regardless of the level of operating earnings. When operating earnings rise or fall, financial leverage produces positive or negative effects on shareholder returns. In evaluating a firm's capital structure and solvency, the analyst must constantly weigh the potential benefits of debt against the risks inherent in its use.

R.E.C. Inc.	2002	2001	2000	1999	1998	Industry Average 2002
Debt to total assets	51.8%	50.1%	49.2%	40.8%	39.7%	48.7%
Long-term debt to total capitalization	31.4%	31.0%	24.1%	19.6%	19.8%	30.4%
Debt to equity	1.07	1.00	.96	.68	.66	.98

The debt ratios for R.E.C. Inc. reveal a steady increase in the use of borrowed funds. Total debt has risen relative to total assets, long-term debt has increased as a proportion of the firm's permanent financing, and external or debt financing has increased relative to internal financing. Given the greater degree of risk implied by borrowing, it is important to determine (1) why debt has increased; (2) whether the firm is employing debt successfully; and (3) how well the firm is covering its fixed charges.

Why has debt increased? The Summary Statement of Cash Flows, discussed in chapter 4 and repeated here as Exhibit 5.4, provides an explanation of borrowing cause. Exhibit 5.4 shows the inflows and outflows of cash both in dollar amounts and percentages.

Exhibit 5.4 shows that R.E.C. Inc. has substantially increased its investment in capital assets, particularly in 2002 when additions to property, plant, and equipment accounted for 82% of the total cash outflows. These investments have been financed largely by borrowing, especially in 2001 when the firm had a sluggish operating performance and no internal cash generation. Operations supplied 73% of R.E.C. Inc.'s cash in 2000 and 62% in 2002, but the firm had to borrow heavily in 2001 (98% of cash inflows). The impact of this borrowing is seen in the firm's debt ratios.

How effectively is R.E.C. Inc. using financial leverage? The answer is determined by calculating the *financial leverage index (FLI),* as follows:

$$\frac{\text{Return on equity}}{\text{Adjusted return on assets*}} = \text{Financial leverage index}$$

When the FLI is greater than 1, which indicates that return on equity exceeds return on assets, the firm is employing debt beneficially. A FLI of less than 1 means the firm is not using debt successfully. For R.E.C. Inc., the FLI is calculated as follows:

	2002	2001	2000
$\dfrac{\text{Return on equity}}{\text{Adjusted return on assets}^{\dagger}}$	$\dfrac{20.45}{11.35} = 1.8$	$\dfrac{15.61}{9.50} = 1.6$	$\dfrac{17.53}{9.57} = 1.8$

$*\dfrac{\text{Net earnings} + \text{interest expense } (1 - \text{tax rate})}{\text{Total assets}} = \text{Adjusted return on assets}$

†ROA Adjusted: $\dfrac{9,394 + 2,585\,(.55)}{95,298} = 11.35\%$ $\dfrac{5,910 + 2,277(.57)}{75,909} = 9.50\%$ $\dfrac{5,896 + 1,274\,(.55)}{66,146} = 9.97\%$

$\dfrac{\text{Average tax rate: Income tax/}}{\text{earnings before tax}}$ $\dfrac{7,686}{17,080} = 45.0\%$ $\dfrac{4,457}{10,367} = 43.0\%$ $\dfrac{4,824}{10,720} = 45.0\%$

EXHIBIT 5.4

R.E.C. INC.
SUMMARY ANALYSIS STATEMENT OF CASH FLOWS
(IN THOUSANDS)

	2002	2001	2000
Inflows (thousands)			
Operations	$10,024	$ 0	$5,629
Sales of other assets	295	0	0
Sales of common stock	256	183	124
Additions of short-term debt	0	1,854	1,326
Additions of long-term debt	5,600	7,882	629
Total	$16,175	$ 9,919	$7,708
Outflows (thousands)			
Operations	$ 0	$ 3,767	$ 0
Purchase of property, plant and equipment	14,100	4,773	3,982
Reductions of short-term debt	30	0	0
Reductions of long-term debt	1,516	1,593	127
Dividends paid	1,582	1,862	1,841
Total	$17,228	$11,995	$5,950
Change in cash and marketable securities	($1,053)	($2,076)	$1,758
Inflows (percent total)			
Operations	62.0%	0.0%	73.0%
Sales of other assets	1.8	0.0	0.0
Sales of common stock	1.6	1.8	1.6
Additions of short-term debt	0.0	18.7	17.2
Additions of long-term debt	34.6	79.5	8.2
Total	100.0%	100.0%	100.0%
Outflows (percent of total)			
Operations	0.0%	31.4%	0.0%
Purchase of property, plant and equipment	81.8	40.0	66.9
Reductions of short-term debt	0.2	0.0	0.0
Reductions of long-term debt	8.8	13.2	2.1
Dividends paid	9.2	15.4	31.0
Total	100.0%	100.0%	100.0%

The FLI for R.E.C. Inc. of 1.8 in 2002, 1.6 in 2001, and 1.8 in 2000 indicates a successful use of financial leverage for the three-year period when borrowing has increased. The firm has generated sufficient operating returns to more than cover the interest payments on borrowed funds.

How well is R.E.C. Inc. covering fixed charges? The answer requires a review of the coverage ratios.

R.E.C. Inc.	2002	2001	2000	1999	1998	Industry Average 2002
Times interest earned	7.44	5.18	8.84	13.34	12.60	7.2
Fixed charge coverage	2.09	2.01	2.27	2.98	3.07	2.5
Cash flow adequacy	4.25	(1.65)	2.46	3.10	2.87	*

*Not available

Given the increased level of borrowing, the times interest earned ratio has declined over the five-year period but remains above the industry average. R.E.C. Inc. leases the majority of its retail outlets so the fixed charge coverage ratio, which considers lease payments as well as interest expense, is the more relevant ratio. This ratio has also decreased, as a result of store expansion and higher payments for leases and interest. Although below the industry average, the firm is still covering all fixed charges by more than two times out of operating earnings, and coverage does not at this point appear to be a problem. The fixed charge coverage ratio is a ratio to be monitored closely in the future, however, particularly if R.E.C. Inc. continues to expand. The cash flow adequacy ratio has averaged 2.2 over the past five years, indicating that R.E.C. Inc. has the ability to cover maturities of long-term debt as well as dividends with cash from operations.

OPERATING EFFICIENCY AND PROFITABILITY

The analysis now turns to a consideration of how well the firm has performed in terms of overall operating efficiency and profitability, beginning with the evaluation of several key ratios.

R.E.C. Inc.	2002	2001	2000	1999	1998	Industry Average 2002
Fixed asset turnover	7.41	8.06	8.19	10.01	10.11	8.72
Total asset turnover	2.26	2.02	2.13	2.87	2.95	2.43

As noted earlier, R.E.C. Inc. has increased its investment in fixed assets as a result of home office and store expansion. The asset turnover ratios reveal a downward trend in the efficiency with which the firm is generating sales from investments in fixed and total assets. The total asset turnover rose in 2002, progress traceable to improved management of inventories and receivables. The fixed asset turnover ratio is still declining, a result of expanding offices and retail outlets, but should improve if the expansion is successful.

R.E.C. Inc.	2002	2001	2000	1999	1998	Industry Average 2002
Gross profit margin	40.00%	39.95%	42.00%	41.80%	41.76%	37.25%
Operating profit margin	8.93%	7.72%	8.00%	10.98%	11.63%	7.07%
Net profit margin	4.36%	3.86%	4.19%	5.00%	5.20%	3.74%
Cash flow margin	4.65%	(2.46)%	4.00%	4.39%	3.92%	*

*Not available

Profitability—after a relatively poor year in 2001 due to economic recession, adverse ski conditions, and the costs of new store openings—now looks more promising. Management adopted a growth strategy reflected in aggressive marketing and the opening of 18 new stores in 2001 and 25 in 2002. With the exception of the cash flow margin, the profit margins are all below their 1998 and 1999 levels but have improved in 2002 and are above industry averages. The cash flow margin, as a result of strong cash generation from operations in 2002, was at its highest level of the five-year period.

The gross profit margin was stable, a positive sign in light of new store openings featuring many "sale" and discounted items to attract customers, and the firm managed to improve its operating profit margin in 2002. The increase in operating profit margin is especially noteworthy because it occurred during an expansionary period with sizable increases in operating expenses, especially lease payments required for new stores. The net profit margin also improved in spite of increased interest and tax expenses and a reduction in interest revenue from marketable security investments.

R.E.C. Inc.	2002	2001	2000	1999	1998	Average 2002
Return on assets	9.86%	7.79%	8.91%	14.35%	15.34%	9.09%
Return on equity	20.45%	15.61%	17.53%	24.25%	25.46%	17.72%
Cash return on assets	10.52%	(4.96)%	8.64%	15.01%	15.98%	*

*Not available

After declining steadily through 2001, return on assets, return on equity, and cash return on assets rebounded strongly in 2002. The return on assets and return on equity ratios measure the overall success of the firm in generating profits, whereas the cash return on assets measures the firm's ability to generate cash from its investment and management strategies. It would appear that R.E.C. Inc. is well positioned for future growth. As discussed earlier, it will be important to monitor the firm's management of inventories, which account for half of total assets and have been problematic in the past. The expansion will necessitate a continuation of expenditures for advertising, at least at the current level, in order to attract customers to both new and old areas. R.E.C. Inc. has financed much of its expansion with debt, and thus far its shareholders have benefited from the use of debt through financial leverage.

R.E.C. Inc. experienced a negative cash flow from operations in 2001, another problem that bears watching in the future. The negative cash flow occurred in a year of only modest sales and earnings growth:

R.E.C. Inc.	2002	2001	2000	1999	1998
Sales growth	40.9%	8.7%	25.5%	21.6%	27.5%
Earnings growth	59.0%	.2%	5.2%	16.9%	19.2%

Sales expanded rapidly in 2002 as the economy recovered and the expansion of retail outlets began to pay off. The outlook is for continued economic recovery.

RELATING THE RATIOS—THE DU PONT SYSTEM

Having looked at individual financial ratios as well as groups of financial ratios measuring short-term liquidity, capital structure and long-term solvency, and operating efficiency and profitability, it is helpful to complete the evaluation of a firm by considering the interrelationship among the individual ratios. That is, how do the various pieces of financial measurement work together to produce an overall return? The *Du Pont system* helps the analyst see how the firm's decisions and activities over the course of an accounting period—which is what financial ratios are measuring—interact to produce an overall return to the firm's shareholders, the return on equity. The summary ratios used are the following:

$$\underset{\text{Net profit margin}}{\overset{(1)}{}} \times \underset{\text{Total asset turnover}}{\overset{(2)}{}} = \underset{\text{Return on investment}}{\overset{(3)}{}}$$

$$\frac{\text{Net income}}{\text{Sales}} \times \frac{\text{Sales}}{\text{Assets}} = \frac{\text{Net income}}{\text{Assets}}$$

$$\underset{\text{Return on investment}}{\overset{(3)}{}} \times \underset{\text{Financial leverage}}{\overset{(4)}{}} = \underset{\text{Return on equity}}{\overset{(5)}{}}$$

$$\frac{\text{Net income}}{\text{Assets}} \times \frac{\text{Assets}}{\text{Equity}} = \frac{\text{Net income}}{\text{Equity}}$$

By reviewing this series of relationships, the analyst can identify strengths and weaknesses as well as trace potential causes of any problems in the overall financial condition and performance of the firm.

The first three ratios reveal that the (3) return on investment (profit generated from the overall investment in assets) is a product of the (1) net profit margin (profit generated from sales) and the (2) total asset turnover (the firm's ability to produce sales from its assets). Extending the analysis, the remaining three ratios show how the (5) return on equity (overall return to shareholders, the firm's owners) is derived from the product of (3) return on investment and (4) financial leverage (proportion of debt in the capital structure). Using this system, the analyst can evaluate changes in the firm's condition and performance, whether they are indicative of improvement or deterioration or some combination. The evaluation can then focus on specific areas contributing to the changes.

Evaluating R.E.C. Inc. using the Du Pont system over the five-year period 1998 to 2002 would show the following relationships:

Du Pont system applied to R.E.C. Inc.

	(1)		(2)		(3)		(4)		(5)
	NPM	×	TAT	=	ROI	×	FL	=	ROE
1998	5.20	×	2.95	=	15.34	×	1.66	=	25.46
1999	5.00	×	2.87	=	14.35	×	1.69	=	24.25
2000	4.19	×	2.13	=	8.92	×	1.97	=	17.57
2001	3.86	×	2.02	=	7.80	×	2.00	=	15.60
2002	4.36	×	2.26	=	9.85	×	2.07	=	20.39

As discussed earlier in the chapter, return on equity is below earlier year levels but has improved since its low point in 2001. The Du Pont system helps provide clues as to why these changes have occurred. Both the profit margin and the asset turnover are lower in 2002 than in 1998 and 1999. The combination of increased debt (financial leverage) and the improvement in profitability and asset utilization has produced an improved overall return in 2002 relative to the two previous years. Specifically, the firm has added debt to finance capital asset expansion and has used its debt effectively. Although debt carries risk and added cost in the form of interest expense, debt has the positive benefit of financial leverage when debt is employed successfully, which is the case for R.E.C. Inc. The 2002 improvement in inventory management has impacted the firm favorably, showing up in the improved total asset turnover ratio. The firm's ability to control operating costs while increasing sales during expansion has improved the net profit margin. The overall return on investment is now improving as a result of these combined factors.

PROJECTIONS, PRO FORMA STATEMENTS, AND MARKET RATIOS

Some additional analytical tools and financial ratios are relevant to financial statement analysis, particularly for investment decisions and long-range planning. Although an in-depth discussion of these tools is beyond the scope of this chapter, we provide an introductory treatment of projections, pro forma financial statements, and several investment-related financial ratios.

The investment analyst, in valuing securities for investment decisions, must project the future earnings stream of a business enterprise. References that provide earnings forecasts are found in the "Other Sources" section earlier in the chapter..

Pro forma financial statements are projections of financial statements based on a set of assumptions regarding future revenues, expenses, level of investment in assets, financing methods and costs, and working capital management. Pro forma financial statements are utilized primarily for long-range planning and long-term credit decisions. A bank considering the extension of $1.5 million in new credit to R.E.C. Inc. would want to look at the firm's pro forma statements assuming the loan is granted and determine—using different scenarios regarding the firm's performance—whether cash flow from operations would be sufficient to service the debt. R.E.C. Inc.'s CEO, who is making a decision about new store expansion, would develop pro forma statements based on varying estimates of performance outcomes and financing alternatives.

Four market ratios of particular interest to the investor are earnings per common share, the price-to-earnings ratio, the dividend payout ratio, and dividend yield. Earnings per common share is net income for the period divided by the weighted average number of common shares outstanding. One million dollars in earnings will look different to the investor if there are 1 million shares of stock outstanding or 100,000 shares. The earnings per share ratio provides the investor with a common denominator to gauge investment returns.

The *basic earnings per share* computations for R.E.C. Inc. are made as follows:

	2002	2001	2000
$\dfrac{\text{Net earnings}}{\text{Average shares outstanding}}$	$\dfrac{9,394,000}{4,792,857} = 1.96$	$\dfrac{5,910,000}{4,581,395} = 1.29$	$\dfrac{5,896,000}{4,433,083} = 1.33$

The price-to-earnings ratio (P/E ratios) relates earnings per common share to the market price at which the stock trades, expressing the "multiple" that the stock market places on a firm's earnings. For instance, if two competing firms had annual earnings of $2.00 per share, and Company 1 shares sold for $10.00 each and Company 2 shares were selling at $20.00 each, the market is placing a different value on the same $2.00 earnings: a multiple of 5 for Company 1 and 10 for Company 2. The P/E ratio is the function of a myriad of factors, which include the quality of earnings, future earnings potential, and the performance history of the company.

The *price-to-earnings ratio* for R.E.C. Inc. would be determined as follows:

	2002	2001	2000
$\dfrac{\text{Market price of common stock}}{\text{Earnings per share}}$	$\dfrac{30.00}{1.96} = 15.3$	$\dfrac{17.00}{1.29} = 13.2$	$\dfrac{25.00}{1.33} = 18.8$

The P/E ratio is higher in 2002 than 2001 but below the 2000 level. This could be due to developments in the market generally and/or because the market is reacting cautiously to the firm's good year. Another factor could be the reduction of cash dividend payments.

The *dividend payout ratio* is determined by the formula cash dividends per share divided by earnings per share:

	2002	2001	2000
$\dfrac{\text{Dividends per share}}{\text{Earnings per share}}$	$\dfrac{.33}{1.96} = 16.8\%$	$\dfrac{.41}{1.29} = 31.8\%$	$\dfrac{.41}{1.33} = 30.8\%$

R.E.C. Inc. reduced its cash dividend payment in 2002. It is unusual for a company to reduce cash dividends because this decision can be read as a negative signal regarding the future outlook. It is particularly uncommon for a firm to reduce dividends during a good year. The explanation provided by management is that the firm has adopted a new policy that will result in lower dividend payments in order to increase the availability of internal funds for expansion; management expects the overall long-term impact to be extremely favorable to shareholders and has committed to maintaining the $.33 per share annual cash dividend.

The *dividend yield* shows the relationship between cash dividends and market price:

	2002	2001	2000
$\dfrac{\text{Dividends per share}}{\text{Market price of common stock}}$	$\dfrac{.33}{30.00} = 1.1\%$	$\dfrac{.41}{17.00} = 2.4\%$	$\dfrac{.41}{25.00} = 1.6\%$

The R.E.C. Inc. shares are yielding a 1.1% return based on the market price at year-end 2002; an investor would likely choose R.E.C. Inc. as an investment more for its long-term capital appreciation than for its dividend yield.

SUMMARY OF ANALYSIS

The analysis of any firm's financial statements consists of a mixture of steps and pieces that interrelate and affect each other. No one part of the analysis should be interpreted in isolation. Short-term liquidity impacts profitability; profitability begins with sales, which relate to the liquidity of assets. The efficiency of asset management influences the cost and availability of credit, which shapes the capital structure. Every aspect of a firm's financial condition, performance, and outlook affects the share price. The last step of financial statement analysis is to integrate the separate pieces into a whole, leading to conclusions about the business enterprise. The specific conclusions drawn will be affected by the original objectives established at the initiation of the analytical process.

The major findings from the analysis of R.E.C. Inc.'s financial statements can be summarized by the following strengths and weaknesses.

STRENGTHS
1. Favorable economic and industry outlook; firm well-positioned geographically to benefit from expected economic and industry growth.
2. Aggressive marketing and expansion strategies.
3. Recent improvement in management of accounts receivable and inventory.
4. Successful use of financial leverage and solid coverage of debt service requirements.
5. Effective control of operating costs.
6. Substantial sales growth, partially resulting from market expansion and reflective of future performance potential.
7. Increased profitability in 2002 and strong, positive generation of cash flow from operations.

WEAKNESSES
1. Highly sensitive to economic fluctuations and weather conditions.
2. Negative cash flow from operating activities in 2001.
3. Historical problems with inventory management and some weakness in overall asset management efficiency.
4. Increased risk associated with debt financing.

The answers to specific questions regarding R.E.C. Inc. are determined by the values placed on each of the strengths and weaknesses. In general, the outlook for the firm is promising. R.E.C. Inc. appears to be a sound credit risk with attractive investment potential. The management of inventories, a continuation of effective cost controls, and careful timing of further expansion will be critically important to the firm's future success.

MAP
This book began with the notion that financial statements should serve as a map to successful business decision making, even though the user of financial statement data would confront mazelike challenges in seeking to find and interpret the necessary information. The chapters have covered the enormous volume of material found in corporate financial reporting, the complexities and confusions created by accounting rules and choices, the potential for management manipulations of financial statement results, the distortions caused by inflation, and the difficulty in finding necessary information. The exploration of financial statements has required a close examination of the form and content of each financial statement presented in corporate annual reporting as well as the development of tools and techniques for analyzing the data. It is the hope of the authors that readers of this book will find that financial statements are a map, leading to sound and profitable business decisions.

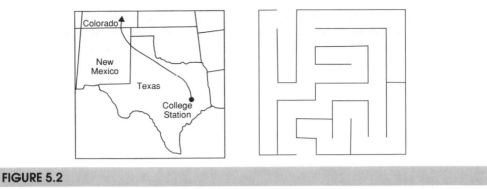

FIGURE 5.2

SELF-TEST

Solutions are provided in appendix D.

_____ 1. What is the first step in an analysis of financial statements?
    (a) Check the auditor's report.
    (b) Check references containing financial information.
    (c) Specify the objectives of the analysis.
    (d) Do a common size analysis.

_____ 2. What is a creditor's objective in performing an analysis of financial statements?
    (a) To decide whether the borrower has the ability to repay interest and principal on borrowed funds.
    (b) To determine the firm's capital structure.
    (c) To determine the company's future earnings stream.
    (d) To decide whether the firm has operated profitably in the past.

_____ 3. What is an investor's objective in financial statement analysis?
    (a) To determine if the firm is risky.
    (b) To determine the stability of earnings.
    (c) To determine changes necessary to improve future performance.
    (d) To determine whether an investment is warranted by estimating a company's future earnings stream.

_____ 4. What information does the auditor's report contain?
    (a) The results of operations.
    (b) An unqualified opinion.
    (c) An opinion as to the fairness of the financial statements.
    (d) A detailed coverage of the firm's liquidity, capital resources, and operations.

_____ 5. Which of the following would not result in a qualified auditor's report?
    (a) The failure to use generally accepted accounting principles.
    (b) Financial statements that present fairly the financial position, results of operations, and changes in financial position.
    (c) The inconsistent application of accounting principles.
    (d) Uncertainties regarding the outcome of significant factors affecting the ongoing operations of the firm.

_____ 6. Which of the following is not required to be discussed in the Management Discussion and Analysis of the Financial Condition and Results of Operations?
  (a) Liquidity.
  (b) Capital resources.
  (c) Operations.
  (d) Earnings projections.

_____ 7. What type of information found in supplementary schedules are required for inclusion in an annual report?
  (a) Segmental data.
  (b) Inflation data.
  (c) Material litigation and management photographs.
  (d) Management remuneration and segmental data.

_____ 8. What is Form 10-K?
  (a) A document filed with the AICPA, containing supplementary schedules showing management remuneration and elaborations of financial statement disclosures.
  (b) A document filed with the SEC by companies selling securities to the public, containing much of the same information as the annual report as well as additional detail.
  (c) A document filed with the SEC containing key business ratios and forecasts of earnings.
  (d) A document filed with the SEC containing nonpublic information.

_____ 9. What information can be gained from sources such as Industry Norms and Key Business Ratios, Annual Statement Studies, Analyst's Handbook, and Industry Surveys?
  (a) The general economic condition.
  (b) Forecasts of earnings.
  (c) Elaborations of financial statement disclosures.
  (d) A company's relative position within its industry.

_____ 10. Which of the following is not a tool or technique used by a financial statement analyst?
  (a) Common size financial statements.
  (b) Trend analysis.
  (c) Random sampling analysis.
  (d) Industry comparisons.

_____ 11. What are common size financial statements?
  (a) Statements that express each account on the balance sheet as a percentage of total assets and each account on the income statement as a percentage of net sales.
  (b) Statements that standardize financial data in terms of trends.
  (c) Statements that relate the firm to the industry in which it operates.
  (d) Statements based on common sense and judgment.

_____ 12. Which of the following is not revealed on a common size balance sheet?
  (a) The debt structure of a firm.
  (b) The capital structure of a firm.

      (c) The dollar amount of assets and liabilities.

      (d) The distribution of assets in which funds are invested.

_____ 13. What is a serious limitation of financial ratios?

      (a) Ratios are screening devices.

      (b) Ratios can be used only by themselves.

      (c) Ratios indicate weaknesses only.

      (d) Ratios are not predictive.

_____ 14. What is the most widely used liquidity ratio?

      (a) Quick ratio.

      (b) Current ratio.

      (c) Inventory turnover.

      (d) Debt ratio.

_____ 15. What is a limitation common to both the current and the quick ratio?

      (a) Accounts receivable may not be truly liquid.

      (b) Inventories may not be truly liquid.

      (c) Marketable securities are not liquid.

      (d) Prepaid expenses are potential sources of cash.

_____ 16. Why is the quick ratio a more rigorous test of short-run solvency than the current ratio?

      (a) The quick ratio considers only cash and marketable securities as current assets.

      (b) The quick ratio eliminates prepaid expenses for the numerator.

      (c) The quick ratio eliminates prepaid expenses for the denominator.

      (d) The quick ratio eliminates inventories from the numerator.

_____ 17. What does an increasing collection period for accounts receivable suggest about a firm's credit policy?

      (a) The credit policy is too restrictive.

      (b) The firm is probably losing qualified customers.

      (c) The credit policy may be too lenient.

      (d) The collection period has no relationship to a firm's credit policy.

_____ 18. Which of the following statements about inventory turnover is false?

      (a) Inventory turnover measures the efficiency of the firm in managing and selling inventory.

      (b) Inventory turnover is a gauge of the liquidity of a firm's inventory.

      (c) Inventory turnover is calculated with either cost of goods sold or net sales in the numerator.

      (d) A low inventory turnover is generally a sign of efficient inventory management.

_____ 19. Which of the following is not a reason for a high inventory turnover ratio?

      (a) Stockpiling inventory.

      (b) Decrease in prices.

      (c) Understocking inventory.

      (d) Shortage of materials.

_____ 20. What do the asset turnover ratios measure?

      (a) The liquidity of the firm's current assets.

      (b) Management's effectiveness in generating sales from investments in assets.

    (c) The overall efficiency and profitability of the firm.

    (d) The distribution of assets in which funds are invested.

____ 21. Which of the following ratios would not be used to measure the extent of a firm's debt financing?

    (a) Debt ratio.

    (b) Debt to equity.

    (c) Times interest earned.

    (d) Long-term debt to total capitalization.

____ 22. Why is the amount of debt in a company's capital structure important to the financial analyst?

    (a) Debt implies risk.

    (b) Debt is less costly than equity.

    (c) Equity is riskier than debt.

    (d) Debt is equal to total assets.

____ 23. Why is the fixed charge coverage ratio a broader measure of a firm's coverage capabilities than the times interest earned ratio?

    (a) The fixed charge ratio indicates how many times the firm can cover interest payments.

    (b) The times interest earned ratio does not consider the possibility of higher interest rates.

    (c) The fixed charge ratio includes lease payments as well as interest payments.

    (d) The fixed charge ratio includes both operating and capital leases while the times interest earned ratio includes only operating leases.

____ 24. Which profit margin measures the overall operating efficiency of the firm?

    (a) Gross profit margin.

    (b) Operating profit margin.

    (c) Net profit margin.

    (d) Return on equity.

____ 25. Which ratio or ratios measure the overall efficiency of the firm in managing its investment in assets and in generating return to shareholders?

    (a) Gross profit margin and net profit margin.

    (b) Return on investment.

    (c) Total asset turnover and operating profit margin.

    (d) Return on investment and return on equity.

____ 26. What does a financial leverage index greater than one indicate about a firm?

    (a) The unsuccessful use of financial leverage.

    (b) Operating returns more than sufficient to cover interest payments on borrowed funds.

    (c) More debt financing than equity financing.

    (d) An increased level of borrowing.

____ 27. What does the price to earnings ratio measure?

    (a) The "multiple" which the stock market places on a firm's earnings.

    (b) The relationship between dividends and market prices.

    (c) The earnings for one common share of stock.

    (d) The percentage of dividends paid to net earnings of the firm.

Use the following data to answer questions 28 through 31:

JDL CORPORATION SELECTED FINANCIAL DATA
DECEMBER 31, 20X9

Current assets	$150,000
Current liabilities	100,000
Inventories	50,000
Accounts receivable	40,000
Net sales	900,000
Cost of goods sold	675,000

____ 28. JDL's current ratio is:
   (a) 1.0 to 1.
   (b) 0.7 to 1.
   (c) 1.5 to 1.
   (d) 2.4 to 1.

____ 29. JDL's quick ratio is:
   (a) 1.0 to 1.
   (b) 0.7 to 1.
   (c) 1.5 to 1.
   (d) 2.4 to 1.

____ 30. JDL's average collection period is:
   (a) 6 days.
   (b) 11 days.
   (c) 16 days.
   (d) 22 days.

____ 31. JDL's inventory turnover is:
   (a) 1.25 times.
   (b) 13.5 times.
   (c) 3.0 times.
   (d) 37.5 times.

Use the following data to answer questions 32 through 35:

RQM CORPORATION SELECTED FINANCIAL DATA
DECEMBER 31, 20X9

Net sales	$1,800,000
Cost of goods sold	1,080,000
Operating expenses	315,000
Net operating income	405,000
Net income	195,000
Total stockholders' equity	750,000
Total assets	1,000,000
Cash flow from operating activities	25,000

____ 32. RQM's gross profit margin, operating profit margin, and net profit margin, respectively, are:

(a) 40.00%, 22.50%, 19.50%
(b) 60.00%, 19.50%, 10.83%
(c) 60.00%, 22.50%, 19.50%
(d) 40.00%, 22.50%, 10.83%

_____ 33. RQM's return on equity is:
(a) 26%
(b) 54%
(c) 42%
(d) 19%

_____ 34. RQM's return on investment is:
(a) 22.5%
(b) 26.5%
(c) 19.5%
(d) 40.5%

_____ 35. RQM's cash flow margin is:
(a) 1.4%
(b) 2.5%
(c) 10.8%
(d) 12.8%

STUDY QUESTIONS AND PROBLEMS

5.1 Eleanor's Computers is a retailer of computer products. Using the financial data provided, complete the financial ratio calculations for 20X7. Advise management of any ratios that indicate potential problems and provide an explanation of possible causes of the problems.

	20X5	20X6	20X7	Industry Averages 20X7
Current ratio	1.71X	1.65X		1.70X
Quick ratio	.92X	.89X		.95X
Average collection period	60 days	60 days		65 days
Inventory turnover	4.20X	3.90X		4.50X
Fixed asset turnover	3.20X	3.33X		3.00X
Total asset turnover	1.40X	1.35X		1.37X
Debt ratio	59.20%	61.00%		60.00%
Times interest earned	4.20X	3.70X		4.75X
Gross profit margin	25.00%	23.00%		22.50%
Operating profit margin	12.50%	12.70%		12.50%
Net profit margin	6.10%	6.00%		6.50%
Return on total assets	8.54%	8.10%		8.91%
Return on equity	20.93%	20.74%		22.28%

Balance Sheet at 12/31/X7

Cash	$ 125,000
Accounts receivable	275,000
Inventory	325,000
Current assets	$ 725,000
Fixed assets (net)	$ 420,000
Total Assets	$1,145,000
Accounts payable	$ 150,000
Notes payable	225,000
Accrued liabilities	100,000
Current liabilities	475,000
Long-term debt	400,000
Total liabilities	$ 875,000
Equity	270,000
Total liabilities and equity	$1,145,000

Income Statement for Year Ended 12/31/X7

Sales	$1,500,000
Cost of goods sold	1,200,000
Gross profit	$ 300,000
Operating expenses	100,000
Operating profit	$ 200,000
Interest expense	72,000
Earnings before tax	128,000
Income tax (0.4)	51,200
Net Income	$ 76,800

5.2 Luna Lighting, a retail firm, has experienced modest sales growth over the past three years but has had difficulty translating the expansion of sales into improved profitability. Using three years' financial statements, you have developed the following ratio calculations and industry comparisons. Based on this information, suggest possible reasons for Luna's profitability problems.

	X9	X8	X7	Industry X9
Current	2.3X	2.3X	2.2X	2.1X
Average collection period	45d	46d	47d	50d
Inventory turnover	8.3X	8.2X	8.1X	8.3X
Fixed asset turnover	2.7X	3.0X	3.3X	3.5X
Total asset turnover	1.1X	1.2X	1.3X	1.5X
Debt ratio	50%	50%	50%	54%
Times interest earned	8.1X	8.2X	8.1X	7.2X
Fixed charge coverage	4.0X	4.5X	5.5X	5.1X
Gross profit margin	43%	43%	43%	40%
Operating profit margin	6.3%	7.2%	8.0%	7.5%
Net profit margin	3.5%	4.0%	4.3%	4.2%
Return on assets	3.7%	5.0%	5.7%	6.4%
Return on equity	7.4%	9.9%	11.4%	11.8%

5.3 Aggieland Autos is an automobile dealership. Using the financial data presented in the next pages, complete the problems listed next.

Required:

(a) Calculate figures for the common size income statement and balance sheet for 20X9.

(b) Calculate cash flow from operating activities for 20X9.

(c) Calculate the relevant financial rations for 20X9.

(d) Analyze the data, and list the strengths and weaknesses of the company. What recommendations would you make to Aggie Al for improving the company?

Aggieland Autos Background

Aggieland Autos is celebrating its tenth anniversary as a profitable company. "Aggie Al," the owner and business manager, has guided the company from a small used car lot to the second largest car dealer in the community. Bob Cole (sales manager), who has been with the company for three years, oversees two salesmen. The firm also employs a mechanic and a bookkeeper.

Aggieland autos sells new and used cars, trucks, and vans. A service center generates a minor portion of profits for the company; the main purpose of the service center is to meet warranty requirements set by the auto manufacturer. The building that houses the service center is currently leased for $1,000 per month. This has increased from $950 per month in 20X8 and 20X7. Accounts receivable are typically sold to a finance company within three weeks of the sale of a vehicle to the customer.

Aggie Al has hired you as a consultant because of your expertise in financial statement analysis. Al would like an assessment of the financial strengths and weaknesses of the business and has provided you with the last three years' balance sheets and income statements.

AGGIELAND AUTO
BALANCE SHEET AT DECEMBER 31,

	20X9	20X8	20X7
Cash	$ 88,531	$ 104,287	$ 117,910
Accounts receivable	117,793	107,009	106,500
Inventory	675,550	564,450	427,526
Total Current Assets	$ 881,874	$ 775,746	$ 651,936
Gross property, plant, and equipment	$ 430,000	$ 420,000	$ 420,000
Accumulated depreciation	(130,000)	(97,000)	(65,000)
Net property, plant, and equipment	300,000	323,000	355,000
Total Assets	$1,181,874	$1,098,746	$1,006,936
Notes payable	$ 192,632	$ 155,000	$ 103,500
Current maturities of long-term debt	30,000	30,000	30,000
Accounts payable	180,000	160,550	157,000
Accrued expenses	45,400	58,804	71,436
Total Current Liabilities	$ 448,032	$ 404,354	$ 361,936
Long-term debt	370,000	400,000	430,000
Total Liabilities	$ 818,032	$ 804,354	$ 791,936
Equity	363,842	294,392	215,000
Total Liabilities and Equity	$1,181,874	$1,098,746	$1,006,936

AGGIELAND AUTOS
INCOME STATEMENT FOR YEARS ENDING DECEMBER 31,

	20X9	*20X8*	*20X7*
Sales	$1,650,000	$1,452,000	$1,304,000
Cost of goods sold	1,344,750	1,161,600	1,043,200
Gross Profit	$ 305,250	$ 290,400	$ 260,800
Depreciation	33,000	32,000	35,000
Lease payments	12,000	11,400	11,400
Other operating expenses	60,500	56,600	53,600
Operating Profit	$ 199,750	$ 190,400	$ 160,800
Interest expense	84,000	58,080	39,120
Earnings Before Tax	$ 115,750	$ 132,320	$ 121,680
Income tax	46,300	52,928	48,672
Net Income	$ 69,450	$ 79,392	$ 73,008

AGGIELAND AUTOS
COMMON SIZE BALANCE SHEET (PERCENT)

	20X9	*20X8*	*20X7*
Cash		9.49	11.71
Accounts receivable		9.74	10.58
Inventory		51.37	42.46
Total Current Assets		70.60	64.74
Gross property, plant, and equipment		38.23	41.71
Accumulated depreciation		(8.83)	(6.46)
Net property, plant, and equipment		29.40	35.26
Total Assets		100.00	100.00
Notes payable		14.11	10.28
Current maturities of long-term debt		2.73	2.98
Accounts payable		14.61	15.59
Accrued expenses		5.35	7.09
Total Current Liabilities		36.80	35.94
Long-term debt		36.41	42.70
Total Liabilities		73.21	78.65
Equity		26.79	21.35
Total Liabilities and Equity		100.00	100.00

AGGIELAND AUTOS
COMMON SIZE INCOME STATEMENT
(PERCENT)

	20X9	20X8	20X7
Sales		100.00	100.00
Cost of goods sold		80.00	80.00
Gross Profit		20.00	20.00
Depreciation		2.20	2.68
Lease payments		0.79	0.87
Other operating expenses		3.90	4.11
Operating Profit		13.11	12.33
Interest expense		4.00	3.00
Earnings Before Tax		9.11	9.33
Income tax		3.65	3.73
Net income		5.47	5.60

AGGIELAND AUTOS
RATIO ANALYSIS

	20X9	20X8	20X7	Industry Average
Current ratio		1.92X	1.80X	1.70X
Quick ratio		0.52X	0.62X	0.40X
Cash-flow liquidity ratio		0.17X	0.54X	0.61X
Average collection period		27 days	29 days	14 days
Inventory turnover		2.06X	2.44X	4.5X
Total asset turnover		1.32X	1.30X	3.70X
Fixed asset turnover		4.50X	3.67X	6.50X
Debt ratio		73.21%	78.65%	68.80%
Debt to equity		2.73X	3.68X	2.20X
Long-term debt to total capitalization		57.60%	66.67%	34.09%
Times interest earned		3.28X	4.11X	2.50X
Fixed charge coverage		2.90X	3.41X	2.40X
Gross profit margin		20.00%	20.00%	15.20%
Operating profit margin		13.11%	12.33%	9.00%
Net profit margin		5.47%	5.60%	3.00%
Cash flow margin		(2.42%)	6.08%	7.12%
Return on equity		26.97%	33.96%	35.58%
Return on investment		7.23%	7.25%	11.10%

AGGIELAND AUTOS
CASH FLOW FROM OPERATING ACTIVITIES

	20X9	*20X8*	*20X7*
Net income		$ 79,392	$73,008
Depreciation		32,000	35,000
Accounts receivable		(509)	(7,900)
Inventories		(136,924)	(27,500)
Accounts payable		3,550	2,400
Accrued expenses		(12,632)	4,300
Cash Flow from Operating Activities		($35,123)	$79,308

5.4 Friendly Frank's Mobile Homes is a retailer of new and used mobile homes. Frank started his company seven years ago and has been very pleased with its rapid growth. There have been a few cash flow problems associated with the growth. The problems got so bad during 20X7 that Frank put $20,300 of additional capital into the company. Frank realizes that some financial problems still exist. Having heard of your expertise in the subject of financial statement analysis, he would like you to provide a financial analysis of the firm.

Required:

(a) Calculate figures for the common size balance sheet and income statement for 20X7.

(b) Calculate the relevant financial ratios for 20X7.

(c) Calculate cash flow from operating activities for 20X7.

(d) Calculate the net trade cycle for 20X7.

(e) Analyze the data and list the strengths and weaknesses of the company. Discuss any recommendations you would make to Frank to improve the company.

FRIENDLY FRANK'S MOBILE HOMES
BALANCE SHEETS

	20X7	20X6	20X5
Assets			
Cash	$ 71,000	$ 67,000	$ 63,800
Accounts receivable (net)	73,000	54,000	32,000
Inventory	927,000	678,000	475,700
Prepaid expenses	25,000	24,000	15,000
Current Assets	$1,096,000	$ 823,000	$586,500
Gross fixed assets	$ 412,000	$ 310,000	$232,500
Accumulated depreciation	(49,000)	(27,000)	(15,000)
Net Fixed Assets	363,000	283,000	217,500
Total Assets	$1,459,000	$1,106,000	$804,000
Liabilities			
Accounts payable	$ 90,000	$ 81,000	$ 42,100
Notes payable	685,000	498,000	321,800
Current maturities of long-term debt	30,000	25,000	15,000
Accrued expenses	121,000	82,000	54,300
Current Liabilities	$ 926,000	$ 686,000	$433,200
Long-term debt	219,000	155,000	131,000
Total Liabilities	$1,145,000	$ 841,000	$564,200
Equity	314,000	265,000	239,800
Total Liabilities and Equity	$1,459,000	$1,106,000	$804,000

FRIENDLY FRANK'S MOBILE HOMES
INCOME STATEMENTS

	20X7	20X6	20X5
Net sales	$3,210,000	$2,515,000	$1,947,000
Cost of goods sold	2,529,000	1,952,000	1,489,000
Gross Profit	681,000	563,000	458,000
Depreciation expense	22,000	12,000	9,000
Lease expense	12,000	10,000	9,600
Other operating expenses	549,000	468,200	390,400
Operating Profit	$ 98,000	$ 72,000	$ 49,000
Interest expense	57,000	36,000	22,000
Earnings Before Tax	41,000	36,000	27,000
Income Tax (.3)	12,300	10,800	8,100
Net Income	$ 28,700	$ 25,200	$ 18,900

FRIENDLY FRANK'S MOBILE HOMES
COMMON SIZE BALANCE SHEET
(AS A PERCENTAGE OF TOTAL ASSETS)

	20X7	20X6	20X5
Assets			
Cash		6.06	7.93
Accounts receivable (net)		4.88	3.98
Inventory		61.30	59.17
Prepaid expenses		2.17	1.87
Current Assets		74.41	72.95
Gross fixed assets		28.03	28.92
Accumulated depreciation		(2.44)	(1.87)
Net Fixed Assets		25.59	27.05
Total Assets		100.00	100.00
Liabilities			
Accounts payable		7.32	5.24
Notes payable		45.03	40.02
Current maturities of long-term debt		2.26	1.87
Accrued liabilities		7.41	6.75
Current Liabilities		62.03	53.88
Long-term debt		14.01	16.29
Total Liabilities		76.04	70.17
Equity		23.96	29.83
Total Liabilities and Equity		100.00	100.00

FRIENDLY FRANK'S MOBILE HOMES
COMMON SIZE INCOME STATEMENTS
(AS A PERCENTAGE OF NET SALES)

	20X7	20X6	20X5
Net Sales		100.00	100.00
Cost of Goods Sold		77.61	76.48
Gross Profit		22.39	23.52
Depreciation expense		.48	.46
Lease expense		.43	.49
Other operating expenses		18.62	20.05
Operating Profit		2.86	2.52
Interest expense		1.43	1.13
Earnings Before Tax		1.43	1.39
Income tax		.43	.42
Net Income		1.00	.97

FIRENDLY FRANK'S MOBILE HOMES
RATIO ANALYSIS

Ratio	20X7	20X6	20X5	Industry Average
Current		1.20X	1.35X	1.20X
Quick		0.21X	0.26X	0.20X
Cash-flow liquidity		(0.09X)	(0.05X)	0.50X
Average collection period		8 days	6 days	4 days
Inventory turnover		2.88X	3.13X	3.30X
Fixed asset turnover		8.89X	8.95X	11.30X
Total asset turnover		2.27X	2.42X	2.50X
Debt ratio		76.04%	70.17%	75.10%
Long-term debt to total capitalization		36.91%	35.33%	29.30%
Debt to equity		3.17X	2.35X	3.50X
Times interest earned		2.00X	2.23X	2.40X
Fixed charge coverage		1.77X	1.85X	1.50X
Gross profit margin		22.39%	23.52%	23.10%
Operating profit margin		2.86%	2.52%	2.00%
Net profit margin		1.00%	0.97%	1.10%
Cash flow margin		(5.15%)	(4.48%)	4.30%
Return on investment		2.28%	2.35%	2.75%
Return on equity		9.51%	7.88%	11.04%

FRIENDLY FRANK'S MOBILE HOMES
CASH FLOW FROM OPERATING ACTIVITIES

	20X7	20X6	20X5
Net Income		$ 25,200	$ 18,900
+ Depreciation expense		12,000	9,000
		37,200	27,900
Change in accounts receivable		(22,000)	(15,000)
Change in inventory		(202,300)	(122,300)
Change in prepaid expenses		(9,000)	1,000
Change in accounts payable		38,900	7,100
Change in accrued expenses		27,700	14,100
Cash Flow from Operating Activities		($129,500)	($ 87,200)

FRIENDLY FRANK'S MOBILE HOMES
NET TRADE CYCLE

	20X7	20X6	20X5
Accounts receivable		7.73 days	5.92 days
Average daily sales			
plus			
Inventory		97.05 days	87.96 days
Average daily sales			
minus			
Accounts payable		(11.59) days	(7.78) days
Average daily sales			
equals			
Cash conversion cycle		93.19 days	86.10 days

5.5 Determine the effect on the current ratio, the quick ratio, net working capital (current assets less current liabilities), and the debt ratio (total liabilities to total assets) of each of the following transactions. Consider each transaction separately and assume that prior to each transaction the current ratio is 2X, the quick ratio is 1X, and the debt ratio is 50%. The company uses an allowance for doubtful accounts. Use I for increase, D for decrease, and N for no change.

	Current Ratio	Quick Ratio	Net Working Capital	Debt Ratio
(a) Borrows $10,000 from bank on short-term note				
(b) Writes off a $5,000 customer account				
(c) Issues $25,000 in new common stock for cash				
(d) Purchases for cash $7,000 of new equipment				
(e) $5,000 inventory is destroyed by fire				
(f) Invests $3,000 in short-term marketable securities				
(g) Issues $10,000 long-term bonds				
(h) Sells equipment with book value of $6,000 for $7,000				
(i) Issues $10,000 stock in exchange for land				
(j) Purchases $3,000 inventory for cash				
(k) Purchases $5,000 inventory on credit				
(l) Pays $2,000 to supplier to reduce account payable				

5.6 Laurel Street, president of Uvalde Manufacturing Inc. is preparing a proposal to present to her board of directors regarding a planned plant expansion that will cost $10 million. At issue is whether the expansion should be financed with debt (a long-term note at First National Bank of Uvalde with an interest rate of 15%) or through the issuance of common stock (200,000 shares at $50 per share). Uvalde Manufacturing currently has a capital structure of:

Debt (12% interest)	40,000,000
Equity	50,000,000

The firm's most recent income statement is presented next:

Sales	$100,000,000
Cost of goods sold	65,000,000
Gross profit	35,000,000
Operating expenses	20,000,000
Operating profit	15,000,000
Interest expense	4,800,000
Earnings before tax	10,200,000
Income tax expense (40%)	4,080,000
Net income	$ 6,120,000
Earnings per share (800,000 shares)	$7.65

Laurel Street is aware that financing the expansion with debt will increase risk but could also benefit shareholders through financial leverage. Estimates are that the plant expansion will increase operating profit by 20%. The tax rate is expected to stay at 40%. Assume a 100% dividend payout ratio.

Required:

(a) Calculate the debt ratio, time interest earned, earnings per share, and the financial leverage index under each alternative, assuming the expected increase in operating profit is realized.

(b) Discuss the factors the board should consider in making a decision.

5.7 C. Alexander, president of Country Creamery, has approached your bank to discuss the firm's credit needs for 20X5. Country Creamery currently has a $120,000 line of credit ($100,000 outstanding at year end) and would like to increase the line by the amount necessary to support its borrowing requirement. Alexander has provided the bank with Country Creamery's balance sheet at 12/31/X4 and income statement for 20X4.

Balance Sheet as 12/31/X4

Cash	$ 30,000	Accounts payable	$270,000
Accounts receivable	250,000	Notes payable	100,000
Inventory	200,000	Accrued wages payable	50,000
Fixed assets (net)	320,000	Long-term debt	220,000
Total Assets	$800,000	Equity	160,000
		Total Liabilities and Equity	$800,000

Income Statement for Year Ending 12/31/X4

Sales		$2,650,000
Cost of goods sold		1,974,250
Gross profit		675,750
Operating expenses		
Depreciation	$ 50,000	
Other	519,750	569,750
Operating profit		106,000
Interest expense		38,400
Earnings before tax		67,600
Income tax (25%)		16,900
Net Income		$ 50,700

Country Creamery has made the following projections for 20X5: sales increase 20%; cost of goods sold percentage 75%; depreciation expense increase by $18,500; other operating expenses increase 15%; interest expense increase 20%; tax rate will remain at 25%. Country Creamery plans to invest $92,500 in new cheese making equipment and will retire $30,000 of long-term debt. Country Creamery has provided a partial pro forma balance sheet at 12/31/X5.

Cash	$ 40,000	Accounts payable	$315,000
Accounts receivable	290,000	Notes payable	?
Inventory	274,000	Accrued wages payable	40,000
Fixed assets (net)	344,000	Long-term debt	190,000
Total Assets	$948,000	Equity	?
		Total Liabilities and Equity	$948,000

Required:

(a) Prepare a pro forma 20X5 income statement.

(b) Prepare a schedule of cash inflows and cash outflows for 19X5. Assuming Country Creamery must maintain a cash balance of $40,000, what is the firm's estimated total borrowing requirement for the line of credit? (To prepare the schedule of cash inflows and outflows you must convert the revenue and expenses on the income statement to a cash basis.)

(c) Complete the pro forma balance sheet.

(d) Determine cash flow from operating activities for 20X5, and prepare a statement of cash flows.

(e) To help assess Country Creamery's credit potential, calculate the company's net trade cycle for 20X4 and 20X5 and analyze the change in the trade cycle.

(f) Compute the following ratios for 20X4 and 20X5: current, quick, average, collection period, inventory turnover, debt, times interest earned.

(g) Analyze the preceding data and make a recommendation regarding the credit request. Explain the reasons for your decisions.

5.8 Dandy Corporation manufactures and markets electronics for the home and office. Distribution is through 5,928 company-owned stores and 3,090 dealer/franchise locations in approximately 100 countries. Dandy has the largest number of retail electronics outlets in the world.

Products offered include telephone equipment; radios; scanners; citizens band radios; security devices; electronic kits and games; clocks and parts; and audio, video, and computer parts.

Dandy plays a major role in the computer marketplace, and the firm has recently begun to emphasize its telephone products. Their newest type of store is the Ding-a-ling Telephone Center, which specializes in business telephone system sales, leasing, and installation. A number of Ding-a-ling Telephone Centers are combined with or adjacent to the Computer Centers. About 36% of the products in the Dandy catalog are manufactured, assembled, or packaged in their plants.

In the 20X7 fiscal year, Dandy made three substantial expenditures of cash. The acquisition of Cosman Industries required cash of $91,500,000. (Cosman is a manufacturer/ wholesaler of consumer electronic stands, racks, desks, and accessories.) Open market purchases of 2,785,000 shares for the treasury totaled $92,535,000. Also, the company used $150 million of cash to finance part of its $355 million purchase and retirement of 10 million shares of common stock. The remainder was financed through long-term debt.

Required:

(a) Calculate the 20X7 ratios and cash flow from operating activities for Dandy Corporation.

(b) Analyze the following:

Short-term liquidity

Capital structure and long-term solvency

Operating efficiency and profitability

(c) Discuss possible reasons for the trend in return on equity.

DANDY CORPORATION
DISTRIBUTION OF SALES

Class of Product	20X7	20X6	20X5	20X4	20X3
Radios, phonographs, TVs	8.6%	8.6%	9.4%	11.6%	12.1%
CB radios, walkie-talkies, scanners, PA systems	5.5	4.9	6.0	6.8	9.3
Audio equipment, tape recorders	17.8	18.2	21.5	25.4	29.5
Electronic parts, batteries, test equipment	13.7	13.2	13.9	14.5	15.8
Toys, antenna, security devices, times, calculators	11.9	12.5	12.0	14.1	12.6
Telephones and intercoms	8.9	8.0	6.5	5.8	5.6
Microcomputers, software, and peripherals	33.6	34.6	30.7	21.8	15.1
	100.0	100.0	100.0	100.0	100.0

RATIO ANALYSIS

Ratio	20X7	20X6	20X5	20X4	20X3	Industry Average*
Current		4.42	4.07	3.48	3.15	2.50
Quick		1.47	1.19	0.96	0.57	0.80
Cash-flow liquidity		1.45	1.09	1.35	0.70	N/A
Average collection period (days)		16.00	15.00	9.00	7.00	11.00
Inventory turnover		1.19	1.23	1.37	1.37	2.30
Fixed asset turnover		9.76	9.03	8.88	8.38	17.50
Total asset turnover		1.59	1.66	1.81	1.95	2.80
Debt		0.29	0.34	0.39	0.60	0.62
Long-term debt to total capitalization		0.14	0.18	0.22	0.48	0.25
Debt to equity		0.41	0.51	0.64	1.51	2.90
Times interest earned		22.30	19.20	14.85	8.69	9.93
Fixed charge coverage		4.91	4.60	4.25	3.37	8.69
Gross profit margin		0.59	0.59	0.58	0.57	0.31
Operating profit margin		0.22	0.21	0.20	0.17	0.08
Net profit margin		0.11	0.11	0.10	0.08	0.04
Cash flow margin		0.05	0.04	0.08	0.08	N/A
Return on investment		17.60	18.04	18.10	15.60	9.20
Return on equity		24.85	27.24	29.68	39.00	11.30
Cash flow from operating activities		$136,061	85,877	134,127	108,330	N/A

*Retail specialty stores for 20X7.

CONSOLIDATED INCOME STATEMENTS
(IN THOUSANDS EXCEPT PER SHARE AMOUNTS)
THREE YEARS ENDED JUNE 30

	20X7	20X6	20X5
Net sales	$2,784,479	$2,513,297	$2,061,212
Costs and expenses			
Cost of products sold	1,184,531	1,008,187	826,842
Selling, general, and administrative	899,885	823,274	690,646
Rent	114,942	106,970	89,732
Depreciation and amortization	46,079	38,679	29,437
Earnings before interest and tax	539,042	536,187	424,555
Interest expense	(27,905)	(24,044)	(22,114)
Interest income	23,542	15,139	20,946
Income from continuing operations before interest and tax	534,679	527,282	423,387
Provision for income taxes	242,808	248,761	199,302
Net income	$ 291,871	$ 278,521	$ 224,085
Income per share	$ 2.75	$ 2.67	$ 2.17

DANDY CORPORATION
CONSOLIDATED BALANCE SHEETS
(IN THOUSANDS)

	6/30/X7	6/30/X6
Assets		
Cash and short-term investments	$ 154,655	$ 279,743
Accounts receivable	122,910	107,530
Inventories	910,530	844,097
Other current assets	40,456	31,928
Total current assets	1,228,551	1,263,298
Property and equipment, net of accumulated depreciation	288,854	257,620
Other assets	135,039	60,990
Total Assets	$1,652,444	$1,581,908
Liabilities and Stockholders' Equity		
Notes payable	$ 51,036	$ 55,737
Accounts payable	88,961	64,640
Accrued expenses	130,386	115,054
Income taxes payable	5,003	50,668
Total current liabilities	275,386	286,099
Long-term debt	347,548	138,420
Deferred income taxes	22,502	17,682
Other noncurrent liabilities	18,312	18,835
Total other liabilities	388,362	174,937
Stockholders' Equity		
Common stock, $1 par	95,645	105,645
Additional paid-in capital	75,413	68,111
Retained earnings	914,297	969,626
Foreign currency translation effects	(21,672)	(16,197)
Treasury stock at cost	(74,987)	(6,213)
Total stockholders' equity	$988,696	$1,120,872
Total liabilities and equity	$1,652,444	$1,581,908

5.9   Writing Skills Problem

R.E.C. Inc.'s staff of accountants finished preparing the financial statements for 2002 and will meet next week with the company's CEO as well as the Director of Investor Relations and representatives from the marketing and art departments to design the current year's annual report.

Required: Write a paragraph in which you present the main idea(s) you think the company should present to shareholders in the annual report.

5.10   Internet Problem

Search the Internet for information on cash flow ratios. Write a short report summarizing the information you find. When you do your search, you will most likely find thousands of matches. Choose several that relate to calculating and using cash flow ratios for analysis purposes.

5.11 Annual Report Problem

The 1998 PETsMART Annual Report can be found at the following Web site: www.prenhall.com/fraser

(a) Using the PETsMART Annual Report, prepare common size balance sheets and common size income statements for all years presented. Calculate key financial ratios.

(b) Using the library, find industry averages to compare to the calculations in (a).

(c) Write a report to the management of PETsMART. Your report should include an evaluation of short-term liquidity, capital structure and long-term solvency, operating performance and efficiency, and market measures. In addition, strengths and weaknesses should be identified, and your opinion of the investment potential and the creditworthiness of the firm should be conveyed to management.

Hint: Use the information from the Annual Report Problems at the end of chapters 1 through 4 to complete this problem.

First Team Sports, Inc. Mini-Case

First Team Sports, Inc. is a worldwide leader in the rapidly growing market for in-line skates and related products. Sales in 55 countries outside of the United States contributed 16% to revenues in 1996, an increase of 158% over 1995 international sales.

The company has developed and patented the Disc Brake System, which enables skaters to stop more easily, more gradually, and with more control. The Gretzky 802 line of roller hockey skates and accessories was introduced in 1996. Wayne Gretzky remained the most visible endorser of the company.

According to the president and CEO, John Egart, 1997 should be another year of growth for the company for the following reasons:

- There is opportunity for continued industry growth as the number of in-line skaters continues to increase.
- Worldwide markets continue to expand.
- There has been strong acceptance of new product lines.
- The average selling price will most likely increase due to the mix of higher-priced products and the fact that many experienced skaters are beginning to upgrade.
- There is ongoing emergence of new niches and sports. The National In-Line Hockey Association predicts that participation in roller hockey will triple that of ice hockey by the year 2000.
- The company has deepened its penetration to specialty stores and the mass-merchant market continues to grow.
- New competition will lead to more product promotion resulting in more visibility and awareness for in-line skating.

REQUIRED:

1. Analyze the firm's financial statements and supplementary information. Your analysis should include the preparation of common size financial statements, key financial ratios with industry comparisons, and an evaluation of short-term liquidity, capital structure and long-term solvency, operating performance and efficiency, and market measures.
2. Using your analysis, offer support for investment in First Team Sports, Inc. common stock.
3. Using your analysis, offer reasons for not investing in First Team Sports, Inc. common stock.

Ratio	Industry Average
Current ratio	1.8X
Quick ratio	0.9X
Cash flow liquidity ratio	0.5X
Average collection period	62 days
Accounts receivable turnover	5.9X
Inventory turnover	3.2X
Net trade cycle	112 days
Fixed asset turnover	9.9X
Total asset turnover	1.8X
Debt ratio	57.3%
Long-term debt to total capitalization	12.9%
Times interest earned	3.6X
Cash flow adequacy	7.2X
Gross profit margin	34.7%
Operating profit margin	7.1%
Net profit margin	3.5%
Cash flow margin	7.5%
Return on investment	12.7%
Return on equity	25.9%
Cash return on assets	14.1%
PE ratio	14.0

CONSOLIDATED BALANCE SHEETS

	February 29, 1996	*February 28, 1995*
ASSETS		
CURRENT ASSETS		
Cash and cash equivalents	$ 2,166,863	$ 601,394
Receivables:		
Trade, less allowance for doubtful accounts 1996—$489,000; 1995—$562,000	16,228,666	16,854,825
Refundable income taxes	155,146	46,146
Inventory	22,813,850	20,838,171
Prepaid expenses	960,079	888,734
Deferred income taxes	827,000	501,000
Total current assets	43,151,604	39,730,270
PROPERTY AND EQUIPMENT, AT COST		
Land	600,000	
Building	4,825,740	
Production equipment	4,069,078	2,558,748
Office furniture and equipment	1,509,120	650,479
Warehouse equipment	315,509	118,898
Leasehold improvements	—	155,738
Vehicles	46,925	62,306
	11,366,372	3,546,169
Less accumulated depreciation and amortization	1,511,689	926,284
	9,854,683	2,619,885
OTHER ASSETS		
License agreements, less accumulated amortization 1996—$2,459,000; 1995—$1,807,000	2,645,268	3,296,830
Other	306,247	216,768
	2,951,515	3,513,598
	$55,957,802	$45,863,753

CONSOLIDATED BALANCE SHEETS

	February 29, 1996	February 28, 1995
Liabilities and Shareholders' Equity		
Current Liabilities		
Note payable to bank	$ 5,268,000	$ 9,064,000
Current maturities of long-term debt	943,060	936,644
Trade accounts payable	9,462,883	9,015,376
Accrued expenses	2,532,676	2,605,160
Total current liabilities	18,206,619	21,621,180
Long-Term Debt		
Less current maturities	6,880,360	3,053,494
Deferred Income Taxes	440,000	339,000
Deferred Revenue	600,000	
Commitments		
Shareholders' Equity		
Common stock, par value $.01 per share; authorized 10,000,000 shares; issued and outstanding 1996—5,721,000 shares; 1995—5,628,184 shares	57,210	56,282
Additional paid-in capital	9,396,802	8,228,843
Retained earnings	20,376,811	12,564,954
Total shareholders' equity	29,830,823	20,850,079
	$55,957,802	$45,863,753

CONSOLIDATED STATEMENTS OF INCOME

Years Ended:	February 29, 1996	February 28, 1995	February 28, 1994
Net Sales			
Net sales	$97,667,448	$85,528,860	$35,534,892
Cost of goods sold	68,499,170	60,128,035	26,049,167
Gross profit	29,168,278	25,400,825	9,485,725
Operating Expenses			
Selling	7,774,248	7,060,747	3,473,717
General and administrative	8,341,008	7,879,569	4,561,333
	16,115,256	14,940,316	8,035,050
Operating income	13,053,022	10,460,509	1,450,675
Other Income (Expense)			
Interest expense	(892,321)	(761,074)	(462,419)
Other, net	(10,844)	(175,678)	12,153
Income before taxes	12,149,857	9,523,757	1,000,409
Federal and state income taxes	4,338,000	3,425,000	365,000
Net income	$ 7,811,857	$ 6,098,757	$ 635,409
Net Income per Common and Common Equivalent Share			
Primary	$1.30	$1.07	$0.12
Fully diluted	1.30	1.03	0.12
Weighted Average Common and Common Equivalent Shares Outstanding			
Primary	6,007,004	5,706,932	5,526,456
Fully diluted	6,010,986	5,912,455	5,526,456

See notes to consolidated financial statements.

CONSOLIDATED STATEMENTS OF CASH FLOWS

Years Ended:	February 29, 1996	February 28, 1995	February 28, 1994
Cash Flows From Operating Activities			
Net income	$7,811,857	$6,098,757	$ 635,409
Adjustments to reconcile net income to net cash provided by (used in) operating activities:			
Depreciation	771,045	569,442	256,171
Amortization of license agreements	651,562	557,173	524,062
Loss on retirement of equipment	13,950	174,256	—
Deferred income taxes	(225,000)	(193,000)	—
Noncash tax expense related to option exercise	667,000	—	—
Changes in assets and liabilities:			
Receivables	626,159	(5,486,640)	(3,945,806)
Inventory	(1,975,679)	(8,504,746)	(4,000,486)
Prepaid expenses	(71,345)	(19,467)	(380,808)
Trade accounts payable	447,507	3,193,893	3,686,703
Accrued expenses	(72,484)	2,083,381	25,338
Income taxes	(109,000)	—	(246,909)
Net cash provided by (used in) operating activities	8,535,572	(1,526,951)	(3,446,326)
Cash Flows from Investing Activities			
Purchases of building and equipment	(7,419,793)	(871,730)	(1,334,436)
Other	(89,479)	(57,321)	(72,346)
Net cash used in investing activities	(7,509,272)	(929,051)	(1,406,782)
Cash Flows from Financing Activities			
Net proceeds on short-term line of credit note	1,079,000	2,490,000	4,329,000
Principal payments on long-term debt	(1,041,718)	(662,335)	(370,885)
Proceeds from exercise of stock options and warrants, net of fractional share payments	501,887	811,744	24,694
Proceeds from long-term borrowings	—	—	999,200
Net cash provided by financing activities	539,169	2,639,409	4,982,009
Increase in cash and cash equivalents	1,565,469	183,407	128,901
Cash and Cash Equivalents			
Beginning	601,394	417,987	289,086
Ending	$2,166,863	$ 601,394	$ 417,987

See notes to consolidated financial statements.

Long-Term Debt

Long-term debt consists of the following:

	February 29, 1996	February 28, 1995
Obligations under license agreements, due in varying installments, with interest imputed at 6.9% to 9.25% though 2001	$2,732,777	$3,441,428
Notes payable to bank under $1 million term credit facility, due in monthly installments of $8,000 to $11,200 to December of 1997, plus interest at the bank's prime rate (8.25% at February 29, 1996), plus 0.25%, collateralized by substantially all corporate assets excluding the land and building	215,643	548,710
Mortgage notes representing line-of-credit debt refinanced as term debt subsequent to year end	4,875,000	
	7,823,420	3,990,138
Less current maturities	943,060	936,644
Long-term portion	$6,880,360	$3,053,494

Aggregate future maturities of long-term debt are as follows:

Years Ending February	
1997	$ 943,060
1998	895,547
1999	963,271
2000	1,068,744
2001	991,243
Thereafter	2,961,555
	$7,823,420

Lease Agreements

Subsequent to year end, the company entered into a lease termination agreement, which released the company from future payments under the aforementioned leases.

Common Stock Data

The range of bid quotations for the Company's Common Stock during fiscal 1995 and fiscal 1996 was as follows:

	High	*Low*
May 31, 1994	$ 6 1/8	$ 4 3/4
August 31, 1994	$ 9 1/2	$ 5 1/2
November 30, 1994	$11	$ 8 7/8
February 28, 1995	$26	$ 9 1/8
May 31, 1995	$25 1/2	$18
August 31, 1995	$31 3/4	$19
November 30, 1995	$21 3/4	$10 3/4
February 29, 1996	$18 3/4	$12 1/4

Dividends

The company has never paid cash dividends and has no present intention to pay cash dividends in the foreseeable future. Under the company's bank line of credit, the company may not pay dividends without the bank's consent.

Cautionary Statements

As provided for under the Private Securities Litigation Reform Act of 1995, the company wishes to caution investors that the following important factors, among others, in some cases have affected and in the future could affect the company's actual results of operation and cause such results to differ materially from those anticipated in forward-looking statements made in this document and elsewhere by or on behalf of the company.

Competition   The company competes with numerous manufacturers of in-line skates domestically and internationally and anticipates future competition from other large and well-established sporting goods manufacturers. Rollerblade, Inc. is the company's primary competitor and has substantially greater resources than the company. The intense competition in the in-line skate market has put pressure on the company's profit margins. The company's ability to remain competitive in the in-line skate market depends on several factors including its ability to: (i) control manufacturing costs and offer products at commercially-acceptable prices; (ii) develop new products and generate market acceptance of such products; and (iii) continue to develop and expand its international business.

Dependence on Key Customers   During the fiscal year ended February 29, 1996, sales to the company's two largest customers accounted for 27% and 12% of the company's revenues for fiscal 1996. Competition from other manufacturers, decreased demand for the company's products or other circumstances may have an adverse impact upon the company's relationship with these customers. Decreased orders from either of these customers could have a material adverse impact on the company's financial results.

Stock Market Volatility   Historically, the company's stock price has been subject to significant volatility. Any deviation in the company's actual results from market expectations has often resulted in significant stock price fluctuations, both positive and negative, and the company has no reason to believe such stock price fluctuations will not continue to occur.

Historical Growth   The company's sales in fiscal 1996 and fiscal 1995 were $97,667,448 and $85,828,860, respectively, representing growth of 14% and 141%, respectively. The company attributes this growth in large part to the growth of the in-line skate market generally. Any decrease in the rate of growth of the in-line skate market can be expected to negatively impact the sales growth of the company. The company has no assurance that its historical sales growth will continue in the future.

L.A. Gear, Inc. Mini-Case

L.A. Gear, Inc. designs, develops, and markets athletic and casual footwear. All of the company's footwear products are manufactured by independent producers located primarily in South Korea, Indonesia, Taiwan, and the People's Republic of China.

The company's products are sold domestically and internationally. Domestic sales account for approximately 80% of total net sales. Advertising and promotion activities are principal elements in the company's marketing strategies. The company maintains an "open stock" inventory, which permits it to ship to retailers on an "at once" basis, but requires the company to maintain large levels of inventory.

The athletic footwear industry is highly competitive. L.A. Gear's primary competitors are Nike, Reebok, and Adidas.

L.A. Gear provides the following table of financial highlights on page 1 of its 1990 annual report:

FINANCIAL HIGHLIGHTS

In thousands, except per share data

For the Years Ended November 30,	1990	1989	1988	1987	1986
Net sales	$902,225	$617,080	$223,713	$70,575	$36,299
Net earnings	31,338	55,059	22,030	4,371	1,745
Net earnings per common share	$1.56	$3.01	$1.29	$.27	$.14
Working capital	180,281	158,879	37,180	20,482	17,028
Total assets	363,955	266,558	128,833	36,794	28,741
Total liabilities	158,078	98,335	87,524	14,675	10,993
Shareholders' equity	205,877	168,223	41,309	22,119	17,748
Net book value per common share	10.61	8.80	2.53	1.37	1.10

As a prospective investor, you are encouraged by the firm's performance. Although earnings have declined in 1990, they are above the levels reported in 1986, 1987, and 1988. Sales are booming, working capital has steadily increased, and the asset base is growing. Net book value per share (assets less liabilities divided by common shares outstanding at year-end) has also risen each year.

The letter to shareholders from the L.A. Gear chairman and president on page 2 of the 1990 annual report summarizes the firm's strengths and weaknesses:

For those of us at L.A. Gear, 1990 will be remembered as a year that brought great accomplishments, and with them, great challenges. Our goals for the period were by no means modest, yet we were able to achieve a great many of them. Sales grew significantly; our international business tripled in volume; and we added key members to our management team to help guide us through the coming decade. In spite of the high points, we definitely experienced growing pains. Changes in business and product mix, price discounting, and national economic pressures all played a part in lowering our profitability. . . .

Like you, we are disappointed with our earnings. As the company's single largest shareholder, I share your profound concerns. It was inevitable that our company would face obstacles, but never have we moved forward with a greater urgency of mission. We are fully committed to taking steps necessary in 1991 to increase long-term profitability.

These include expanding product sourcing, decreasing inventory levels and reducing operating expenses. While the short-term impact of these actions remains uncertain, we believe these measures will strengthen our Company and solidify the base from which to move forward and prosper.

Inspired and confident, you prepare to contact your broker. Before calling, however, you decide to review the L.A. Gear financial statements and develop your own set of financial highlights and company strengths and weaknesses.

REQUIRED:

1. Analyze the firm's financial statements and supplementary information. Your analysis should include the preparation of common size financial statements, key financial ratios with industry comparisons, and an evaluation of short-term solvency, capital structure and long-term solvency, operating performance and efficiency, and market measures.
2. Identify the strengths and weaknesses of the company.
3. Compare your evaluation with the five-year financial highlights and shareholder's letter presented by the company.

Ratio	Industry Average
Current ratio	3.03X
Quick ratio	1.90X
Cash flow liquidity ratio	1.15X
Average collection period	57.2 days
Accounts receivable turnover	6.47X
Inventory turnover	4.30X
Fixed asset turnover	16.77X
Total asset turnover	2.04X
Debt ratio	33.28%
Long-term debt to total capitalization	8.58%
Debt to equity	50.53%
Times interest earned	19.16X
Fixed charge coverage	10.60X
Cash flow adequacy	12.20X
Gross profit margin	39.40%
Operating profit margin	14.87%
Net profit margin	6.74%
Cash flow margin	8.76%
Return on investment	13.06%
Return on equity	19.21%
PE ratio	16.83%
Cash return on assets	11.00
Net trade cycle	83 days

L.A. GEAR, INC. AND SUBSIDIARIES
CONSOLIDATED STATEMENTS OF EARNINGS

	Year Ended November 30,		
	1990	1989	1988
Net sales	$902,225,000	$617,080,000	$223,713,000
Cost of sales	591,740,000	358,482,000	129,103,000
Gross profit	310,485,000	258,598,000	94,610,000
Selling, general and administrative expenses	240,596,000	154,449,000	53,168,000
Interest expense, net	18,515,000	12,304,000	4,102,000
Earnings before income taxes	51,374,000	91,845,000	37,340,000
Income tax expense	20,036,000	36,786,000	15,310,000
Net Earnings	$ 31,338,000	$ 55,059,000	$ 22,030,000
Earnings per common share	$ 1.56	$ 3.01	$ 1.29
Weighted average shares outstanding	20,041,000	18,308,000	17,110,000

L.A. GEAR, INC. AND SUBSIDIARIES
CONSOLIDATED BALANCE SHEETS

	November 30,	
	1990	*1989*
Assets		
Current assets:		
Cash	$ 3,291,000	$ 353,000
Accounts receivable, net of allowance for doubtful accounts and merchandise returns	156,391,000	100,290,000
Inventory	160,668,000	139,516,000
Prepaid expenses and other current assets	16,912,000	12,466,000
Deferred tax charges	1,097,000	4,589,000
Total current assets	338,359,000	257,214,000
Property and equipment, at cost, net of accumulated depreciation and amortization of $4,975,000 and $1,809,000 in 1990 and 1989, respectively	23,624,000	8,079,000
Other assets	1,972,000	1,265,000
	$363,955,000	$266,558,000
Liabilities and Shareholders' Equity		
Current liabilities:		
Line of credit	$ 94,000,000	$ 37,400,000
Accounts payable	22,056,000	25,619,000
Accrued expenses and other current liabilities	39,672,000	17,627,000
Accrued compensation	2,350,000	16,906,000
Income taxes payable	—	783,000
Total current liabilities	158,078,000	98,335,000
Shareholders' equity:		
Common stock, no par value. Authorized 80,000,000 shares; issued and outstanding 19,395,170 shares at November 30, 1990 and 19,108,753 shares at November 30, 1989	91,179,000	84,863,000
Preferred stock, no stated value. Authorized 3,000,000 shares; no shares issued	—	—
Retained earnings	114,698,000	83,360,000
Total shareholders' equity	205,877,000	168,223,000
Commitments and contingencies		
	$363,955,000	$266,558,000

L.A. GEAR, INC. AND SUBSIDIARIES
CONSOLIDATED STATEMENTS OF CASH FLOWS

	Year Ended November 30,		
	1990	*1989*	*1988*
Cash flows from operating activities:			
Net earnings	$31,338,000	$55,059,000	$22,030,000
Adjustments to reconcile net cash used in operating activities:			
Depreciation and amortization	3,394,000	1,199,000	446,000
Issuance of stock to employee as compensation	—	558,000	—
(Increase) decrease in:			
Accounts receivable	(56,101,000)	(50,764,000)	(34,378,000)
Inventory	(21,152,000)	(72,960,000)	(50,743,000)
Prepaids and other current assets	(4,446,000)	(9,083,000)	(2,432,000)
Deferred taxes	3,492,000	(3,555,000)	(1,020,000)
Increase (decrease) in:			
Accounts payable	(3,563,000)	17,871,000	7,197,000
Accrued expenses, accrued compensation and other current liabilities	7,489,000	16,204,000	8,319,000
Income taxes payable	(783,000)	(3,434,000)	3,894,000
Net cash used in operating activities	(40,332,000)	(48,905,000)	(46,687,000)
Cash flows from investing activities:			
Capital expenditures	(18,939,000)	(6,168,000)	(2,546,000)
Other assets	(707,000)	(246,000)	(406,000)
Net cash used in investing activities	(19,646,000)	(6,414,000)	(2,952,000)
Cash flows from financing activities:			
Exercise of stock options and warrants	908,000	1,309,000	495,000
Tax benefit arising from the exercise of incentive stock options	5,408,000	1,372,000	—
Proceeds from issuance of common stock	—	68,616,000	—
Borrowings under credit agreements	56,600,000	(19,830,000)	50,104,000
Net cash provided by financing activities	62,916,000	51,467,000	50,599,000
Net cash flow	2,938,000	(3,852,000)	960,000
Cash at beginning of year	353,000	4,205,000	3,245,000
Cash at end of year	$ 3,291,000	$ 353,000	$ 4,205,000

COMMITMENTS AND CONTINGENCIES

The Company occupies certain facilities, including the home office and distribution centers, and uses certain equipment under operating leases. Rental expense for 1990, 1989 and 1988 amounted to approximately $10,603,000, $3,296,000, and $1,752,000, respectively.

COMMON STOCK, DIVIDEND POLICY

The company's stock is traded on the New York Stock Exchange. To date, the company has not paid dividends on its Common Stock. Under the terms of the bank agreement, as amended, the Company is prohibited from declaring dividends on its Common Stock. At January 31, 1991, there were 3,294 shareholders of record.

	February 28,		May 31,		August 31,		November 30,	
	1990	1989	1990	1989	1990	1989	1990	1989
Price range of common stock:								
High	$35.38	$17.56	$50.13	$26.32	$31.25	$33.75	$16.88	$45.75
Low	$23.38	$10.00	$26.88	$15.07	$12.88	$25.75	$10.63	$29.94

A Guide to Earnings Quality

The assessment of earnings quality is a critical element in the analysis of financial statements. The earnings statement encompasses a number of areas that provide management with opportunities for influencing the outcome of reported earnings in ways that may not best represent economic reality or the future operating potential of a firm. These include:

- Accounting choices, estimates, and judgments.
- Changes in accounting methods and assumptions.
- Discretionary expenditures.
- Nonrecurring transactions.
- Nonoperating gains and losses.
- Revenue and expense recognitions that do not match cash flow.

In evaluating a business firm, it is essential that the financial statement analyst consider the *qualitative* as well as the *quantitative* components of earnings for an accounting period. The higher the quality of financial reporting, the more useful is the information for business decision making. The analyst should develop an earnings figure that is reflective of the future ongoing potential of the firm. This process requires a consideration of qualitative factors and necessitates, in some cases, an actual adjustment of the reported earnings figure.

The purpose of this appendix is to provide the financial statement user with a step-by-step guide that links the items on an earnings statement with the key areas in the financial statement data that affect earnings quality. (See Exhibit A.1.)

The list does not, by any means, include all of the items that affect earnings quality. Rather, the examples illustrate some of the qualitative issues that are most commonly encountered in financial statement data. Another purpose of the appendix is to provide the financial statement user with an approach to use in analyzing and interpreting the qualitative factors. The checklist represents an attempt to provide a framework for the analysis of earnings quality rather than a complete list of its components.

Although the examples in this book deal primarily with the financial reporting of wholesale, retail, and manufacturing firms, the concepts and techniques presented can also apply to other types of industries. For instance, there is a discussion in this appendix of the provision for doubtful accounts as it impacts earnings quality. The same principles, on a larger scale, would apply to the provision for loan loss reserves for financial institutions. Almost all of the items on the checklist—other than those directly related to cost of goods sold—would apply to most types of business firms including service-oriented companies.

Using the Checklist

Each item on the checklist in Exhibit A.1 will be discussed and illustrated with examples from the 2002 ABC Corporation Annual Report. ABC Corporation, a manufac-

---

EXHIBIT A.1 A Checklist for Earnings Quality

I. Sales
  1. Allowance for doubtful accounts
  2. Price vs. volume changes
  3. Real vs. nominal growth

II. Cost of Goods Sold
  4. Cost-flow assumption for inventory
  5. Base LIFO layer reductions
  6. Loss recognitions on write downs of inventory (also see item 13)

III. Operating Expenses
  7. Discretionary expenses
     Research and development
     Repair and maintenance
     Advertising and marketing
  8. Depreciation (depletion, amortization)
     Methods
     Estimates
  9. Pension accounting—interest rate assumptions

IV. Nonoperating Revenue and Expense
  10. Gains (losses) from sales of assets
  11. Interest income
  12. Equity income
  13. Loss recognitions on write downs of assets (also see item 6)
  14. Accounting changes
  15. Extraordinary items

V. Other Issues
  16. Material changes in number of shares outstanding
  17. Acquisitions and dispositions
  18. Reserves

---

turer of steel products, has diversified its operations through the acquisition of an oil and gas company.

I. SALES

1. Allowance for doubtful accounts

Most companies sell products on credit. Revenue is recognized on the income statement when the sales are made, and accounts receivable are carried on the balance sheet until the cash is collected. Because some customer accounts are never satisfied, the balance sheet includes an allowance for doubtful accounts. A discussion of sales, accounts receivable, and the allowance for doubtful accounts is provided in chapters 2 and 3.

The allowance account, which is deducted from the balance sheet accounts receivable account, should reflect the volume of credit sales, the firm's past experience with customers, the customer base, the firm's credit policies, the firm's collection practices, economic conditions, and changes in any of these factors. There should be a consistent relationship, all other things being equal, between the rate of change in sales, accounts receivable, and the allowance for doubtful accounts. If the amounts are changing at different rates or in different directions—for example, if sales and accounts receivable are increasing, but the allowance account is decreasing or is increasing at a much smaller rate—the analyst should be alert to the potential for manipulation through the allowance account. Of course, there could also be a plausible reason for such a change.

The relevant items needed to relate sales growth with accounts receivable and the allowance for doubtful accounts are found on the income statement (sales) and balance sheet (accounts receivable and allowance for doubtful accounts.)[1]

The following is an excerpt from the 2002 ABC Corporation Consolidated Statement of Income and Consolidated Balance Sheet.

(In millions)	2002	2001	Percentage Change
Sales	$19,283	$19,104	00.9
Receivables	1,570	1,650	(04.8)
Less allowance for doubtful accounts	(12)	(39)	(62.2)
Receivables (net)	1,558	1,611	

Between 2002 and 2001, sales for ABC increased slightly (by .9%), and accounts receivable decreased slightly (by 4.8%). During the same period, the allowance for doubtful accounts decreased considerably (by 69.2%). Because the allowance account involves estimations by management of accounts that will not be collected during the next accounting period, the analyst would want to determine whether the firm is justified in reducing the account by such a large percentage relative to gross receivables and sales because this reduction has a positive impact on pretax earnings (of $27 million). If the account is manipulated to increase earnings, then the quality of reported earnings is lessened. On the other hand, there may be a reasonable explanation for the large reduction—such as a change in customer base or economic conditions.

2. Price vs. volume changes

If a company's sales are increasing (or decreasing), it is important to determine whether the change is a result of price, volume, or a combination of both factors. Are sales growing because the firm is increasing prices or because more units or being sold, or both? It would seem that, in general, higher quality earnings would be the product of both volume and price increases (during inflation). The firm would want to sell more units and keep prices increasing at least in line with the growth rate of general inflation.

Information regarding the reasons for sales growth (or decline) is one of the areas covered in a firm's management discussion and analysis section of the annual or 10-K report, discussed in chapter 1. To relate sales growth to reasons for sales growth, use sales data from the income statement and the volume/price discussion from the management discussion and analysis section.

---

[1] The underlying liquidity of accounts receivable is also extremely important in assessing earnings quality. This topic is covered in chapters 4 and 5.

From the ABC Consolidated Statement of Income:

	2002	2001	2000
Sales (millions)	$19,283	$19,104	$17,539

The following is an excerpt from the ABC Management Discussion and Analysis of Financial Condition and Results of Operations:

> Sales increased to $19.3 billion in 2002 from $19.1 billion in 2001 and $17.5 billion in 2000. The increase from 2001 reflects higher steel shipment levels, increased refined hydrocarbon liftings, partially offset by lower selling prices for steel, crude oil, natural gas and refined products. The increase in sales in 2001 from 2000 reflected higher steel shipment levels and net selling prices, increased volumes of liquid hydrocarbon liftings from the South Brazos field and increased shipments and prices for most chemical products.

A determination can be made from this information that the slight sales growth in 2002 was the result of volume increases, offset by a price decline; in 2001, the sales growth resulted from both price and volume increases.

3. Real vs. nominal growth

A related issue is whether sales are growing in "real" (inflation-adjusted) as well as "nominal" (as reported) terms. Disclosures regarding inflation accounting, no longer required, are discussed in chapter 1. The change in sales in nominal terms can be readily calculated from the figures reported on the income statement. An adjustment of the reported sales figure with the Consumer Price Index (CPI) (or some other measure of general inflation) will enable the analyst to make a comparison of the changes in real and nominal terms. To make the calculation to compare real with nominal sales, begin with the sales figures reported in the income statement, and adjust years prior to the current year with the CPI or some other price index.

Sales (millions)	2002	2001	Percentage Change
As reported (nominal)	$19,283	$19,104	0.937
Adjusted (real)	19,283	19,786	(2.542)
Using average CPI (1967 = 100)			
(2002 CPI/2001 CPI) × 2001 Sales = Adjusted sales			
(322.2/311.1) × $19,104 = $19,786			

Sales, when adjusted for general inflation, actually decreased in 2002. An alternative approach would be to compare the growth in nominal sales—an increase of .9%—with the change in the CPI—an increase from 311.1 to 322.2 of 3.6%. Either way, it is apparent that ABC sales growth did not keep pace with the rate of general inflation. The point made in the previous section is that prices actually decreased for many product lines.

II. COST OF GOODS SOLD

4. Cost-flow assumption for inventory

During periods of inflation, the LIFO cost-flow assumption for inventory accounting, described in chapter 2, produces lower earnings than FIFO or average cost. But

LIFO results in the matching of current costs with current revenues and therefore produces higher quality earnings than either FIFO or average cost unless the firm operates in an industry with volatile or falling prices. The inventory accounting system used by the company is described in the note to the financial statement that details accounting policies or the note discussing inventory. The following excerpt is from Note 1, Summary of Principal Accounting Policies from the ABC Corporation annual report:

> Inventories—The cost of inventories is determined primarily under the last-in, first-out (LIFO) method. . . .

The quality of ABC's earnings is enhanced by the LIFO choice. Cash flow is also helped because LIFO ordinarily produces lower taxable earnings and thus lower tax payments. The LIFO system, however, generally results in undervalued inventory on the balance sheet during inflation because the ending inventory balance is determined by the older, lowest cost items. Companies using LIFO disclose the current value of the inventory or the amount by which inventory is undervalued in a note to the financial statements, such as the following for ABC Corporation:

> Current acquisition costs are estimated to exceed inventory values at December 31 by approximately $1.05 billion in 2002 and $1.18 billion in 2001.

5. Base LIFO layer reductions

If a company using the LIFO method reduces inventory during the accounting period and liquidates the base LIFO layer, as discussed in chapter 2, there will be an increase in earnings as a result. When this situation occurs, LIFO has the opposite earnings effect from what is described in item 4. When LIFO liquidations occur, earnings are enhanced. A base LIFO layer reduction reduces the quality of earnings in the sense that there is an improvement in operating profit from what would generally be considered a negative occurrence: inventory reductions. The base LIFO layer reduction and its effect on earnings is quantified in a note to the financial statements.

> Cost of sales has been reduced and operating income increased by $143 million in 2002, $180 million in 2001, and $402 million in 2000 as a result of liquidations of LIFO inventories.

In considering the future, ongoing potential of the company, it would be appropriate to exclude from earnings the effect of LIFO liquidations because a firm would not want to continue benefiting from inventory shrinkages.

6. Loss recognitions on write-downs of inventories

The principle of conservatism in accounting requires that firms carry inventory in the accounting records at the lower of cost (as determined by the cost flow assumption such as LIFO, FIFO, average cost) or market. If the value of inventory falls below its original cost, the inventory is written down to market value. Market generally is determined by the cost to replace or reproduce the inventory but should not exceed the net realizable amount (selling price less completion and disposal costs) the company could generate from selling the item. The amount of the write-down will affect comparability, thus quality, of the profit margins from period to period.

Firms also write down the carrying cost of property, plant, and equipment when there is a permanent impairment in value, and certain investments in marketable equity securities (according to the provisions of FASB 115 discussed in chapter 2) are carried at market value.

When the write-down of inventory is included in cost of goods sold, the gross profit margin is affected in the year of the write-down. The following is an example from one of ABC's competitors, XYZ Corporation:

> Gross profit as a percent of sales and operating revenues was 54.5% in fiscal 2002 compared to 57.3% in 2001. During the past two years, the percentage has been adversely impacted by the unsettled conditions in the foreign steel market which created heavy discounting. During the third quarter of fiscal 2002, the company determined that certain products needed to be permanently reduced in price because of changes in pricing structure within the industry and sharp declines in material prices. The cost of goods sold included inventory write-downs of approximately $33 million in recognition of these changes.

In comparing the gross profit margin between periods, the analyst should be aware of the impact on the margin that occurs from such write-downs.

III. OPERATING EXPENSES

7. Discretionary expenses

A company can increase earnings by reducing variable operating expenses in a number of areas such as the repair and maintenance of capital assets, research and development, and advertising and marketing. If such discretionary expenses are reduced primarily to benefit the current year's reported earnings, the long-run impact on the firm's operating profit may be detrimental and thus the quality lowered. The analyst should review the trends of these discretionary expenses and compare them with the firm's volume of activity and level of capital investment. Amounts of discretionary expenditures are disclosed in notes, such as the following for ABC Corporation:

(In millions)	2002	2001	2000
Repairs and maintenance	$1,158	$1,176	$1,281
Research and development	54	61	84

ABC reduced expenditures both for the maintenance and repair of plant and equipment and for research and development. These reductions occurred during a period of growing sales and increased investments in capital assets:

(In millions)	2002	2001	2000
Sales	$19,283	$19,104	$17,539
Property, plant, equipment	23,735	23,670	21,807

The analyst would want to determine the reasons for such reductions in discretionary expenses and assess the long-run effect of these policies on profitability.

8. Depreciation

The amount of annual depreciation expense recognized for an accounting period, as discussed in chapter 1, depends upon the choice of depreciation method and estimates regarding the useful life and salvage value of the asset being depreciated. Most companies use the straight-line method rather than an accelerated method for reporting purposes because it produces a smoother earnings stream and higher earnings in the early years of the depreciation period. The straight-line method, however, is lower in quality in most cases because it does not reflect the economic reality of product usefulness in that most machinery and equipment do not wear evenly over the depreciation period. Depreciation policy is explained in notes to the financial statements:

> Property, plant and equipment. Depreciation is generally computed on the straight-line method, based upon the estimated lives of assets.

Similarly, the analyst would want to review depletion for firms operating in the extractive industries and amortization for intangible assets. Depletion of the cost of mineral properties, other than oil and gas, is based on rates that are expected to amortize the cost over the estimated tonnage of materials to be removed. ABC reports the following:

> Depreciation and depletion of oil and gas producing properties are computed at rates applied to the units of production on the basis of proved oil and gas reserves as determined by the corporation geologists and engineers[2] . . . The purchase price exceeded the value of the net tangible assets acquired by $60 million. This intangible asset is being amortized on a straight line basis over 15 years.

The intangible asset being amortized by ABC is goodwill, discussed in chapter 2, which arises in business combinations when the acquiring company pays more than the fair market value for the net tangible assets acquired. Goodwill is carried on the balance sheet as a noncurrent asset. Other intangible assets that are amortized include patents, trademarks, copyrights, and leasehold improvements.

As high-technology companies replace traditional companies such as those in manufacturing, the analysis of goodwill may change. Many analysts have begun to discount or ignore amortization charges of goodwill in newer, technological companies. The reasoning is that the most valuable assets of these new companies are intangible assets such as the employees and the brand names created by the company. These assets do not appear on the balance sheet, yet they are the reason that large premiums are paid by the acquiring company. FASB has even suggested that in the future companies may include two net income figures in their annual reports—the traditional one and one that ignores goodwill.[3]

---

[2] It is also important to note that ABC uses the successful efforts method of accounting for oil and gas exploration and development. This means that the firm carries as a balance sheet asset only the cost of successful exploration and development. Costs of unsuccessful efforts are expensed in the year they occur. The other acceptable method, but one that is lower in quality, is the full cost method, by which companies capitalize—carry on the balance sheet—all costs, whether or not they resulted in productive operations.

[3] Anne Tergesen, "Which Number Is the Real McCoy?" *Business Week,* October 11, 1999.

9. Pension accounting—interest rate assumptions

Although a detailed explanation of pension accounting is beyond the scope of this book, it is important to be aware of some basic pension accounting principles as they impact earnings quality. The reader is referred to the discussion of disclosure requirements for postretirement benefits other than pensions in chapter 2.

Pension accounting is based on expectations regarding the benefits that will be paid when employees retire and on the interest that pension assets will earn over time. The provisions for pension accounting are specified in Statement of Financial Accounting Standards No. 87, "Employers' Accounting for Pensions."[4]

If a company changes, based on actuarial estimates, the interest rate assumptions used in pension accounting, this change affects the amount of annual pension expense and the present value of the pension benefits. If the assumed rate of interest is increased, pension cost is reduced and earnings increased. For example, if you need $5,000 in 20 years, the amount you would have to invest today would be different if your investment earned 6% or 8%. At 6% you would have to invest $1,560 to accumulate to $5,000 at annual compound interest in 20 years; if the interest rate were increased to 8%, you would only have to contribute $1,075.[5] Also, the present value of the benefits to be paid in the future is affected by increasing the interest rate. The present value of $5,000 to be paid in 20 years is $1,560 at a 6% discount rate and $1,075 at an 8% rate.

To summarize the effects of a change in the pension interest rate assumption, if the assumed interest rate is lowered, the annual pension cost will increase and the present value of the benefits will also increase; if the assumed interest rate is increased, pension cost and the present value of the benefits are reduced.

FASB Statement No. 87 requires companies with a defined benefit pension plan—a plan that states the benefits to be received by employees after retirement or the method of determining such benefits—to disclose the following:

1. A description of the plan, including employee groups covered, type of benefit formula, funding policy, and types of assets held.
2. The amount of pension expense showing separately the service cost component, the interest cost component, the actual return on assets for the period, and the net total of other components.[6]
3. A schedule reconciling the funded status of the plan with amounts reported in the company's balance sheet.
4. The weighted average discount rate and rate of compensation increase used to measure the projected benefit obligation and the weighted average expected long-term rate of return on plan assets.
5. The amounts and types of securities included in plan assets.

---

[4] For a detailed discussion of FASB Statement 87, see L. Revsine, "Understanding Financial Accounting Standard 87," *Financial Analysts Journal,* January-February 1989.

[5] $5,000 (.312 = $1,560; $5,000 × .215 = $1,075) (factors for present value of single sum for 20 periods, 6% and 8%).

[6] The service cost represents the increase during the year in the discounted present value of payable benefits, resulting from employees' working an additional year; interest cost arises from the passage of time and increases interest expense; return on plan assets reduces pension expense; other components include net amortization and deferrals and are related to the choice of discount and interest rates. The same rate must be used to compute service cost and interest cost, but a different rate can be used to compute the expected rate of return on pension plan assets.

A *liability* is recognized if the pension expense recognized to date is greater than the amount funded; an *asset* is reported if the pension expense to date is less than the amount funded. An *additional liability* is recognized if the accumulated benefit obligation is greater than the fair market value of plan assets less the balance in the accrued pension liability account or plus the balance in the deferred pension asset account.

A portion of the footnote disclosure relating to employees' benefit plans from the ABC Annual Report is provided:

> The company and certain of its subsidiaries have defined benefit plans for regular full-time employees. Cost for the company's defined benefit plans includes the following components:

(In millions)	2002	2001	2000
Service cost (benefits earned during period)	$11.9	$ 9.7	$ 7.7
Interest cost on projected benefit obligation	10.0	8.9	7.2
Investment loss (gain) on plan assets	(9.9)	(19.7)	6.1
Net amortization and deferral	(.2)	10.9	(14.1)
Net pension cost	$11.8	$ 9.8	$ 6.9

> The plans' assets are diversified in stocks, bonds, real estate, short-term, and other investments. The plans' funded status was as follows:

	2002	2001
Plan assets at market value	$117.2	107.7
Projected benefit obligation	(133.0)	(119.1)
Total projected obligation (in excess of) plan assets	(15.8)	(11.3)
Unamortized transitional net assets	(2.3)	(2.5)
Unamortized net	6.6	12.0
Unrecognized prior service cost	.5	.5
Net pension liability	(11.0)	(1.2)

> The discount rate and rate of future compensation increases used in determining the projected benefit obligation and costs were 9% and 6%, respectively, and the expected long-term rate of return on plan assets was 9% at December 31, 2002, 2001, and 2000.

For ABC, the net pension cost is calculated as service cost, plus interest cost, plus or minus the investment gain or loss, less the net amortization and deferral. The net pension liability is the amount by which the projected benefit obligation exceeds the plan assets at fair value, plus the unamortized transitional net assets, less the unamortized net gain and the unrecognized prior service cost.

FASB Statement No. 87 has substantially improved the accounting methods and disclosure requirements for pension accounting, but pension accounting remains an important qualitative issue. A change in interest rate assumptions is important because it represents an accounting estimate that affects annual pension cost and the relationship between pension assets and the present value of pension benefits. When a firm changes its interest rate assumptions, there is an impact on pension expense as well as the status of the plan. Although FASB Statement No. 87 included explicit criteria for selecting interest rates, it still allows some management discretion.[7] ABC Corporation had no changes in interest rate assumptions over the three year period.

IV. NONOPERATING REVENUE AND EXPENSE

10. Gains (losses) from sales of assets

As discussed in chapter 1, when a company sells a capital asset, such as property or equipment, the gain or loss is included in net income for the period. The sale of a major asset is sometimes made to increase earnings and/or to generate needed cash during a period when the firm is performing poorly. Such transactions are not part of the normal operations of the firm and should be excluded from net income when considering the future operating potential of the company.

Gains and losses on asset sales are disclosed in financial statement notes, such as the following from ABC Corporation:

(In millions)	*2002*	*2001*
Other income includes:		
Gain on disposal of assets	$55	$265

The total income before taxes, extraordinary gains, and accounting changes for ABC was $797 million in 2002 and $980 million in 2001. The nonoperating gains from sales of assets thus accounted for 7% and 27% of pretax ordinary income.

11. Interest income

Interest income is also nonoperating in nature except for certain types of firms such as financial institutions. Interest income results primarily from short-term temporary investments in marketable securities to earn a return on cash not immediately needed in the business. These security investments were explained in chapter 2. In the assessment of earnings quality, the analyst should be alert to the materiality and variability in the amount of interest income because it is not part of operating income. Interest income is disclosed on the face of the income statement or in notes to the financial statements. An excerpt from ABC's notes:

(In millions)	*2002*	*2001*
Interest income	$59	$91

Using the pretax, ordinary income figures from item 10 for ABC, it can be determined that interest income contributed 7% in 2002 and 9% in 2001 to earnings before taxes, extraordinary items, and accounting changes. The two nonoperating sources combined—asset sales and interest income—accounted for 14% in 2002 and 36% in 2001. Because these income items are material to the financial statements as a whole and fluctuate significantly between periods, they are important in analyzing earnings quality. A large and varying proportion of ABC income is the result of nonoperating sources.

---

[7] An interesting article on the effect of interest rate assumptions is Susan Pulliam, "Hopeful Assumptions Let Firms Minimize Pension Contributions," *The Wall Street Journal,* September 2, 1993.

12. Equity income

Use of the equity method to account for investments in unconsolidated subsidiaries, discussed and illustrated in chapter 3, permits the investor to recognize as investment income the investor's percentage ownership share of the investee's reported income rather than recognizing income only to the extent of cash dividends actually received. The net effect is that the investor, in most cases, records more income than is received in cash. Detail on such investments is provided in the notes, such as the following for ABC:

(In millions)	2002	2001
Net income (loss) from ABC's share in equity method entities	$63	$35
Dividends received from equity method entities	$31	$30

In each year, ABC reported more earnings on the earnings statement than was received in dividends. Cash flow from operations, discussed in chapter 4, excludes the amount by which investment income recognized exceeds cash received: $32 million in 2002 and $5 million in 2001 for ABC. It would also be appropriate to eliminate this noncash portion of earnings for comparative purposes.

13. Loss recognition on write-downs of assets

As was discussed in item 6, the write-down of asset values, following the principle of carrying assets at the lower of cost or market value, affects the comparability and thus the quality of financial data. (Also note the provisions of FASB Statement No. 115, discussed in chapter 2, for *unrealized gains and losses* on investments in debt and equity securities.) The reasons for the write-downs would also be important in assessing the quality of the financial data. Information on asset write-downs is presented in notes to the financial statements.

ABC reported the following:

The following unusual items resulted in favorable (unfavorable) effects on income:

(In millions)	2002	2001
Provisions for estimated shutdown costs	$15	$ 0
Adjustment to provision for occupational disease claims	$24	$ 0
Revaluation of assets	$ 0	($47)
	$39	($47)

ABC received a positive earnings boost in 2002 from the upward revaluation of provisions made in earlier periods to recognize the shutdown of plant facilities and the provision for potential black lung disease claims. A loss was recorded in 2001 from the write-down of assets. These amounts should be reviewed and excluded from earnings to make comparisons with other years when assessing future operating potential.

14. Accounting changes

Accounting changes are explained and quantified in financial statement notes. ABC reported the following change in accounting principles:

In 2002, the Corporation adopted a change in accounting for petroleum revenue tax payable to the United Kingdom. The newly adopted method of accounting for this income tax is based on the estimated effective tax rate over the life of the Brazos field. This method recognizes certain unique tax allowances proportionally over the income from the field rather than when realized for tax return purposes. Management considers the new method to be a preferred accounting practice under the circumstances, resulting in a better matching of expense with revenue and a better measurement of the deferred tax liability. The cumulative effect of the change on prior years is $45 million, net of United States income tax. The effect on the income for the year 2002 is as follows:

(In millions except per share data)	*2002*
Total income before extraordinary gain	$15
Per share—basic	.14
—diluted	.12
Net income	$60
Per share—basic	.54
—diluted	.47

The cumulative effect of the change, net of tax—$45 million—is shown separately on the income statement and should be eliminated in making comparisons with future and prior years' earnings because prior years' earnings were computed using a different accounting method.

15. Extraordinary items

Extraordinary items are gains and losses that are both unusual and infrequent in nature. They are shown separately, net of tax, on the income statement. Because very few transactions meet the definition of extraordinary, it is rare to see such items on an earnings statement. Most of those that do appear are the result of early debt extinguishments.

In-substance defeasance, a common type of early debt extinguishment, is of particular importance in the analysis of earnings quality because of the gain that is included in income and also because debt, which is still outstanding, is removed from the books. FASB Statement No. 76, "Extinguishment of Debt," permits firms to purchase at a discount[8] riskless securities (U.S. government securities or securities backed by the U.S. government), place the securities in an irrevocable trust designated to meet the interest and principal payments on the outstanding debt, recognize a gain for the difference between the principal amount of the debt and the price paid for the riskless securities in the open market, and eliminate the original liability.

For example, assume that on January 1, 2001, Topco Corporation issues $100,000 principal amount of 10-year, 8% bonds, with interest payable semiannually on June 30 and December 31. On January 1, 2005, Topco executes an in-substance defeasance by purchasing at a discount for $75,000 (because market rates of interest have risen and

---

[8] During a period when market rates of interest have risen and bond prices have fallen.

bond prices have fallen) U.S. government securities that match in maturity, interest, and principal the Topco bonds. Topco places the U.S. government securities in an irrevocable trust to meet the interest payment on the bonds and the principal amount at maturity. Topco recognizes an extraordinary gain of $25,000 (net of tax) and eliminates the $100,000 as a liability, even though it is still a legal liability.

Defeasance transactions are explained in notes to the financial statements, such as the following for ABC in 2002:

> In 2002 the Corporation extinguished $399 million principal amount of debt, resulting in a net extraordinary gain of $51 million, after income tax of $43 million. The debt securities extinguished included all outstanding 4–5/8% Sinking Fund Debentures due 2009—$168 million, all outstanding 7–3/4% Sinking Fund Debentures due 2012—$34 million and $59 million principal amount of Environmental Improvement Bonds. All of these securities, which were still outstanding at December 31, 2002, were extinguished by placing securities into separate irrevocable trusts that will make the scheduled principal and interest payments. Other extinguishments of debt in 2002 included the repurchase of $85 million principal amount of Environmental Improvement Bonds and $53 million principal amount of various other debt securities.
>
> In 2001 the Corporation repurchased debt securities with a total principal amount of $242 million, resulting in an extraordinary gain of $79 million, net of income tax of $6 million.

ABC eliminated $339 million debt from the balance sheet and recorded a gain in the earnings statement of $51 million in 2002; the firm eliminated $242 million debt and posted a $79 million gain in 2001. In the process ABC has tied up enormous sums of liquid assets that will be unavailable for other purposes for many years. It is also possible that the trustee holding the securities could default and the original liability would be reinstated on the balance sheet.[9] The gain recognized from an in-substance defeasance should be eliminated from earnings when evaluating a firm's future operating potential.

V. OTHER ISSUES

16. Material changes in number of shares outstanding

The number of common stock shares outstanding and thus the computation of earnings per share can change materially from one accounting period to the next. These changes result from such transactions as treasury stock purchases and the purchase and retirement of a firm's own common stock.

17. Acquisitions and dispositions

Acquisitions and dispositions of other companies and/or major lines of business can have a significant impact on the comparability of financial reporting. The treat-

---

[9] For more reading on this topic, see B. R. Guamnitz. and J. E. Thompson, "In-Substance Defeasance: Costs, Yes; Benefits, No," *Journal of Accountancy,* March 1987.

ment of goodwill, discussed in item 8, is one of the qualitative factors that results from acquisitions. Ongoing restructuring of a company can also be a signal of underlying problems. Large charges classified as restructuring charges are sometimes used by companies to clean up their balance sheet. These charges are often referred to as "Big Bath" charges. The analyst should review the footnote disclosures carefully to assess whether the restructuring charges are associated with a significant reorganization of the company rather than ordinary business expenses. Companies that erroneously classify ordinary business expenses as restructuring charges hope that analysts will ignore what appears to be a one-time charge. In addition, any reversal of these charges in later years causes the company to recognize a gain that lowers the quality of earnings once again.

In-process research and development charges are one-time charges taken at the time of an acquisition. The charged amounts are part of the acquisition price that the acquiring company determines are not yet viable research and development because they are still in process. These charges can be written off immediately under current accounting rules. Any revenue gains from the research in the future will cause higher earnings that have not been matched to the expenses that created them.

18. Reserves

Companies often create reserve accounts to set aside funds today to cover some known future cost. In the 1990s, the SEC, under the leadership of Arthur Levitt, sent a message to Corporate America that continued abuse of reserve accounts would not be tolerated. The abuse occurs when companies create reserve accounts for the purpose of setting aside funds in good years (i.e., reducing net income) and then shifting the reserve amounts to the income statement in poor years. The net effect is to smooth out earnings from year to year.

In assessing the quality of a company's reported earnings, it is helpful to consider not only the issues presented in the checklist but any other factors that the analyst believes may cause the reported earnings figure to misrepresent the ongoing future operating potential of the firm.

What Are the Real Earnings?

What is the appropriate earnings figure for ABC in 2002? There are numerous possible answers to this question—perhaps as many as there are readers. ABC reported a bottom line net income figure of $409 million in 2002. At a minimum, the following adjustments should be considered:

(IN MILLIONS)

1. Start with total income before taxes, extraordinary gain, and cumulative effect of the change in accounting principle (from the income statement) $797

2. Deduct:

   Base LIFO layer reductions (item 5)   (143)

   Gain on disposal of assets (item 10)   (55)

   Amount by which equity income exceeds cash received (item 12)   (32)

Unusual items (item 13)	(39)
Provision for taxes[10] (from income statement)	(484)
Adjusted income	$ 44

In addition, consider other items discussed in the appendix—for example, the following reductions between 2001 and 2002:

- $27 million in the allowance for doubtful accounts;
- $7 million in research and development expenditures;
- $18 million in maintenance and repair of plant and equipment;
- $32 million in interest income.

Comparable adjustments would also be required for previous years' earnings figures in order to make relevant comparisons. The ultimate objective in the analysis of earnings quality is to arrive at a performance measure that best reflects both financial reality and the future operating potential of the firm.

---

[10] It would also be appropriate to adjust the tax provision for the tax effect of items excluded from income; this information is not available for ABC.

The Analysis of Segmental Data

Beginning in calendar year 1998, companies were required by the provisions of FASB Statement No. 131, "Disclosures about Segments of an Enterprise and Related Information," to disclose supplementary financial data for each reportable segment. FASB Statement No. 131 also covers reporting requirements for foreign operations, sales to major customers, and disclosures required for enterprises that have only one reportable segment. Segmental disclosures are valuable to the financial analyst in identifying areas of strength and weakness within a company; proportionate contribution to revenue and profit by each division; the relationship between capital expenditures and rates of return for operating areas; and segments that should be deemphasized or eliminated. The information on segments is presented as a supplementary section in the notes to the financial statements, as part of the basic financial statements, or in a separate schedule that is referenced to and incorporated into the financial statements.

An *operating segment* is defined by FASB Statement No. 131 as a component of a business enterprise:

1. That engages in business activities from which it may earn revenues and incur expenses,
2. Whose operating results are regularly reviewed by the company's chief operating decision maker to make decisions about resources allocated to the segment and assesses its performance, and
3. For which discrete financial information is available.

A segment is considered to be reportable if any one of three criteria is met:

1. Revenue is 10% or more of combined revenue, including intersegment revenue.
2. Operating profit or loss is 10% or more of the greater of combined profit of all segments with profit or combined loss of all segments with loss.
3. Segment assets exceed 10% or more of combined assets of all segments.

The following information must be disclosed according to FASB Statement No. 131:

1. *General Information.* The "management approach" is used to identify operating segments in the enterprise. The management approach is based on the way that management organizes the segments within the company for making operating decisions and assessing performance. A company must identify how it is organized and what factors were used to identify operating segments and describe the types of products and services from which each operating segment derives its revenues.
2. *Information about Profit or Loss.* A company must report a measure of profit or loss for each reportable segment. In addition, certain amounts must be disclosed if the specified amounts are included in information reviewed by the chief oper-

ating decision maker. For companies basing profit or loss on pretax income from continuing operations, the following amounts must be disclosed[1]:

- Revenues (separated into sales to external customers and intersegment sales)
- Interest revenue
- Interest expense
- Depreciation, depletion, and amortization expense

3. *Information about Assets.* A company must report a measure of the total operating segments' assets. Only assets included in reports to the chief operating decision maker should be included. The total capital expenditures that have been added to long-lived assets must also be reported for each operating segment.

The total of the operating segments' revenues, profit or loss, assets, and any other items reported shall be reconciled to the company's total consolidated amounts for each of these items.

The following analysis of Motorola's segment disclosures provides an illustration of how to interpret segmental data.

Exhibit B.1 illustrates an excerpt from the general information and the geographic area information disclosed by Motorola Inc. in the Company's 1998 Annual Report. Exhibit B.2 illustrates the revenue, profit (loss), assets, capital expenditures, depreciation expense, interest revenue, interest expense, and net interest for Motorola's five reportable segments: Cellular Products, Semiconductor Products, Land Mobile Products, Messaging, Information and Media Products, and Other Products. Segmental reporting does not include complete financial statements, but it is feasible to perform an analysis of the key financial data presented.

Refer first to Exhibit B.1. The majority of Motorola's sales are from the United States; however, a decrease in domestic sales has occurred in 1998, whereas sales in the United Kingdom and other nations have increased each year.

Referring to Exhibit B.2, notice that total revenue for Motorola has declined in 1998, but more significant is that the company is generating overall operating losses in 1998 compared to operating profits in 1997 and 1996.

In order to analyze the performance for each segment, six tables have been prepared from computations based on the figures provided in Exhibit B.2. Table B.1 shows the percentage contribution to total revenue by segment.

Note the change in trends over the three-year period. Cellular Products not only continues to be the largest revenue producer, but also is contributing proportionately more each year to total revenues. Land Mobile Products has also increased its relative contribution to total revenue over the three-year period from 1996 to 1998. Semiconductor Products and Messaging, Information, and Media Products, on the other hand, have contributed less to revenue each of the past three years. Other Products appears to be a stable revenue producer.

Table B.2 reveals the contribution by segment to operating income and provides a basis for assessing the ability of a segment to translate revenue into profit. Land

---

[1] If more complex profit measures are used, the company must also disclose any unusual items, equity income, income tax expense, extraordinary items, and other significant noncash items.

EXHIBIT B.1 Information by Segment and Geographic Region

The company implemented Statement of Financial Accounting Standards No. 131, "Disclosures about Segments of an Enterprise and Related Information," as of January 1, 1998. This statement establishes standards for the way public business enterprises report information about operating segments in annual financial statements and in interim financial reports issued to shareholders. This statement is not require to be applied to interim financial statements in the initial year of application. The company has restated the previously reported annual segment operating results to conform to the statement's management approach.

The company's operations are predominantly in the wireless communication, semiconductor technology, and advanced electronics industries and involve the design, manufacture, and sale of a diversified line of products. The company's reportable segments have been determined based on the nature of the products offered to customers, which include, but are not limited to, cellular phones and systems; semiconductors (including discrete semiconductors and integrated circuits); two-way radios and personal communications equipment and systems; and pagers and data communications equipment and systems. Automotive, defense, and space electronic products are part of the Other Products segment

Segment operating results are measured based on profit (loss) before tax adjusted, if necessary, for certain segment specific items. Intersegment and intergeographic sales are accounted for on an arm's length pricing basis.

Geographic area information

Years ended December 31 1996	Net Sales			Assets		
	1998	1997	1996	1998	1997	
United States	$20,397	$21,809	$20,614	$14,932	$14,000	$12,797
United Kingdom	5,709	5,254	4,571	2,083	2,098	1,816
Other nations	12,812	12,778	12,312	8,804	7,966	6,788
Adjustments and eliminations (568)	(9,520)	(10,047)	(9,524)	(851)	(651)	
Geographic totals	$23,398	$29,794	$27,973	24,968	23,413	20,833
General corporate				3,760	2,865	3,243
Consolidated totals				$28,728	$27,278	$24,076

Mobile Products was the leading contributor to operating profit in 1998. Cellular Products also contributed positively to operating profits in 1998. The other three segments generated significant operating losses, with Semiconductor Products contributing the most to the overall operating loss. Notice that both Semiconductor Products and Messaging, Information, and Media Products generated less overall revenue from 1996 to 1998; operating profits in these divisions were positive in 1996, but declined each year thereafter until both segments generated losses in 1998. Other Products, which consistently produced more than 14% of revenue, is also on a downward trend with regard to operating profit. This segment generated losses in both 1997 and 1998.

EXHIBIT B.2 Motorola Inc. and Subsidiaries Segment Information (Dollars in Millions)

	Net Sales			Operating Profit (Loss) Before Tax					
Years ended December 31	*1998*	*1997*	*1996*	*1998*		*1997*		*1996*	
Cellular Products	$12,483	$11,934	$10,804	$482	3.9%	$1,283	10.8%	$1,162	10.8%
Semiconductor Products	7,314	8,003	7,858	(1,225)	(16.8)%	168	2.1%	186	2.4%
Land Mobile Products	5,397	4,926	4,008	729	13.5%	542	11.0%	452	11.3%
Messaging, Information and Media Products	2,633	3,793	3,958	(699)	(26.5)%	41	1.1%	46	1.2%
Other Products	4,385	4,326	4,061	(544)	(12.4)%	(85)	(2.0)%	30	0.7%
Adjustments and eliminations	(2,814)	(3,188)	(2,716)	14	(0.5)%	(48)	1.5%	(29)	1.1%
Segment totals	$29,398	$29,794	$27,973	(1,243)	(4.2)%	1,901	6.4%	1,847	6.6%
General corporate				(131)		(85)		(77)	
Earnings (loss) before income taxes				$(1,374)	(4.7)%	$1,816	6.1%	$1,775	6.3%

	Assets			Capital Expenditures			Depreciation Expense		
Years ended December 31	*1998*	*1997*	*1996*	*1998*	*1997*	*1996*	*1998*	*1997*	*1996*
Cellular Products	$9,282	$8,021	$6,314	$607	$900	$673	$411	$534	$474
Semiconductor Products	8,232	7,947	7,889	1,783	1,153	1,416	1,178	1,169	1,160
Land Mobile Products	2,720	2,538	2,130	270	228	159	183	168	162
Messaging, Information and Media Products	2,043	2,391	2,506	97	149	275	164	219	243
Other Products	3,111	2,974	2,256	199	178	196	216	191	221
Adjustments and eliminations	(420)	(458)	(262)	—	—	—	—	—	—
Segment totals	24,968	23,413	20,833	2,956	2,608	2,719	2,152	2,281	2,260
General corporate	3,760	3,865	3,243	265	266	254	45	48	48
Consolidated totals	$28,728	$27,278	$24,076	$3,221	$2,874	$2,973	$2,197	$2,329	$2,308

	Interest Income			Interest Expense			Net Interest		
Years ended December 31	*1998*	*1997*	*1996*	*1998*	*1997*	*1996*	*1998*	*1997*	*1996*
Cellular Products	$7	$2	$1	$90	$41	$57	$(83)	$(39)	$(56)
Semiconductor Products	12	12	15	116	71	103	(104)	(59)	(88)
Land Mobile Products	2	5	2	20	14	16	(18)	(9)	(14)
Messaging Information and Media Products	15	18	22	22	28	36	(7)	(10)	(14)
Other Products	5	2	2	21	5	—	(16)	(3)	2
Segment totals	41	39	42	269	159	212	(228)	(120)	(170)
General corporate	44	46	22	32	57	37	12	(11)	(15)
Consolidated totals	$85	$85	$64	$301	$216	$249	$(216)	$(131)	$(185)

TABLE B.1 Contribution by Segment to Revenue (Percentages)

	1998	1997	1996
Cellular Products	42.46	40.06	38.62
Semiconductor Products	24.88	26.86	28.09
Land Mobile Products	18.36	16.53	14.33
Messaging, Information, and Media Products	8.95	12.73	14.15
Other Products	14.92	14.52	14.52
Adjustments and eliminations	(9.57)	(10.70)	(9.71)
Total revenue	100.00%	100.00%	100.00%

TABLE B.2 Contribution by Segment to Operating Income (Percentages)

	1998	1997	1996
Cellular Products	38.78	67.49	62.91
Semiconductor Products	(98.55)	8.84	10.07
Land Mobile Products	58.65	28.51	24.47
Messaging, Information, and Media Products	(56.24)	2.16	2.49
Other Products	(43.77)	(4.47)	1.63
Adjustments and eliminations	1.13	(2.53)	(1.57)
Total operating profit	100.00%	100.00%	100.00%

TABLE B.3 Operating Profit Margin by Segment (Percentages)

	1998	1997	1996
Cellular Products	3.86	10.75	10.76
Semiconductor Products	(16.75)	2.10	2.37
Land Mobile Products	13.51	11.00	11.28
Messaging, Information, and Media Products	(26.55)	1.08	1.16
Other Products	(12.41)	(1.96)	0.74

Operating Profit Margin (operating profit divided by revenue) is presented for each segment in Table B.3. The operating profit margin shows the percent of every sales dollar that is converted to (before-tax) profit. The profit margin is highest in all three years from Land Mobile Products. Cellular Products is the only other segment with positive operating profit margin in 1998; however, its profit margin has declined from more than 10% in 1996 and 1997 to 3.86% in 1998. Profit margins in the other three segments have declined each year since 1996, and in 1998 no longer generate profits.

Table B.4 is a percentage breakdown of capital expenditures by segment. Motorola has chosen to invest heavily in Semiconductor Products, especially in 1998. This investment has not so far resulted in increased revenues; instead revenues

TABLE B.4 Capital Expenditures by Segment (Percentages)

	1998	1997	1996
Cellular Products	20.54	34.51	24.75
Semiconductor Products	60.32	44.21	52.08
Land Mobile Products	9.13	8.74	5.85
Messaging, Information, and Media Products	3.28	5.71	10.11
Other Products	6.73	6.83	7.21
Total capital expenditures	100.00%	100.00%	100.00%

declined in 1998. Further investigation is warranted to determine if a shift in this area is occurring and whether the potential for renewed profitability will occur in the future. In addition, the company has chosen to significantly reduce capital expenditures in Cellular Products in 1998. Although revenues have not been hurt by this decline, the operating profit has dropped in this segment from 67% to just under 39% in 1998.

To determine the reasons for these changes, one would most likely want to read the Management Discussion and Analysis section of the Motorola Annual Report for 1998. Capital expenditures are increasing each year in Land Mobile Products, which has resulted in a positive effect on both revenue and profit in this segment. The declining investment in the Messaging, Information, and Media Products and Other Products segments may account for the declining profits in these two segments.

It is important to examine the relationship between investment and return, and this information is provided in Table B.5, which shows return on investment by segment (operating profit divided by identifiable assets). Land Mobile Products consistently generates solid and increasing return on investment each year. The significant deterioration in all other segments is an alarming development. Of greatest concern is that Motorola is clearly investing heavily in Semiconductor Products yet not realizing positive returns.

Table B.6 compares a ranking of segments in 1998 by segment assets with percentage contribution to operating income, operating profit margin, and return on investment. Cellular Products is the largest segment when considering total investment in assets. Of concern, however, is that despite its contribution to revenues, both operating profit margin and return on investment in this segment are deteriorating. Land Mobile Products appears to be the only healthy segment in the company. Semiconductor

TABLE B.5 Return on Investment by Segment (Percentages)

	1998	1997	1996
Cellular Products	5.19	16.00	18.40
Semiconductor Products	(14.88)	2.11	2.36
Land Mobile Products	26.80	21.36	21.22
Messaging, Information, and Media Products	(34.21)	1.71	1.84
Other Products	(20.01)	(2.86)	1.33

TABLE B.6 Ranking of Segments in 1998

	Percentage of Total Segment Assets	Percent Contribution to Operating Profit	Operating Profit Margin	Return on Investment
Cellular Products	37.18	38.78	3.86	5.19
Semiconductor Products	32.97	(98.55)	(16.75)	(14.88)
Other Products	12.46	(43.77)	(12.41)	(20.01)
Land Mobile Products	10.89	58.65	13.51	26.80
Messaging, Information, and Media Products	8.18	(56.24)	(26.55)	(34.21)

Products is a problem area for Motorola, as are the Messaging, Information, and Media Products and Other Products segments.

Summary

The analytical tools used to assess the segmental data of Motorola Inc. are applicable to any company with segmental disclosures. Minor variations and/or additions to the tables prepared for Motorola may be appropriate for a particular company, but the basic analysis should include, by segment and for at least a three-year period: (1) percentage contribution to revenue; (2) percentage contribution to operating income; (3) operating profit margin; (4) capital expenditures; (5) return on investment; and (6) an examination of the relationship between the size of a division and its relative contribution.

Appendix C

Understanding Bank Financial Statements

Reading and interpreting the financial statements of commercial banking institutions[1] involves exposure to some financial statement accounts and analytical ratios that are different from those discussed in previous sections of this book. Banks generate profits, if they are successful, by earning more on their assets (loans and investments) than they pay in interest to depositors. In spite of the differences that result from the nature of a bank's operations, however, the underlying concepts of assessing a bank's financial condition and performance are essentially similar because—like their nonbank counterparts—banking institutions attempt to effectively manage the tradeoff between risk and return in order to improve the overall return on equity.

One major positive aspect about the evaluation of bank financial statements is that all insured commercial banking institutions in the U.S.—regardless of type and size of bank and whether or not the bank is privately held or publicly traded—prepare financial statements in a uniform reporting format, and this information is available to banks and to the general public on both a quarterly and an annual basis. Insured banks file required financial data on an established periodic basis with the appropriate regulatory authority (Comptroller of the Currency for national banks, Federal Reserve Board for state banks that are members of the Federal Reserve System, and Federal Deposit Insurance Corporation for other state-chartered banks). The balance sheet and income statement for each bank are compiled and published in a standardized document that also includes financial ratios and other analytical data as well as peer group comparisons. This document, called the *Uniform Bank Performance Report,* is provided free to each banking institution and can be purchased by other users for any insured commercial bank in the U.S. from the Federal Examinations Institution Council.[2]

The format and content of banking information that is provided in the Uniform Bank Performance Report will form the basis for the material presented in this appendix, but comparable data could be developed from a bank's annual or 10-K report. Only the balance sheet and income statement are covered in the appendix because they are the two statements presented in the report; the statement of cash flows is less important to the analysis of depository institutions, given the nature of its assets (loans and investments) and liabilities (deposits).

The appendix will include a discussion of the financial statements of Metrobank, a large urban bank. The reporting format is a condensed version of the statements presented in the Uniform Bank Performance Report; the analytical ratios and peer group data are drawn from the report. The financial ratios and analytical approach used for

---

[1] For more information about this topic, see Donald R. Fraser and Lyn M. Fraser, *Evaluating Commercial Bank Performance, A Guide to Financial Analysis,* Bankers Publishing Company, Rolling Meadows, IL, 1990.

[2] For order information, contact the FDIC Disclosure Group, UBPR, Department 0649, Washington DC 20073–0649.

Metrobank will also apply to smaller banks and rural banks. Like the analysis of any business firm, however, the analyst would need to be aware of the characteristics of the bank in its particular operating environment, economic conditions, and the issues—such as the quality of financial reporting and the need to consider intangible, unquantifiable information—that were discussed in chapter 1.

The analyst should also be alert to any changes in accounting principles that affect banking institutions; for example, FASB Statement No. 115, "Accounting for Certain Investments in Debt and Equity Securities" (discussed in chapter 2), has major implications for the commercial banking industry by requiring banks to value many of their securities at current market prices, effective for fiscal years beginning after December 15, 1993. Specifically, the rule requires that trading securities—debt and equity securities held for current resale—be reported at fair value with unrealized gains and losses included in earnings. Securities classified as available for sale are also reported at fair value with unrealized gains and losses included as a separate component of stockholders' equity. Debt securities held to maturity continue to be reported at amortized cost. Banks also are affected by FASB Statements No.107 and No. 119, which require the disclosure of the fair value of financial instruments, and by FASB Statements No. 114 and No. 118, which require banks to value impaired or troubled loans at current value.

Balance Sheet

The balance sheet for Metrobank, an urban bank in a peer group of banks with total assets in excess of $10 billion, is presented in Exhibit C.1.

ASSETS

For most banks, loans are the largest asset category and would be the counterpart to inventory and accounts receivable for a retail firm. Loans are listed by type—real estate, commercial, individual, and agricultural. This section also includes leases because lease arrangements sometimes substitute for direct lending. From gross loans and leases, deductions are made for unearned income and the allowance account. Unearned income is income—for example, the amount deducted from a discounted note—that will be recognized on the income statement over the life of a loan. The loan and lease allowance account is comparable to a nonbank business firm's allowance for doubtful accounts, but it is generally much more significant for banks because loan losses are the major source of risk and loss at banking institutions. The adequacy of this account is directly relevant to any assessment of bank risk. Bank management, with certain guidelines from the regulatory authorities, estimates an amount for uncollectible loans and leases; losses are charged against this account, and any recoveries are added to it. This allowance account is counted as primary capital in meeting a bank's capital requirement for regulation.

Investments for banks consist primarily of debt securities because banks are generally prohibited from investing in equity securities. These investments consist of U.S. government securities, municipal (states and political subdivisions) securities, interest-bearing balances due from banks, federal funds (interbank loans of cash reserves), and trading account assets (securities that banks hold for resale and for underwriting municipal issues).

Net loans and leases and total investments comprise a bank's earning assets.

EXHIBIT C.1

METROBANK BALANCE SHEET*
ASSETS, LIABILITIES, AND CAPITAL ($MILLIONS) AT DECEMBER 31,

	2002	2001
Assets		
Loans		
Real estate	1,248	1,382
Commercial	3,244	4,088
Individual	489	270
Agricultural	40	50
Other domestic loans and leases	271	493
Foreign loans and leases	683	622
Gross loans and leases	5,975	6,905
Less: unearned income	30	36
Loans and leases allowance	258	265
Net loans and leases	5,687	6,603
U.S. Treasury, agency securities	892	844
Municipal securities	455	494
Other securities	510	1,034
Fed funds sold	1,905	911
Trading account assets	25	3
Total investments	3,789	3,387
Total earning assets	9,477	9,990
Cash due from banks	987	977
Premises, fixed assets	289	297
Other real estate owned	135	134
Other assets	265	239
Total assets	11,154	11,638
Average assets	11,675	11,509
Liabilities and Capital		
Demand deposits	1,960	2,055
Now and ATS	394	350
MMDA, other savings	1,126	946
Nonbrokered time <$100M	775	707
Core deposits	4,255	4,057
Brokered deposits	87	94
Nonbrokered time >$100M	1,141	1,435
Foreign deposits	892	930
Total deposits	6,374	6,517
Fed funds, other borrowings	3,834	4,235
Volatile liabilities	5,954	6,694
Other liabilities	256	229
Total liabilities	10,464	10,980
Subordinated notes, debentures	35	35
Common and preferred capital	655	623
Total liabilities and capital	11,154	11,638

*Totals may not add due to rounding.

The remaining assets include cash (currency and coin) and noninterest balances due from other depository institutions; premises, furniture, fixtures, and any other long-lived assets (net of depreciation); and other real estate, such as foreclosed property from problem loans.

In addition to total assets, a figure for average assets is provided in the report.

LIABILITIES

The major liabilities for banks are different types of deposit accounts that are used to fund lending and investing. These accounts vary according to interest payment, maturity, check-writing, and insurability.

CAPITAL

Subordinated notes and debentures, actually debt, are counted as capital because this type of long-term debt, with claims subordinated to the claims of depositors, has the maturity and permanence of capital and can qualify as capital in meeting regulatory requirements. One weakness of the Uniform Bank Performance Report is that the remaining capital accounts (common and preferred stock, additional paid-in capital, retained earnings, and other categories) are lumped together as one reported item, making it difficult to trace changes in the capital account from period to period. The income statement shows the amount of cash dividends declared and the change in the retained earnings account for the period.

Income Statement

Exhibit C.2 shows the income statement for Metrobank for the three years ending December 31, 2002. (The Uniform Bank Performance Report always provides five periods of data, and this lengthier period will be used for the analysis of Metrobank.)

Because loans are the largest category of assets for most banks, interest on loans is the major source of income. The reader will notice the designation "TE" next to the figure for "income for loans and leases" and other amounts on the income statement. Some bank income, for example, interest on loans and investments relating to state and political subdivisions, is tax-exempt. A tax benefit is estimated, using a prescribed formula, and added to income in order to improve the comparability of interest income among banks.

Income on securities is the next revenue item, followed by other interest income, which includes interest on balances due from banks, income on federal funds, and income on assets held in trading accounts.

The various categories of interest expense reflect interest paid on designated types of liabilities—foreign deposits, large negotiable certificates of deposits, other deposits, fed funds, and other borrowings.

Net interest income is the difference between total interest income and total interest expense.

Noninterest income includes trust activities, service charges, gains/losses on trading account activities, and foreign transactions.

Other expenses are those for overhead (salaries and employee benefits, expenses of premises) and the provision for loan and lease losses.

EXHIBIT C.2

METROBANK INCOME STATEMENT
REVENUE AND EXPENSES ($ MILLIONS) AT DECEMBER 31

	2002	2001	2000
Interest income:			
Income on loans and leases (TE)	590.4	550.4	574.5
Income on investments (TE)	154.4	149.6	144.5
Other interest income	269.4	134.4	162.0
Total interest income (TE)	1,014.2	834.4	881.1
Interest expense:			
Foreign deposits	60.3	74.3	67.2
CDs over $100M	117.8	102.4	114.0
Other deposits	143.8	124.4	121.0
Fed funds	396.6	237.6	271.2
Total interest expense	754.0	577.6	608.2
Net interest expense (TE)	260.2	256.8	272.8
Noninterest income	173.6	134.6	143.9
Adjusted operating income (TE)	433.8	391.4	416.7
Overhead expenses	285.6	245.0	262.9
Provision loan/lease loss	51.0	59.0	61.0
Pretax operating income (TE)	97.2	87.4	92.8
Securities gains/losses	15.6	1.9	1.4
Pretax net operating income	112.8	89.3	94.2
Income taxes (TE)	38.8	30.8	31.9
Net operating income	74.0	58.5	62.3
Net extraordinary items	0	0	0
Net income	74.0	58.5	62.3
Cash dividends declared	26.0	70.0	60.0
Retained earnings	48.0	−11.5	2.3
Memo: Net international income	10.0	3.8	5.9

Any gains or losses on the sale, exchange, redemption, or retirement of securities (other than trading account assets) are shown as a separate category on the income statement because they are not considered a part of normal banking operations.

Applicable income tax includes the total estimated federal, state, local, and foreign income taxes on income.

The remainder of the income statement shows net income, cash dividends declared, the change in retained earnings for the period, and net international income (included as a memo item).

Analysis

The reader should be aware that there are many more analytical tools available in Uniform Bank Performance Report and in banking textbooks than will be covered in this appendix. An attempt has been made to select seventeen financial ratios that will be useful in evaluating the financial condition and performance of any commercial banking institution, with the understanding that other analytical information can be drawn upon to provide depth and detail in particular circumstances. To the extent possible, the ratios selected are compatible with those used in chapter 5 for nonbank business firms.

The reader should also recognize that there is no set of analytical tools that will accurately predict a bank's success or failure. These ratios should be used in conjunction with the absolute dollar amounts shown in the financial statements as well as with considerable common sense and critical judgment.

Following a brief description of the financial ratios, a five-year analysis of Metrobank will be provided. As the result of rounding in the financial data presented, the actual ratio calculations in the Uniform Bank Performance Report are somewhat different from those that would be calculated from the numbers on the Metrobank balance sheet and income statement.

Exhibit C.3 shows the seventeen financial ratios, based on the calculations as they are made in the report, for Metrobank over the five-year period, 1998 to 2002. Comparable peer group averages, also from the report, are presented for 2002.

SUMMARY RATIOS
1. Net income/average equity is return on equity (ROE), an overall measure of the bank's ability to generate return to its shareholders.
2. Net income/average assets is return on investment (ROI) or return on assets (ROA), revealing the bank's effectiveness in earning a profit from its lending, investing, and other income-generating activities.
3. Equity capital/assets is a summary measure of bank risk. The higher the proportion of capital relative to assets, the less is overall risk. Keep in mind that risk, in and of itself, is not necessarily bad and, in fact, can multiply overall returns to shareholders, as discussed in chapter 5. The objective of bank management is to manage risk effectively.

PROFITABILITY
The following are ratios that consider the proportion of a bank's major categories of revenue and expense in relation to a common denominator. They provide perspective on specific sources of revenue and expense over time and in comparison with the bank's peer group.

4. Interest income/average assets
5. Interest expense/ average assets
6. Net interest income/average assets
7. Non-interest income/average assets
8. Overhead expense/average assets
9. Provision for loan and lease loss/average assets

EXHIBIT C.3 Metrobank Financial Ratios

	2002	2001	2000	1999	1998	Peer 2002
Summary						
1. Net income/equity (ROE)	11.51	9.36	9.95	−12.40	8.14	18.50
2. Net income/average assets (ROA)	.63	.51	.55	−.70	.49	.91
3. Equity capital/assets	5.87	5.36	5.42	5.63	5.48	5.40
Profitability						
Percent of average assets:						
4. Interest income	8.61	7.29	7.71	7.50	7.81	9.48
5. Interest expense	6.40	5.05	5.33	5.13	5.60	6.43
6. Net interest income	2.21	2.24	2.39	2.36	2.21	3.21
7. Noninterest income	1.47	1.18	1.26	1.00	0.08	1.69
8. Overhead expense	2.43	2.14	2.30	2.81	2.46	3.05
9. Provision loan and lease loss	0.43	0.52	0.53	1.24	1.12	0.56
Risk						
10. Growth rate—assets	−4.16	5.95	4.36	−2.99	−1.00	4.47
11. Growth rate—capital	3.53	1.42	1.58	6.99	8.81	4.61
12. Cash dividends/net income	35.14	119.55	99.37	NA	39.71	40.70
13. Net loss/total loans and leases	1.02	.42	.75	.82	1.15	.86
14. Earnings coverage net loss (X)	2.09	4.30	2.67	.73	1.61	3.46
15. Loss reserve/total loans and leases	4.33	3.86	4.30	3.53	2.63	2.72
16. Net loans and leases/assets	50.99	56.74	50.12	61.26	61.00	60.41
17. Interest rate gap	−7.66					6.50

RISK

The following help assess the relationship between assets and equity.

10. Growth rate of assets
11. Growth rate of primary capital
12. Cash dividends/net operating income

In general, the higher the proportion of assets relative to capital, the greater is a bank's risk. Because of the importance of this relationship between assets and capital, it is helpful to compare the growth rate of assets and capital[3] over time. If a bank's assets are growing rapidly, there is a potential that the growth may be coming from the extension of riskier loans. Because core deposits generally increase at steady rates, volatile liabilities likely provide the funding sources for this asset growth, thus adding risk. This increased risk would be moderated by a comparable growth in capital.

---

[3] The *Uniform Bank Performance Report* uses primary capital, which includes common equity, the loan and lease loss reserve, permanent and convertible preferred stock, qualifying mandatory convertible debt and minority interest in consolidated subsidiaries, less intangible assets.

The relationship between dividends and income provides information about how much capital will remain for the bank's internal growth; the higher the dividend payout, the lower is the potential for internal capital growth.

The following are all elements of credit risk.

13. Net loss/total loans and leases
14. Earnings coverage of net loss (expressed in "times")
15. Loss reserves/total loans and leases

Loan losses are a major cause of bank failures, underscoring the importance of assessing credit risk.

The net loss is gross loan and lease charge-offs, less gross recoveries. Looking at net loss relative to total loans and leases shows the proportion of a bank's loan-lease portfolio that have been written off during the period.

Earnings coverage of net loss is a measure of the bank's ability to cover its loan losses from operating income.

Loss reserve relative to loans and leases considers the adequacy of the provision for potential losses.

The following is a measure of liquidity.

16. Net loans and leases/assets

Because loans and leases hold the greatest potential for bank losses, their proportion relative to assets helps assess the degree of liquidity in the asset base (keeping in mind that loans are also the primary source of bank profitability).

The following is a commonly used measure of interest rate risk.

17. Interest rate gap

Interest rate risk is the effect on bank profitability of changes in interest rates. Banks earn interest on loans and investments; they pay interest to depositors. When interest rates change, there may be an effect on income if a bank holds rate sensitive assets and liabilities. If, for example, a bank holds more rate sensitive assets than liabilities when interest rates rise, profits will be improved because the bank will receive more in increased interest revenue than it will pay out in rising costs. The reverse would be true during a period of falling interest rates. The interest rate gap is the difference between rate-sensitive assets and liabilities; holding more rate-sensitive assets than liabilities is called a positive gap, and an excess of rate-sensitive liabilities over assets results in a negative gap.[4]

METROBANK

Exhibit C.3 presents a five-year summary of the seventeen ratios and a peer group comparison for all insured commercial banks having assets in excess of $10 billion.

---

[4] The interest rate gap is estimated from data in the *Uniform Bank Performance Report* using the section on "Maturity and Repricing Distribution." The calculation is made by deducting the percent of interest bearing liabilities repriced within three months from the percent of interest bearing assets repriced within the past three months.

Suggestion to the reader

Before reading the remainder of the appendix, look at the balance sheet (Exhibit C.1), income statement (Exhibit C.2), and financial ratios/peer group comparisons (Exhibit C.3) for Metrobank. Make a note of any significant trends in the figures presented and attempt to explain those trends. List Metrobank's strengths and weaknesses. Compare your analysis with the one provided in this section.

Looking first at the three summary ratios, it would appear that Metrobank, though still far below its peer group, has improved overall performance—both over the five-year period and in the most recent year—as measured by the return on equity and return on assets. Metrobank accomplished the improvement in ROE while simultaneously reducing its overall level of risk, as indicated by the increase in equity/assets. This means that profitability has increased by relatively more than the reduction in risk. (See discussion of the leverage multiplier in chapter 5.)

The gains in profitability are *not* the result of improvement in net interest income. Although interest income relative to average assets has risen, interest expense has risen more rapidly. The year 2002 was a year of increasing interest rates in the economy. The interest rate gap (shown as the last ratio in Exhibit C.3) is negative for Metrobank, which means that the bank has more interest rate–sensitive liabilities than assets. A negative gap will impair profitability during a period of rising interest rates, and this was the case for Metrobank.

Metrobank accomplished its overall gains partly through an increase in noninterest income. For many banks, these traditionally less significant income sources—such as trust activities, various types of service charges, and trading account profits or losses—have become increasingly important during the era of deregulation. Banks have sought new sources of income as competition has increased pricing pressures on interest earning assets and liabilities. Apparently Metrobank is benefiting from such activities.

Another reason for the overall improvement in net income is a $15.6 million gain from securities transactions (see income statement). The analyst should bear in mind that this is a fluctuating source of income and is not part of normal banking operations.

Considering the various measures of risk, Metrobank has decreased its asset base (due to a reduction in all categories of loans except loans to individuals), while accomplishing internal capital growth as the result of a reduction in the dividend payout ratio. Note that in 2001 Metrobank paid more in dividends that it generated in income. The ratio in 2000 was close to 100%, and the ratio in 1999 does not compute because the bank reported a loss. The 2002 dividend policy would appear to be much more sensible from the standpoint of capital risk.

Credit risk measures indicate an increase in loan and lease losses relative to the loan-lease base and a reduction in earnings coverage of loan losses. The bank shows improvement in the loss allowance relative to the loan-lease base because gross loans and leases have decreased by more than the loan and lease loss allowance. Metrobank has reduced the provision for loan lease/average assets at a time when loan losses have increased. Credit risk would appear to be a potential problem for Metrobank. From the information presented it is difficult to assess why the bank is experiencing the increased losses, but it is certainly an issue that would warrant further scrutiny by the analyst. The Uniform Bank Performance Report shows net losses by type of loan.

From this information (not presented here) it is evident that the major source of the losses is real estate loans, which may continue to be a problem for Metrobank because real estate loans comprise more than 20% of the loan portfolio.

The bank appears to be improving its liquidity. The proportion of loans and leases to assets has declined and is substantially below the peer group. Given the problems associated with credit risk, this trend is probably a positive one.

The strengths for Metrobank are improved profitability, the reduction of overall risk achieved largely through internal capital growth, and improved liquidity.

The bank's weaknesses are credit risk, evidenced by problems with loan-lease losses; a negative interest rate gap in a period of increasing interest rates; and the fact that much of the improvement in income production was the result of securities gains, a potentially nonrecurring activity.

Solutions to Self-Tests

CHAPTER 1

1. (d)	8. (d)	15. (a)	(6) a
2. (d)	9. (c)	16. (d)	(7) d
3. (d)	10. (b)	17. (1) c	(8) b
4. (b)	11. (c)	(2) b	(9) d
5. (a)	12. (b)	(3) a	(10) a or b
6. (d)	13. (c)	(4) c	
7. (b)	14. (d)	(5) b	

CHAPTER 2

1. (b)	16. (a)	(i) NC	(n) 6
2. (a)	17. (c)	(j) NC	(o) 8
3. (b)	18. (b)	24. (a) 4	25. (a) 7
4. (c)	19. (b)	(b) 5	(b) 1
5. (b)	20. (d)	(c) 8	(c) 5
6. (a)	21. (d)	(d) 7	(d) 9
7. (d)	22. (c)	(e) 1	(e) 4
8. (c)	23. (a) NC	(f) 2	(f) 6
9. (b)	(b) C	(g) 2	(g) 10
10. (c)	(c) C	(h) 5	(h) 2
11. (d)	(d) C	(i) 8	(i) 3
12. (a)	(e) NC	(j) 5	(j) 8
13. (c)	(f) C	(k) 3	
14. (b)	(g) C	(l) 2	
15. (d)	(h) C	(m) 1	

CHAPTER 3

1. (c)	12. (a)	(e) 5	(2) d
2. (b)	13. (a)	(f) 14	(3) a
3. (a)	14. (c)	(g) 1	(4) c
4. (c)	15. (d)	(h) 6	(5) d
5. (d)	16. (c)	i) 11	(6) a
6. (a)	17. (b)	(j) 2	(7) e
7. (c)	18. (a)	(k) 10	(8) c
8. (d)	19. (a) 4	(l) 12	(9) c
9. (d)	(b) 9	(m) 3	(10) b
10. (b)	(c) 13	(n) 7	(11) d
11. (b)	(d) 8	20. (1) c	(12) c

CHAPTER 4

1. (d)	10. (b)	19. (b)	28. A
2. (a)	11. (b)	20. (d)	29. A
3. (b)	12. (c)	21. (c)	30. S
4. (a)	13. (a)	22. (b)	31. (a)
5. (c)	14. (d)	23. A	32. (b)
6. (d)	15. (d)	24. S	33. (a)
7. (b)	16. (c)	25. S	34. (d)
8. (c)	17. (d)	26. A	
9. (c)	18. (d)	27. S	

CHAPTER 5

1. (c)	10. (c)	19. (a)	28. (c)
2. (a)	11. (a)	20. (b)	29. (a)
3. (d)	12. (c)	21. (c)	30. (c)
4. (c)	13. (d)	22. (a)	31. (b)
5. (b)	14. (b)	23. (c)	32. (d)
6. (d)	15. (a)	24. (b)	33. (a)
7. (a)	16. (d)	25. (d)	34. (c)
8. (b)	17. (c)	26. (b)	35. (a)
9. (d)	18. (d)	27. (a)	

Summary of Financial Ratios

Ratio	Method of Computation	Significance
Current	$\dfrac{\text{Current assets}}{\text{Current liabilities}}$	Measures short-term liquidity, the ability of a firm to meet needs for cash as they arise.
Quick or acid-test	$\dfrac{\text{Current assets} - \text{inventory}}{\text{Current liabilities}}$	Measures short-term liquidity more rigorously than the current ratio by eliminating inventory, usually the least liquid current asset.
Cash flow liquidity	$\dfrac{\text{Cash} + \text{marketable securities} + \text{cash flow from operating activities}}{\text{Current liabilities}}$	Measures short-term liquidity by considering as cash resources (numerator) cash plus cash equivalents plus cash flow from operating activities.
Average collection period	$\dfrac{\text{Accounts receivable}}{\text{Net sales}/\,365}$	Indicates days required to convert receivables into cash.
Accounts receivable turnover	$\dfrac{\text{Net sales}}{\text{Accounts receivable}}$	Indicates how many times receivables are collected during a year, on average.
Inventory turnover	$\dfrac{\text{Cost of goods sold}}{\text{Inventories}}$	Measures efficiency of the firm in managing and selling inventory.
Fixed asset turnover	$\dfrac{\text{Net sales}}{\text{Net property, plant, and equipment}}$	Measures efficiency of the firm in managing fixed assets.
Total asset turnover	$\dfrac{\text{Net sales}}{\text{Total assets}}$	Measures efficiency of the firm in managing all assets.
Debt ratio	$\dfrac{\text{Total liabilities}}{\text{Total assets}}$	Shows proportion of all assets that are financed with debt.
Long-term debt to total capitalization	$\dfrac{\text{Long-term debt}}{\text{Long-term debt} + \text{stockholders' equity}}$	Measures the extent to which long-term debt is used for permanent financing.
Debt to equity	$\dfrac{\text{Total liabilities}}{\text{Stockholders' equity}}$	Measure debt relative to equity base.

Times interest earned

$$\frac{\text{Operating profit}}{\text{Interest expense}}$$

Measures how many times interest expense is covered by operating earnings.

Fixed charge coverage

$$\frac{\text{Operating profit} + \text{lease payments}}{\text{Interest expense} + \text{lease payments}}$$

Measures coverage capability more broadly than times interest earned by including lease payments as a fixed expense.

Cash flow adequacy

$$\frac{\text{Cash flow from operating activities}}{\text{Average annual long-term debt maturities}}$$

Measures how many times average annual payments of long-term are covered by operating debt cash flow.

Gross profit margin

$$\frac{\text{Gross profit}}{\text{Net sales}}$$

Measures profit generated after consideration of cost of products sold.

Operating profit margin

$$\frac{\text{Operating profit}}{\text{Net sales}}$$

Measures profit generated after consideration of operating expenses.

Net profit margin

$$\frac{\text{Net profit}}{\text{Net sales}}$$

Measures profit generated after consideration of all expenses and revenues.

Cash flow margin

$$\frac{\text{Cash flow from operating activities}}{\text{Net sales}}$$

Measures the ability of the firm to generate cash from sales.

Return on investment

$$\frac{\text{Net earnings}}{\text{Total assets}}$$

Measures overall efficiency of firm in managing assets and generating profits.

Return on equity

$$\frac{\text{Net earnings}}{\text{Stockholders' equity}}$$

Measures rate of return on stockholders' (owners') investment.

Cash return on assets

$$\frac{\text{Cash flow from operating activities}}{\text{Total assets}}$$

Measures the return on assets on a cash basis.

Earnings per common share

$$\frac{\text{Net earnings}}{\text{Average common shares outstanding}}$$

Shows return to common stock shareholder for each share owned.

Price to earnings

$$\frac{\text{Market price of common stock}}{\text{Earnings per share}}$$

Expresses a multiple that the stock market places on a firm's earnings.

Dividend payout

$$\frac{\text{Dividends per share}}{\text{Earnings per share}}$$

Shows percentage of earnings paid to shareholders.

Dividend yield

$$\frac{\text{Dividends per share}}{\text{Market price of common stock}}$$

Shows the rate earned by shareholders from dividends relative to current price of stock.

Glossary

Accelerated Cost Recovery System: The system established by the Economic Recovery Tax Act of 1981 to simplify depreciation methods for tax purposes and to encourage investment in capital by allowing rapid write-off of asset costs over predetermined periods, generally shorter than the estimated useful lives of the assets. The system remains in effect for assets placed in service between 1981 and 1986 but was modified by the Tax Reform Act of 1986 for assets placed in service after 1986. *See* Modified Accelerated Cost Recovery System.

Accelerated depreciation: An accounting procedure under which larger amounts of expense are apportioned to the earlier years of an asset's depreciable life and lesser amounts to the later years.

Accounting period: The length of time covered for reporting accounting information.

Accounting principles: The methods and procedures used in preparing financial statements.

Accounts payable: Amounts owed to creditors for items or services purchased from them.

Accounts receivable: Amounts owed to an entity, primarily by its trade customers.

Accounts receivable turnover: *See* Summary of financial ratios, appendix E.

Accrual basis of accounting: A method of earnings determination under which revenues are recognized in the accounting period when earned, regardless of when cash is received, and expenses are recognized in the period incurred, regardless of when cash is paid.

Accrued liabilities: Obligations resulting from the recognition of an expense prior to the payment of cash.

Accumulated depreciation: A balance sheet account indicating the amount of depreciation expense taken on plant and equipment up to the balance sheet date.

Acid-test ratio: *See* Summary of financial ratios, appendix E.

Activity ratio: A ratio that measures the liquidity of specific assets and the efficiency of the firm in managing assets.

Additional paid-in-capital: The amount by which the original sales price of stock shares sold exceeds the par value of the stock.

Adverse opinion: Opinion rendered by an independent auditor stating that the financial statements have not been presented fairly in accordance with generally accepted accounting principles.

Allowance for doubtful accounts: The balance sheet account that measures the amount of outstanding accounts receivable expected to be uncollectable.

Amortization: The process of expense allocation applied to the cost expiration of intangible assets.

Annual report: The report to shareholders published by a firm; contains information required by generally accepted accounting principles an/or by specific Securities and Exchange Commission requirements.

Assets: Items possessing service or use potential to owner.

Auditor's report: Report by independent auditor attesting to the fairness of the financial statements of a company.

Average collection period: *See* Summary of financial ratios, appendix E.

Average cost method: A method of valuing inventory and cost of products sold; all costs, including those in beginning inventory, are added together and divided by the total number of units to arrive at a cost per unit.

Balance sheet: The financial statement that shows the financial condition of a company on a particular date.

Balancing equation: Assets = Liabilities + Stockholders' equity.

Basic earnings per share: The earnings per share figure calculated by dividing net earnings available to common shareholders by the average number of common shares outstanding.

Book value: *See* Net book value.

Calendar year: The year starting January 1 and ending December 31.

Capital assets: *See* Fixed assets.

Capital in excess of par value: *See* Additional paid-in-capital.

Capital lease: A leasing arrangement that is, in substance, a purchase by the lessee, who accounts for the lease as an acquisition of an asset and the incurrence of a liability.

Capital structure: The permanent long-term financing of a firm represented by long-term debt, preferred stock, common stock, and retained earnings.

Capitalize: The process whereby initial expenditures are included in the cost of assets and allocated over the period of service.

Cash basis of accounting: A method of accounting under which revenues are recorded when cash is received and expenses are recognized when cash is paid.

Cash conversion cycle: The amount of time (expressed in number of days) required to sell inventory and collect accounts receivable, less the number of days credit extended by suppliers.

Cash equivalents: Security investments that are readily converted to cash.

Cash flow adequacy: *See* Summary of financial ratios, appendix E.

Cash flow from financing activities: On the statement of cash flows, cash generated from/used by financing activities.

Cash flow from investing activities: On the statement of cash flows, cash generated from/used by investing activities.

Cash flow from operating activities: On the statement of cash flows, cash generated/used by operating activities.

Cash flow from operations: The amount of cash generated from/used by a business enterprise's normal, ongoing operations during an accounting period.

Cash flow liquidity ratio: *See* Summary of financial ratios, appendix E.

Cash flow margin: *See* Summary of financial ratios, appendix E.

Cash flow return on assets: *See* Summary of financial ratios, appendix E.

Commercial paper: Unsecured promissory notes of large companies.

Common size financial statements: A form of financial ratio analysis that allows the comparison of firms with different levels of sales or total assets by introducing a common denominator. A common size balance sheet expresses each item on the balance sheet as a percentage of total assets, and a common size income statement expresses each item as a percentage of net sales.

Common stock: Shares of stock representing ownership in a company.

Complex capital structure: Capital structures including convertible securities, stock options, and warrants.

Comprehensive income: The concept that income should include all revenues, expenses, gains, and losses recognized during an accounting period, regardless of whether they are the results of operations.

Conservatism: The accounting concept holding that in selecting among accounting methods the choice should be the one with the least favorable effect on the firm.

Consolidation: The combination of financial statements for two or more separate legal entities when one company, the parent, owns more than 50% of the voting stock of the other company or companies.

Constant dollar approach: An approach to adjust items for inflation by applying the change in a general price index; also called general price level.

Contra-asset account: An account shown as a deduction from the asset to which it relates in the balance sheet.

Convertible securities: Securities that can be converted or exchanged for another type of security, typically common stock.

Cost flow assumption: An assumption regarding the order in which inventory is sold; used to value cost of goods sold and ending inventory.

Cost method: A procedure to account for investments in the voting stock of other companies under which the investor recognizes investment income only to the extent of any cash dividends received.

Cost of goods sold: The cost to the seller of products sold to customers.

Cost of goods sold percentage: The percentage of cost of goods sold to net sales.

Cost of sales: *See* Cost of goods sold.

Cumulative effect of change in accounting principle: The difference in the actual amount of retained earnings at the beginning of the period in which a change in accounting principle is instituted and the amount of retained earnings that would have been reported at that date if the new accounting principle had been applied retroactively for all prior periods.

Current (assets/liabilities): Items expected to be converted into cash or paid out in cash in one year or one operating cycle, whichever is longer.

Current cost approach: An approach to adjusting items for inflation by applying the specific price change of each asset.

Current maturities of long-term debt: The portion of long-term debt that will be repaid during the upcoming year.

Current ratio: *See* Summary of financial ratios, appendix E.

Debt ratio: *See* Summary of financial ratios, appendix E.

Debt to equity ratio: *See* Summary of financial ratios, appendix E.

Defeasance: An accounting technique for the early extinguishment of debt by which a firm purchases at a discount riskless securities (U.S. government securities or securities backed by the U.S. government), places the securities in an irrevocable trust to meet interest and principal payments on outstanding debt, recognizes a gain for the difference between the principal amount of the debt and the price paid for the riskless securities, and eliminates the original liability.

Deferred credits: *See* Unearned revenue.

Deferred taxes: The balance sheet account that results from temporary differences in the recognition of revenue and expense for taxable income and reported income.

Depletion: The accounting procedure used to allocate the cost of acquiring and developing natural resources.

Depreciation: The accounting procedure used to allocate the cost of an asset, which will benefit a business enterprise for more than a year, over the asset's service life.

Derivatives: Financial instruments that derive their value from an underlying asset or index.

Diluted earnings per share: The earnings per share figure calculated using all potentially dilutive securities in the number of shares outstanding.

Direct method: On the statement of cash flows, a method of calculating cash flow from operating activities that shows cash collections from customers; interest and dividends collected; other operating cash receipts; cash paid to suppliers and employees; interest paid; taxes paid; and other operating cash payments.

Disclaimer of opinion: Independent auditor could not evaluate the fairness of the financial statements and, as a result, expresses no opinion on them.

Discontinued operations: The financial results of selling a major business segment.

Discretionary items: Revenues and expenses under the control of management with respect to budget levels and timing.

Dividend payout ratio: *See* Summary of financial ratios, appendix E.

Dividend yield: *See* Summary of financial ratios, appendix E.

Double-declining balance method: An accounting procedure for depreciation under which the straight-line rate of depreciation is doubled and applied to the net book value of the asset.

Du Pont system: An analytical technique used to evaluate the profitability and return on equity for a firm.

Earnings before income taxes: The profit recognized before the deduction of income taxes.

Earnings before interest and taxes: The operating profit of a firm.

Earnings per common share: *See* summary of financial ratios, appendix E.

Earnings statement: *See* Income statement.

Equity: *See* Stockholders' equity.

Equity method: The procedure used for an investment in common stock when the investor company can exercise significant influence over the investee company; the investor recognizes investment income of the investee's net income in proportion to the percent of stock owned.

Expenses: Cost incurred to produce revenue.

Extraordinary transactions: Items that are unusual in nature and not expected to recur in the foreseeable future.

Financial leverage: The extent to which a firm finances with debt, measured by the relationship between total debt and total assets.

Financial leverage index: The ratio of return on equity to return on assets (adjusted to exclude the effect of the method used to finance assets), which indicates whether financial leverage is being used successfully by a firm. An index of greater than 1 indicates the successful use of financial leverage.

Financial ratios: Calculations made to standardize, analyze, and compare financial data; expressed in terms of mathematical relationships in the form of percentages or times.

Financial statements: Accounting information regarding the financial position of a firm, the results of operations, and the cash flows. Four statements comprise the basic set of financial statements: the balance sheet, the income statement, the statement of stockholder's equity, and the statement of cash flows.

Financing activities: On the statement of cash flows, transactions that include borrowing from creditors and repaying the principal; obtaining resources from owners and providing them with a return on the investment.

Finished goods: Products for which the manufacturing process is complete.

First-in, first-out (FIFO): A method of valuing inventory and cost of goods sold under which the items purchased are assumed to be sold first.

Fiscal year: A 12-month period starting on a date other than January 1 and ending 12 months later.

Fixed assets: Tangible, long-lived assets that are expected to provide service benefit for more than one year.

Fixed asset turnover: *See* Summary of financial ratios, appendix E.

Fixed charge coverage: *See* Summary of financial ratios, appendix E.

Foreign currency translation effects: Adjustment to the equity section of the balance sheet resulting from the translation of foreign financial statements.

Form 10-K: An annual document filed with the Securities and Exchange Commission by companies that sell securities to the public.

General price level adjustment: An approach used to adjust items for inflation by applying the change in a general price index; also called constant dollar.

Generally accepted accounting principles: The accounting methods and procedures used to prepare financial statements.

Goodwill: An intangible asset representing the unrecorded assets of a firm; appears in the accounting records only if the firm is acquired for a price in excess of the fair market value of its net assets.

Gross margin: *See* Gross profit.

Gross profit: The difference between net sales and cost of goods sold.

Gross profit margin: *See* Summary of financial ratios, appendix E.

Historical cost: The amount of cash or value of other resources used to acquire an asset; for some assets, historical cost is subject to depreciation, amortization, or depletion.

Income statement: The financial statement presenting the revenues and expenses of a business enterprise for an accounting period.

Industry comparisons: Average financial ratios compiled for industry groups.

Industry segment: *See* segment.

In-substance defeasance: See Defeasance.

Intangible assets: Assets such as goodwill that possess no physical characteristics but have value for the company.

Integrated disclosure system: A common body of information required by the Securities and Exchange Commission for both the 10-K Report filed with the

Securities and Exchange Commission and the annual report provided to shareholders.

Interim statements: Financial statements issued for periods shorter than one year.

Inventories: Items held for sale or used in the manufacture of products that will be sold.

Inventory turnover: *See* Summary of financial ratios, appendix E.

Investing activities: On the statement of cash flows, transactions that include acquiring and selling or otherwise disposing of (1) securities that are not cash equivalents and (2) productive assets that are expected to benefit the firm for long periods of time; lending money and collecting on loans.

Last-in, first-out (LIFO): A method of valuing inventory and cost of goods sold under which the items purchased last are assumed to be sold first.

Leasehold improvement: An addition or improvement made to a leased structure.

Leverage ratio: A ratio that measures the extent of a firm's financing with debt relative to equity and its ability to cover interest and other fixed charges.

Liabilities: Claims against assets.

Line of credit: A prearranged loan allowing borrowing up to a certain maximum amount.

Liquidity: The ability of a firm to generate sufficient cash to meet cash needs.

Liquidity ratio: A ratio that measures a firm's ability to meet needs for cash as they arise.

Long-term debt: Obligations with maturities longer than one year.

Long-term debt to total capitalization: *See* Summary of financial ratios, appendix E.

Lower of cost or market method: A method of valuing inventory under which cost or market, whichever is lower, is selected for each item, each group, or for the entire inventory.

Management Discussion and Analysis (MD&A) of the Financial Condition and Results of Operation: A section of the annual and 10-K report that is required and monitored by the Securities and Exchange Commission in which management presents a detailed coverage of the firm's liquidity, capital resources, and operations.

Marketable securities: Cash not needed immediately in the business and temporarily invested to earn a return.

Matching principle: The accounting principle holding that expenses are to be matched with the generation of revenues in order to determine net income for an accounting period.

Merchandise inventories: Goods purchased for resale to the public.

Minority interest: Claims of shareholders other than the parent company against the net assets and net income of a subsidiary company.

Modified accelerated cost recovery system (MACRS): A modification of the Accelerated tax recovery system (ACRS) in the Tax Reform Act of 1986 for assets placed in service after 1986.

Monetary assets/liabilities: Items that are stated in terms of current value and do not need to be adjusted for inflation; include cash, marketable securities, and all liabilities other than deferred income.

Multiple-step format: A format for presenting the income statement under which several intermediate profit measures are shown.

Net assets: Total assets less total liabilities.

Net book value of capital assets: The difference between original cost of property, plant, and equipment and any accumulated depreciation to date.

Net earnings: The firm's profit or loss after consideration of all revenue and expense reported during the accounting period.

Net income: *See* Net earnings.

Net profit margin: *See* Summary of financial ratios, appendix E

Net sales: Total sales revenue less sales returns and sales allowances.

Net trade cycle: *See* Cash conversion cycle.

Noncurrent assets/liabilities: Items expected to benefit the firm for/with maturities of more than one year.

Notes payable: A short-term obligation in the form of a promissory note to suppliers or financial institutions.

Notes to the financial statements: Supplementary information to financial statements that explain the firm's accounting policies and provide detail about particular accounts and other information such as pension plans.

Off–balance sheet financing: Financial techniques for raising funds that do not have to be recorded as liabilities on the balance sheet.

Operating activities: On the statement of cash flows, transactions that include delivering or producing goods for sale and providing services; the cash effects of transactions and other events that enter into the determination of income.

Operating cycle: The time required to purchase or manufacture inventory, sell the product, and collect the cash.

Operating expenses: Costs related to the normal functions of a business.

Operating lease: A rental agreement where no ownership rights are transferred to the lessee at the termination of the rental contract.

Operating profit: Sales revenue less the expenses associated with generating sales. Operating profit measures the overall performance of a company on its normal, ongoing operations.

Operating profit margin: *See* Summary of financial ratios, appendix E.

Options: *See* Stock options.

Par value: The floor price below which stock cannot be sold initially.

Plant and equipment: *See* Fixed assets.

Preferred stock: Capital stock of a company that carries certain privileges or rights not carried by all outstanding shares of stock.

Prepaid expenses: Expenditures made in the current or prior period that will benefit the firm at some future time.

Price-earnings ratio: *See* Summary of financial ratios, appendix E.

Principal: The original amount of a liability.

Prior period adjustment: A change in the retained earnings balance primarily resulting from the correction of errors made in previous accounting periods.

Pro forma financial statements: Projections of future financial statements based on a set of assumptions regarding future revenues, expenses, level of investment in assets, financing methods and costs, and working capital management.

Profitability ratio: A ratio that measures the overall performance of a firm and its efficiency in managing assets, liabilities, and equity.

Property, plant, and equipment: *See* Fixed assets.

Prospectus: A formal written description of a mutual fund required by the SEC.

Publicly held companies: Companies that operate to earn a profit and issue shares of stock to the public.

Qualified opinion: An opinion rendered by an independent auditor when the overall financial statements are fairly presented "except for" certain items (which the auditor discloses).

Quality of financial reporting: A subjective evaluation of the extent to which financial reporting is free of manipulation and accurately reflects the financial condition and operating success of a business enterprise.

Quick ratio: *See* Summary of financial ratios, appendix E.

Raw materials: Basic commodities or natural resources that will be used in the production of goods.

Replacement cost: The estimated cost of acquiring new and substantially equivalent property at current prices.

Reported income: The net income published in financial statements.

Restructuring charges: Costs to reorganize a company.

Retained earnings: The sum of every dollar a company has earned since its inception, less any payments made to shareholders in the form of cash or stock dividends.

Return on assets: *See* Return on investment.

Return on equity: *See* Summary of financial ratios, appendix E.

Return on investment: *See* Summary of financial ratios, appendix E.

Revenue: The inflow of assets resulting from the sale of goods or services.

Sales allowance: A deduction from the original sales invoice price.

Sales return: A cancellation of a sale.

Salvage value: The amount of an asset estimated to be recoverable at the conclusion of the asset's service life.

Segment: A component of a business enterprise that sells primarily to outside markets and for which information about revenue and profit is accumulated.

Segment operating expenses: Expenses relating to unaffiliated customers and segment revenue; expenses not directly traceable to segments are allocated to segments on a reasonable basis.

Segment operating profit/loss: Segment revenue less all operating expenses.

Segment revenue: Sales of products and services to unaffiliated customers and intersegment sales, with company transfer prices used to determine sales between segments.

Selling and administrative expenses: Costs relating to the sale of products or services and to the management function of the firm.

Short-term: Generally indicates maturity of less than a year.

Single-step format: A format for presenting the income statement under which all items of revenue are grouped together and then all items of expense are deducted to arrive at net income.

Stated value: The floor price below which stock cannot be sold initially; see also par value.

Statement of cash flows: The financial statement that provides information about the cash inflows and outflows from operating, financing, and investing activities during an accounting period.

Statement of retained earnings: The financial statement that presents the details of the transactions affecting the retained earnings account during an accounting period.

Statement of stockholders' equity: A financial statement that summarizes changes in the shareholders' equity section of the balance sheet during an accounting period.

Stock dividends: The issuance of additional shares of stock to existing shareholders in proportion to current ownership.

Stock options: A contract that conveys the right to purchase shares of stock at a specified price within a specified time period.

Stockholders' equity: Claims against assets by the owners of the business; represents the amount owners have invested including income retained in the business since inception.

Straight-line depreciation: An accounting procedure under which equal amounts of expense are apportioned to each year of an asset's life.

Structural analysis: Analysis looking at the internal structure of a business enterprise.

Summary of financial ratios: *See* appendix E.

Tangible: Having physical substance.

Taxable income: The net income figure used to determine taxes payable to governments.

Temporary differences: Differences between pretax accounting income and taxable income caused by reporting items of revenue or expense in one period for accounting purposes and in an earlier or later period for income tax purposes.

Times interest earned: *See* Summary of financial ratios, appendix E.

Total asset turnover: *See* Summary of financial ratios, appendix E.

Treasury stock: Shares of a company's stock that are repurchased by the company and not retired.

Trend analysis: Evaluation of financial data over several accounting periods.

Unearned revenue: A liability caused by receipt of cash in advance of earning revenue.

Uniform Bank Performance Report: A standardized document for insured banks that includes a balance sheet, income statement, financial ratios, peer group comparisons, and other analytical data.

Units-of-production method: An accounting method under which depreciation expense is based on actual usage.

Unqualified opinion: An opinion rendered by an independent auditor of financial statements stating that the financial statements have been presented fairly in accordance with generally accepted accounting principles.

Unqualified opinion with explanatory language: An opinion rendered by an independent auditor of financial statements stating that the financial statements have been presented fairly in accordance with generally accepted accounting principles, but there are items which the auditor wishes to explain to the user.

Unrealized gains (losses) on marketable equity securities: The gains (losses) disclosed in the equity section resulting from the accounting rule that requires investments in marketable equity securities to be carried at the lower of cost or market value.

Warrant: A certificate issued by a corporation that conveys the right to buy a stated number of shares of stock at a specified price on or before a predetermined date.

Work-in-process: Products for which the manufacturing process is only partially completed.

Working capital: The amount by with current assets exceed current liabilities.

Index